JUSTIFICATION
and the KINGDOM *of* GOD

JUSTIFICATION and the KINGDOM of GOD

The Kingdom of the Covenant

VOLUME ONE

PAUL CHULHONG KANG

Foreword by D. Clair Davis

WIPF & STOCK · Eugene, Oregon

JUSTIFICATION AND THE KINGDOM OF GOD, VOLUME ONE
The Kingdom of the Covenant

Copyright © 2025 Paul ChulHong Kang. All rights reserved. Except for brief quotations in critical publications or reviews, no part of this book may be reproduced in any manner without prior written permission from the publisher. Write: Permissions, Wipf and Stock, 199 W. 8th Ave., Suite 3, Eugene, OR 97401.

Wipf & Stock
An Imprint of Wipf and Stock
199 W. 8th Ave., Suite 3
Eugene, OR 97401

www.wipfandstock.com

PAPERBACK ISBN: 979-8-3852-3367-0
HARDCOVER ISBN: 979-8-3852-3368-7
EBOOK ISBN: 979-8-3852-3369-4

01/16/25

Unless otherwise indicated, Scripture quotations are from the ESV® Bible (The Holy Bible, English Standard Version®), © 2001 by Crossway, a publishing ministry of Good News Publishers. Used by permission. All rights reserved.

Scripture quotations marked (NIV) are taken from the Holy Bible, New International Version®, NIV®. Copyright © 1973, 1978, 1984, 2011 by Biblica, Inc.™ Used by permission of Zondervan. All rights reserved worldwide. www.zondervan.com The "NIV" and "New International Version" are trademarks registered in the United States Patent and Trademark Office by Biblica, Inc.

To Jesus Christ,
who perfectly obeyed the word of our Heavenly Father
to adopt us into his family
and who continually blesses, guides, supports,
comforts, protects, and keeps us safe
(Eph 3:20–21)

and to my best friend and dear wife,
Grace EunHee,
and to my family,
who have supported, helped,
and patiently endured with me all this time

and to the next generation,
those future image bearers of God

Contents

Foreword by D. Clair Davis	ix
Preface	xi
Abbreviations	xv
Author's Introduction	xvii
The Kingdom of the Covenant	1
1 The Kingdom of God Has Already Begun	3
2 The Kingdom of the Covenant	27
3 The Righteousness of the Eternal God	76
4 The Word of God	101
5 Conclusion: God's Word Is the Most Important	188
Bibliography	191
Subject Index	193
Scripture Index	213

Foreword

WE ARE BOTH BLESSED and challenged by Paul Kang's theology of the gospel of Jesus. First of all, Kang constantly and steadfastly reminds us how it is God's word that encourages us with the reality of our Father's saving love and also our need for further personal trust and obedience. We know that all of us Evangelicals believe that deep down but are slow in saying it. So let us all join in now, all of us, and find both steadfast joy and obedience in God's holy word. We have been too long content with telling the world that we're not liberals who doubt everything in the Bible, and now it's high time to remind ourselves and then everyone else that the word is what we live out of, joyfully and gratefully.

Then there is what we can be doing with our justification. We keep saying "faith alone," making it clear that we know we're not doing anything to earn our forgiveness, like some folks used to think. But we push it too far by saying it's totally a legal, forensic way of talking. Then Kang wakes us all up by actually connecting justification with the kingdom of God! Whatever God does connects with everything else he does, as his kind plan for us, his kingdom, fits his forgiveness of our sins. Now that's an eye-opener, seeing Jesus on the cross as the way Father keeps on blessing our lives right now, helping us grow in the restored image of God when we trust and obey his word.

All those theologians do have the same agenda, putting together the pieces of God's love so we can see its beauty overall and in all. But Kang doesn't quit then, he keeps at it, his Lord gets even kinder. He wants more than a unified theology; he wants us to see Jesus who loves us all the time everywhere but especially in justification and the kingdom. Jesus desires that we know and love each other the way he and his Father do, and with Kang that heavenly desire comes to its fulfillment! We know and deeply appreciate all of God's goodness, and Rom 2:4 becomes so real, where

God's kindness leads to our repentance, bringing in us a harvest of our obedient hearts, so much more than just understanding God's ways but also living out his love and merciful kindness.

Paul Kang shows us God's way, the Way. Now we are called to add to it in our theology and also in our love. He shows us God's path to grow in the image of God, and we rejoice to keep on steadfastly moving ahead in it! He opens our eyes wider and wider as we are amazed to see the glory of God, in all his kindness!

Dr. D. Clair Davis
Professor of Church History, Emeritus
Westminster Theological Seminary

Preface

THE JOURNEY OF WRITING the *Justification and Kingdom of God* began with a fundamental yet simple question: "How should we live?" This question led to the exploration of the profound connection between the kingdom of God and the covenant, guiding Christians toward a life rooted in his word.

I have deeply explored the authority and relevance of the Bible throughout my more than twenty years in pastoral ministry and seventeen years in teaching ministry. Despite health challenges and demanding workload that led to doubts about completing this work, God continually reaffirmed the authority and purpose of his word. This journey has become a personal testimony of his desire for us to understand his eternal plans and unfailing love. Surprisingly, the challenges I faced regarding health and workload while writing this set have also sharpened my understanding of the power of the gospel (Rom 1:16–17) and the providence of God (Rom 8:28–29), both of which I have outlined in these volumes.

These volumes examine God's righteousness and its relationship with Adam's sin, justification, and sanctification. By framing these relationships within the concept of the image of God, they reach a critical conclusion:

> The gospel includes not only *the forgiveness of sins* but also *the restoration of the marred image of God*. Furthermore, sanctification—essentially the Christian life—involves *the growth of this restored image*.

These volumes fill a significant practical and theological gap in Christianity concerning the connection between the image of God and the Christian life. To bridge this gap, they offer a biblically grounded understanding of three relational aspects of God's kingdom, aligned with his purpose in creating humanity. For readers to fully understand God's primary purpose in establishing God's kingdom and creating humanity, they must recognize three essential connections:

1. The relationship between God's righteousness and his word
2. The relationship between the perfect righteousness of Christ and the justification of sinners in Jesus Christ
3. The relationship between God's image bearer and the responsibilities of a Christian

Living a godly life depends on a correct understanding of justification through Jesus's perfect obedience, which, by grace alone, restores the marred image of God within us. The tangible transformation of heart and behavior, reflecting faith's fruit, marks the growth of God's restored image in us through Jesus Christ.

To develop the critical conclusion of this set I focused on three key strategies to better discern God's purpose for his kingdom, focusing on obedience and living in his image as revealed in Scripture:

1. Scripture alone (*sola Scriptura*): Answers are drawn exclusively from Scripture, prioritizing clarity over speculation or theological debate. These volumes exclude human assumptions that disregard God's word, which is the ultimate standard of truth in all matters.
2. Redemptive historical interpretation and unity in diversity: This approach highlights Scripture's coherence, countering medieval and Enlightenment views that elevated human reasoning over God's word. Unity in diversity helps us identify Scripture's smaller patterns, while redemptive historical interpretation reveals the larger, cohesive picture.[1]
3. Understanding God's righteousness and God's image: Redemptive history and unity in diversity lead to a clearer view of God's righteousness, his kingdom purposes, and his image in humanity. This

---

1. A good example that illustrates the expression of "unity in diversity" in the New Testament is the saving work of Christ. The New Testament expresses the saving work of Christ (unity) in diverse ways from the perspective of grace, love, atonement, reconciliation, sacrifice, redemption, ransom, and victory (diversity). It talks about grace (Eph 2:8–9), love (Rom 5:5; 8:35–39), atonement (2 Cor 5:21), reconciliation (Rom 5:1, 9–11), sacrifice (Heb 9:26; Eph 5:2; 1 Cor 5:7), redemption (Rom 6:18; Titus 2:14; Col 1:13–14), ransom (Matt 20:28; 1 Tim 2:6; Rom 3:24), and victory (Col 2:13–15; 1 Cor 15:57; Col 1:11) (Kang, *Living Out the Gospel*, 113–38).

understanding underscores that the fulfilment of theology lies in obedience to God's word.

As the image of God grows within us, we fulfill our responsibilities as God's children through prayer and obedience to his word, receiving his blessings along the way. Through faith that works in love and manifests God's love for others, bearing the fruit of the Holy Spirit, we glorify God by displaying his grace and love to the world.

I thank God for the incredible opportunity to write this set. I am deeply grateful to my wife, Grace EunHee, and my daughter, Joyce YunSun, for their unwavering support and prayers that have sustained me throughout this writing journey. I also want to express my heartfelt gratitude to my family—Esther YunJung, Sam YunIl, Randon, HeeJae, WonJae, and JungWon—who have encouraged me in countless ways. I am thankful for the ongoing support and love of my parents, late parents-in-law, Wan, Hyun, and friends of the Gospel Foundation.

Special thanks go to Dr. D. Clair Davis, a mentor whose invaluable guidance has shaped me over the years, and to my friends and colleagues in Christ, who have steadfastly supported and prayed for this work. I also extend my gratitude to my copyeditor Rebecca Abbott, and Wipf and Stock Publishers for their professionalism, expertise, and consistent support throughout this endeavor.

Finally, these volumes underscore that God, who invites us into his family through the perfect obedience of Jesus Christ, desires his children to grow and become like their heavenly Father. My hope is that these volumes will strengthen you, the readers, to grow in wisdom, knowledge, righteousness, holiness, and goodness—all in Jesus Christ—through the commandment to "love one another."

Paul ChulHong Kang

For in it the righteousness of God is revealed from faith for faith, as it is written, "The righteous shall live by faith." (Rom 1:17)
But seek first the kingdom of God and his righteousness, and all these things will be added to you. (Matt 6:33)
And have put on the new self, which is being renewed in knowledge after the image of its creator. (Col 3:10)
Now to him who is able to do far more abundantly than all that we ask or think, according to the power at work within us, to him be glory in the church and in Christ Jesus throughout all generations, forever and ever. Amen. (Eph 3:20–21)

Abbreviations

BDAG   Walter Bauer et al. *A Greek-English Lexicon of the New Testament and Other Early Christian Literature.* 3rd ed. Chicago: University of Chicago Press, 2000. (Danker-Bauer-Arndt-Gingrich)

BDB   Francis Brown et al. *Enhanced Brown-Driver-Briggs Hebrew and English Lexicon.* Oxford: Clarendon Press, 1977

DCH   *Dictionary of Classical Hebrew.* Edited by David J. A. Clines. 9 vols. Sheffield: Sheffield Phoenix Press, 1993–2014

EDNT   *Exegetical Dictionary of the New Testament.* Edited by Horst Balz and Gerhard Schneider. ET. 3 vols. Grand Rapids: Eerdmans, 1990–93

ESV   English Standard Version

Institutes   *The Institutes of the Christian Religion.* John Calvin. Translated by Ford Lewis Battles. 2 vols. Philadelphia: Westminster, 1960

L&N   Louw, Johannes P., and Eugene A. Nida, eds. *Greek-English Lexicon of the New Testament: Based on Semantic Domains.* 2nd ed. New York: United Bible Societies, 1989

NIV   New International Version

TDNT   *Theological Dictionary of the New Testament.* Edited by Gerhard Kittel and Gerhard Friedrich. Translated by Geoffrey W. Bromiley. 10 vols. Grand Rapids: Eerdmans, 1964–76

TLOT   *Theological Lexicon of the Old Testament.* Edited by Ernst Jenni, with assistance from Claus Westermann. Translated by Mark E. Biddle. 3 vols. Peabody, MA: Hendrickson, 1997

Author's Introduction

THE MAIN CORE THEME of this *Justification and Kingdom of God* set is that our righteous, holy, and good God has established a kingdom based on a covenant. This set introduces the kingdom of God in three volumes: *The Kingdom of the Covenant, The Kingdom of Justification, The Kingdom of Faith*. Volumes 1 and 2 introduce the kingdom of God, centered on the work of God's sovereign grace, while volume 3 discusses the responsibility of the citizens of God's kingdom in practicing their faith. Through this discussion, I will endeavor to clearly explain the difference between the kingdom of God and the kingdom of this world.

We need to remember that there are quite a few people in this world who have turned the kingdom of God into a mythical tale. There are those who think that the kingdom of God may come into existence in the distant future. Also, some deny the existence of the kingdom of God. Therefore, I believe there is a need to uproot such misconceptions about the kingdom of God through books like this *Justification and the Kingdom of God*.

First, we need to establish what the kingdom of God is.

The kingdom of God is a kingdom established through the redemptive history of Jesus Christ, built on the covenantal words between God and humans.[1]

> For this is the covenant that I will make with the house of Israel after those days, declares the Lord: I will put my laws into their minds, and write them on their hearts, and I will be their God, and they shall be my people. (Heb 8:10)[2]

---

1. Kline, *Structure of Biblical Authority*, 25, 35–38, 53–57, 68–75, 76–93, 95–102, 146–53, 154–62, 167–203; Frame, *Systematic Theology*, 87–91; Frame, *Doctrine of Christian Life*, 271–79; Vos, *Redemptive History*, 304–16; Ridderbos, *Coming of the Kingdom*.

2. This is a recitation of Jer 31:33.

From eternity to eternity, God the Lord (Ps 90:1–2) has made sinful humans into citizens of the eternal kingdom of God only by his grace. Therefore, the most crucial events in the history of the kingdom of God are the events of the redemptive history, namely, the events of creation, fall, and redemption.[3] Thus, the kingdom of God is a kingdom established by Jesus with his coming as King, built on God's grace and love. Jesus' perfect obedience to the word restored the marred image of God in sinners. Now, sinners can enter the kingdom of God by believing in Jesus, the King. God has blessed fallen humans to become God's children and to be obedient to the word.

Therefore, in *Justification and the Kingdom of God*, the exploration of justification and the kingdom of God leads to an examination of the identity of the citizens of God's kingdom and what it means for those citizens to live in God's kingdom by faith.

In other words, I want us to journey together in search of the answer to the question "How should the citizens of God's kingdom live on earth?" As previously mentioned, this is the writing motivation of *Justification and the Kingdom of God*. For this purpose, we will discuss in depth the meaning of the kingdom of God, the law of the kingdom of God, the identity of its citizens, and how to live by faith in this kingdom.

To briefly provide more detail on each volume:

In volume 1, *The Kingdom of the Covenant*, we will first examine the fact that the kingdom of God is established through the covenant of God.

For this, we will endeavor to find answers to the following questions: What is the covenant of God revealed in the Bible? Why did God give the covenant? And in discussing God's covenant, we will also discuss creation and the fall.

God gave Adam the words of the first covenant. Examining the Adamic covenant helps us understand our current state (self) and the meaning of the image of God within us. While other covenants are important, the Mosaic covenant plays a particularly significant role in understanding the entire Old Testament. The Mosaic law helps us understand the principle by which God governed Israel and the principle by which he governs humanity through his authoritative word. It also clearly shows the reason the Messiah had to come. Therefore, the Mosaic law is

---

3. Frame, *Doctrine of Christian Life*, 271; Frame, *Systematic Theology*, 87–91; Kline, *Structure of Biblical Authority*, 101. Regarding the history of redemption, please see ch. 4 in this vol.

very important for understanding justification, which will be discussed in volume 2, *The Kingdom of Justification*.

For this reason, we will also examine God's righteousness in connection with the Mosaic covenant. The discussion of God's righteousness in volume 1, chapter 3, greatly assists in understanding the word, the law of God. Jesus also came into this world according to the word of the covenant, the law of the kingdom of God, and took on the punishment for the sins of sinners according to the law of righteousness of the kingdom of God. Jesus' redemptive work demonstrates how solemn God's righteousness, as revealed in the law of the kingdom of God, is. God's righteousness is also the legal standard for governing the kingdom of God, the standard for salvation, and the standard for a good life.

In fact, beyond just the Mosaic law, the righteousness of God is well represented throughout the entirety of God's word in the Bible. Above all, we must not forget that God has given us the word of God, the law of the kingdom of God. The word of God in the Bible is the law and the only truth for us. Therefore, in volume 1, chapter 4, we will explore the significant attributes of God's word: God's attributes of lordship; and the power of life, the power of work, and the power of judgment in the word. God has given us his word to represent himself, and he wants us to treat the word as we would treat him (John 1:1–2).

It is not an exaggeration to say that life and death in our life of faith hinge on how we receive the word of God. We Christians can encounter God when we encounter and believe in God's word. The kingdom of the covenant is the kingdom of this word.

In volume 2, *The Kingdom of Justification*, in connection with volume 1, we will strive to find an answer to the following question: What is justification?

Through an in-depth look at justification, the standard for salvation, we will carefully examine Jesus' perfect obedience that satisfied God's righteousness, and through which the justification of sinners or the grace of salvation became possible.

The importance of justification, that is, the significance of the gospel, cannot be overstated. This is because the identity of the citizens of God's kingdom all comes from the gospel. For this reason, in volume 2, chapter 1, we will start with a definition of the gospel and then clarify the relationship between the gospel and justification. Furthermore, we will briefly explore some examples in Christian history where God's grace and the necessity for justification were denied.

Following that, in volume 2, chapter 2, we will take a closer look at the basis of the identity of God's children: How can sinners become children of the righteous God? How can sinners be called righteous?

The answers to these questions are crucial for our identity and the assurance of our faith. As we delve into the topic of justification, we will come to a clearer understanding of the redemptive work of Jesus by discussing the meaning of "perfect obedience." As a result, we will be able to answer the aforementioned questions and gain a good understanding of the significance of justification, the meaning of perfect obedience, and the relationship between the two. Furthermore, we will understand why Jesus' obedience to the punishment of the cross cannot fully meet the requirements for the justification of sinners. This is because only the perfect obedience of Jesus can fully meet the requirements for the justification of sinners.

To properly understand the meaning of Jesus' perfect obedience, it is necessary to view obedience in both a narrow sense (centered on the Mosaic law) and a broader sense. Additionally, we need to explore the relationship between the perfect obedience of Jesus' life and the covenants of the Old Testament. The in-depth discussion on this perfect obedience will enable us to deeply recognize God's great grace and providence, as well as the value of Jesus' obedience and the magnitude of his love for us.

In volume 2, chapter 3, we will examine union with Jesus, the imputation of righteousness, and a justifying faith to further clarify what the perfect righteousness obtained by Jesus through his perfect obedience is. This will provide a clear understanding of the conditions of justification for sinners and help us to firmly establish our identity as God's children. In this process, we will also gain a basic understanding of the restored image of God, as well as the guilt and pollution of sin. Through the discussion and understanding of these concepts, we will see that the kingdom of God is established through the gospel of Jesus and will realize that the gospel is the sole path of grace that leads to entering the kingdom of God.

Furthermore, the restoration of the marred image of God speaks to the present reality of the kingdom of God that has actually come into us. Right here, in this very moment, we will come to realize the present reality of the kingdom of God that has already come within us. At the same time, we will also recognize that this present reality has been endowed with eternal value by the everlasting God. As a result, we will also come to realize that God requires the obedience of faith in our lives as the proper response and responsibility to God's saving grace.

In volume 3, *The Kingdom of Faith*, we will see that the kingdom of God is established upon the word of the covenant and faith that believes in Jesus.

For this, we will seek to find answers to the following questions: What is faith? Why does God give us faith? What does it mean to live by faith? In addition, we will examine in detail the obedience of faith and the responsibility we should show to God, who has granted us the grace of justification.

We should remember that the discussion of *The Kingdom of Faith* cannot be separated from *The Kingdom of the Covenant* and *The Kingdom of Justification*. It is obvious here that the sovereign work of the Holy Spirit continues to govern the kingdom of God. In volume 3, chapter 1, we will discuss the definition of faith, that the object of faith is Jesus Christ, and the content of faith is the word of God. And we will focus on the fact that God's word is the standard for every area of our lives. We will notice that if we stray from the word of God in our life of faith, we move away from God.

Then in volume 3, chapter 2, we will discuss that faith and change are inseparable. God's children must grow according to the image of God, who is righteous, holy, and good. This is because the most important thing in a life of faith is change.

In chapter 2, we will also discuss the growth of God's image by connecting *The Kingdom of the Covenant* and *The Kingdom of Justification*. Growth in the image of God is a special right and responsibility given by God only to those who believe in Jesus. It is essential to understand that growth of God's image manifests as growth in intellectual excellence and moral excellence for a fruitful life. In a narrow sense, this growth signifies the growth of wisdom, knowledge, righteousness, holiness, and goodness, which is the growth of the restored image of God in Jesus. This speaks of the actual change in our hearts and behaviors as we, who are justified and saved by grace and whose marred image of God is restored in Jesus, grow in faith.

In volume 3, chapter 3, we will look at the obedience of faith and the fruit of faith. Understanding the sovereign work of the Holy Spirit is vital even in the fruit of faith. However, we must not forget the importance of our repentance and our obedience according to God's word in bearing the fruit of faith. This is because the Bible teaches repentance and obedience to the word as the most crucial foundation for a fruitful life.

Last, we will look into the characteristics of obedience to the word of God as described in the Bible. Every act of faith and obedience we carry out on this earth through our belief in Jesus holds eternal value to God.

Also, in order to avoid a vague or self-conceived so-called "life of faith as one pleases," it is essential to carefully examine the meaning of faith, the changes in life due to justification, and the fruit of faith. All of these processes will help us stand more firmly on the rock of the word, enjoying the grace of justification with greater strength and living a life of obedience, the response of faith that God wants.

In summary, the understanding of the kingdom of God covered in the *Justification and the Kingdom of God* emphasizes the absolute need for the guidance of the Holy Spirit. God desires to establish a kingdom full of God's children who have grown to be conformed to the image of God. Therefore, for the establishment of God's kingdom, I strongly urge the readers of this series to live a life of obedience to the word by relying on the Holy Spirit.

In this set, we will come to realize that the purpose for which God established his kingdom surpasses all human thoughts and theories (Isa 55:6–9). We will recognize that the secret of the invisible kingdom of God has been revealed and made known in the world by Jesus. The kingdom of God that came with Jesus did not disappear from this earth after Jesus ascended to sit at the right hand of the throne in heaven. The kingdom of God is within the children of God on this earth. This means that now is the opportunity for the children of God to manifest the kingdom of God to the world.

To repeat, the children of God can show the kingdom of God to the world through their life of faith right now. Though the world may not recognize it, the work of God's grace is ongoing, and the kingdom of God, which has come through Jesus Christ, continues within the lives of God's children. When those who receive God's grace, who are justified by faith, believe and obey God's word (Rom 1:17), the people of the world will see the kingdom of God through their lives.

The Kingdom of the Covenant

THE KINGDOM OF GOD is a kingdom of the covenant. This means the following:

- First, the kingdom of God is a kingdom established by the word of the covenant.
- Second, the kingdom of God is a kingdom governed by the word of the covenant that is its law.
- Third, the kingdom of God has the word of the covenant as the standard of life for human words and actions.

To properly view the kingdom of God from the perspective of the covenant, it is necessary to first examine the biblical meaning and purpose of the kingdom of God. We will begin our exploration of the covenant kingdom by discussing significant characteristics of God's kingdom: its eternality and present reality. This discussion will help us reawaken to God, who is the eternal and unchanging truth, and subsequently aid us in insightfully understanding and comprehending his covenant, his righteousness, and his word.

1

The Kingdom of God Has Already Begun

1. THE KINGDOM OF GOD

THE MOST IMPORTANT CHARACTERISTIC of the kingdom of God is, of course, that it is a kingdom built by God. Therefore, the kingdom of God reflects the attributes of God, who personally chooses its citizens. When viewed in terms of our relationship, the most important attributes of God that appear in the kingdom of God can be seen as God's eternity and God's righteousness. The reason is that the Bible promises the eternal value of Jesus' redemptive work accomplished according to the standard of God's unchanging righteousness. Also, the word of God promises eternal results for our faith.

We often forget about God's eternity, but the Bible emphasizes it. As finite beings, we don't quite understand how God created time and how it relates to eternity, but the meaning of eternity is very important to us. It is important because God connects our present time to eternity. The God of the Bible also assigns eternity to salvation and faith. This is why I continue to emphasize in these *Justification and the Kingdom of God* volumes that there is eternal value in the response of faith and the obedience of faith. It is the eternal God who gives eternal meaning to our present words and actions.

God's kingdom is not established by human laws. God, who has faithfully executed his own established laws, created the world and humanity, and governs his kingdom according to these divine laws. This God gives us his word, in which his righteousness is revealed, as the law of God's kingdom. The law of God's righteousness given to mankind is also eternal. Therefore, it is very important to understand the characteristics of God's righteousness revealed in Scripture, because God, who is eternal, created the world and established his kingdom based on his righteousness. We will look at these attributes of God's righteousness in chapter 3 of this volume, and it will be continuously emphasized throughout this set.

God's eternity and God's righteousness will give us assurance of salvation and help us live in faith in the word of God's promises. Because God is eternal and unchanging, the standard of righteousness for our salvation also never changes. In this regard, the citizens of the kingdom of God are those whose problems of unrighteousness have been eternally resolved through the work of God's love.

A. When Did the Eternal Kingdom of God Begin?

How does the Bible introduce the beginning of the eternal kingdom of God?

The eternal kingdom of God began when Jesus Christ came to this earth and proclaimed the gospel (Matt 9:15; 11:11; 13:16–17; 23:13; Mark 10:15; Luke 17:21).[1] The gospel is "the good news of the kingdom" (Matt 9:35) that Jesus has opened the way for us, sinners, to enter the kingdom of God (Matt 9:35). In other words, the gospel is the good news that announces the beginning of the eternal kingdom of God. This is why the kingdom of God is "the focus of the good news" throughout the New Testament (Matt 9:35; 24:14; Luke 8:1; Acts 1:3; 8:12; 19:8; 20:25; 28:23, 31).[2]

Looking at Mark 1:15 can be helpful for us.

> The time is fulfilled, and the kingdom of God is at hand; repent and believe in the gospel. (Mark 1:15)

In this text, Jesus connects the beginning of the kingdom of God with the gospel. He also tells us that the kingdom of God is related to the repentance of human sins. In other words, the kingdom of God will be open to

---

1. Bavinck, *Reformed Dogmatics*, 3:247, 498; 4:715; Vos, *Pauline Eschatology*, 246.
2. Frame, *Systematic Theology*, 95.

those who repent and believe in the gospel. God promises that the eternal kingdom of God will begin for those who believe in Jesus.

In fact, the coming of the kingdom of God through the redemptive work of Jesus has the deepest relationship with human creation. To properly understand this, we need to know that the great work of God's grace began with the creation of humans in God's image. The triune God created Adam, the representative of all humankind in his image (Gen 1:26–28). God gave Adam and all humans the word of God's covenant, requiring obedience of faith to them to obey the word. However, the crisis of the kingdom came when Adam, the representative of all humankind, disobeyed the word of the covenant. Initially, it seemed like the establishment of the kingdom of God failed because of the fall of Adam. At that time, the wise, righteous, holy, and good image of God given to the creatures (humans)—which contained intellectual excellence and moral excellence such as wisdom, righteousness, holiness, and goodness—was also marred.[3] Surprisingly, however, God, who withheld the deserved punishment for Adam's sin, sought the responsibility and punishment from himself. Here, we should note that the establishment of the kingdom of God did not fail, but rather continued to progress.

After the fall of Adam, the eternal God continued to give humans redemptive covenants through God's covenant people, Israel.[4] These covenants of God were given to all sinners through Israel, enabling them to live with the expectation of the restoration of the eternal kingdom of God. And God, as promised, sent Jesus to restore the marred kingdom of God. Through the tremendous sacrifice of Jesus Christ, the eternal kingdom of God was renewed and began anew.

God, who hates sin and judges it, turned the crisis of human fall into an opportunity for the restoration of the marred image of God through his love and grace. He sent Jesus Christ, the Representative of the new covenant, to be punished on behalf of sinners, thereby strengthening the kingdom of God. Thus, the kingdom of God is not a kingdom established by the accomplishment of human efforts, but a kingdom established only by the work of God's grace.[5] This is the amazing and marvelous work of God's grace manifested in the salvation of fallen humanity.

---

3. We will discuss more about the marred image of God in "2-A. Adamic Covenant," in this volume, ch. 2, and the restored image of God in "Justification and the Restored Image of God," in vol. 2, ch. 3.

4. Kline, *Structure of Biblical Authority*, 174–95.

5. Hoekema, *Bible and the Future*, 45.

B. The Coming of the Eternal Kingdom of God and Its Present Reality

In Luke 4:16–22, Jesus proclaimed the coming of the messianic kingdom by reading from Isa 61.[6] The coming of the kingdom of God, as the Old Testament said, was accomplished as "a present and actual reality" through Jesus Christ by "fulfilling" the salvation of sinners who would enter the eternal kingdom of God.[7] This kingdom of God is entered only by faith in Jesus (John 3:16; 17:3). The Holy Spirit actually applies the present reality of the kingdom of God to those who confess their faith in Christ.[8]

Knowing the fact that the coming of the kingdom of God through the fulfillment of salvation has become a present reality is very important in our life of faith. This is very important because our faith in the present reality of the coming of the kingdom of God becomes the decisive foundation of our confidence that changes the goal of our life according to God's will.

The present reality of the kingdom of God was made possible because God gave the "Kingdom of God itself" as a gift of grace to sinners.[9] For those who believe in Jesus Christ and receive the kingdom of God as a gift, Jesus Christ becomes their inheritance. In this way, our citizenship in the kingdom of God begins the moment we believe in Jesus (Phil 3:20).[10] This has been made possible because Jesus, having divine nature and human nature, connected the life of faith on earth with the eternal kingdom of God through his redemptive work. Mark 10:25–26 further clarifies the meaning of Jesus' words "the kingdom of God is at hand; repent and believe in the gospel" (Mark 1:15).

> "It is easier for a camel to go through the eye of a needle than for a rich person to enter the kingdom of God." And they were exceedingly astonished, and said to him, "Then who can be saved?" (Mark 10:25–26)

This text is part of what Jesus taught the disciples in response to a young man's question on eternal life (Mark 10). Mark 10:17–31 is

---

6. Frame, *Systematic Theology*, 90–98.

7. Ridderbos, *Coming of the Kingdom*, 49, 63–64, 47–56, 61–103; Frame, *Systematic Theology*, 92.

8. Bavinck, *Reformed Dogmatics*, 3:498; 4:48; Vos, *Pauline Eschatology*, 259; Hoekema, *Bible and the Future*, 48–52.

9. Frame, *Doctrine of Christian Life*, 284.

10. "But our citizenship is in heaven, and from it we await a Savior, the Lord Jesus Christ" (Phil 3:20).

important to us because it clearly defines the meaning of the present reality of the kingdom of God. It explains that the coming of the kingdom of God does not come at the second coming of Christ, but rather, it comes to you when you believe in Jesus Christ and receive salvation. The passage also indicates that salvation and eternal life are directly related to the present reality of the kingdom of God (John 3:3–8, 16–18). The kingdom of God, hidden in the Old Testament, began to appear in the world through Jesus. This is why Jesus officially proclaimed the coming of the kingdom of God.

Therefore, the teaching of Mark 10:23–31 is very important for those exploring the present reality of the kingdom of God. In Mark 10:23–31, Jesus uses the phrases "to enter the kingdom of God" (10:23), "to be saved" (10:26), and "to have eternal life" (10:30) interchangeably (cf. Matt 19:23–30; Luke 18:18–30; John 3:3–5).[11] The coming of the kingdom of God has already taken place in Jesus Christ. When you believe in Jesus and have eternal life, the kingdom of God comes into your hearts.[12]

> Being asked by the Pharisees when the kingdom of God would come, he answered them, "The kingdom of God is not coming in ways that can be observed, nor will they say, 'Look, here it is!' or 'There!' for behold, the kingdom of God is in the midst of you (or within you)." (Luke 17:20–21)

When we look at these passages together (Mark 1:15; 10:23–31; John 17:3; Luke 17:20–21; 2 Cor 1:22; Rom 5:5; 10:9–10) with John 3:16–21, it helps us better understand the meaning of the present reality of the kingdom of God.

> For God so loved the world, that he gave his only Son, that whoever believes in him should not perish but have eternal life. For God did not send his Son into the world to condemn the world, but in order that the world might be saved through him. Whoever believes in him is not condemned, but whoever does

---

11. In Luke 18:18–30, Jesus uses "to inherit eternal life," "to enter the kingdom of God," and "to be saved" interchangeably when he speaks about eternal life. Jesus also emphasizes that salvation is impossible by human power, but "it is possible with God" (Luke 18:27). This means that salvation is possible only by God's grace. It became possible to enter the kingdom of God by faith alone because of Jesus Christ alone. We will continue to discuss this in vol. 2.

12. The famous parables of the sower, the seed growing, and the mustard seed (Matt 13:1–23, 31–21, 33; Luke 8:4–15; 13:21; Mark 4:1–9, 13–20) are all parable sermons about the kingdom of God. These parables deal with the kingdom of God and the gospel. Ridderbos, *Coming of the Kingdom*, 121–48, 185, 269–77.

not believe is condemned already, because he has not believed in the name of the only Son of God. And this is the judgment: the light has come into the world, and people loved the darkness rather than the light because their works were evil. For everyone who does wicked things hates the light and does not come to the light, lest his works should be exposed. But whoever does what is true comes to the light, so that it may be clearly seen that his works have been carried out in God. (John 3:16–21)

The official kingdom of God has begun with the fulfillment of Christ's redemptive work. Thus, the fulfillment of salvation and the kingdom of God have become the historic present reality to humanity (John 17:3). Whoever believes in Jesus, the eternal kingdom of God comes into their hearts. The moment you believe in Jesus, you enter the eternal kingdom of God. Just as salvation begins by faith in Jesus, so does the kingdom of God. Because of Jesus Christ, the kingdom of God has officially become the present reality.

Remember that salvation began because of Jesus Christ. Therefore, salvation does not begin when Jesus returns. That is, as to soteriology centered on the redemptive work of Jesus, the coming of Jesus Christ is "the single coming" for the completion of "once-for-all salvation."[13]

Atonement, obedience, sacrifice, propitiation, reconciliation, redemption, and ransom—all these terms point to once-for-all salvation. This means that there are not two salvations for sinners, but only one. For the purpose and completion of the "once-for-all salvation" for sinners, there is the first and second coming of Jesus. Just as the coming of the kingdom of God by Jesus' first coming has initiated the present reality of the eternal kingdom of God, salvation has already begun on this earth.

Therefore, the first coming of Jesus was to "prepare" salvation, and the second coming is to "complete" salvation.[14] The same is true of the kingdom of God. Thus, the kingdom of God has already begun and is moving towards its completion. The eternal kingdom of God has begun by the coming of Messiah, and can be known by grace alone through faith alone.[15] Accordingly, the day you believe in Jesus on this earth and enter the eternal kingdom of God becomes the most blessed day of your life.

---

13. Bavinck, *Reformed Dogmatics*, 3:248.

14. Bavinck, *Reformed Dogmatics*, 3:246–48. We can also say that Jesus comes once for the purpose of "salvation" and once for the purpose of "judgment."

15. Ridderbos, *Coming of the Kingdom*, 128.

Moreover, God connects today's words and actions of your faith with the eternity of God's kingdom. This is also the amazing work of God's grace.

C. This Age and the Age to Come

Here, we need to take a moment to look at a misunderstanding regarding the beginning of the eternal kingdom of God. The most representative misunderstanding can be found in eschatology that focuses on "When will Jesus return?" Especially, the interpretation of "this age" and "the age to come" in Matt 12:32 is a typical example of seeking the beginning of the kingdom of God.

If we interpret Matt 12:32 as referring to the first and second comings of Jesus, there does not appear to be a major problem. However, problems may arise when analyzing the beginning of the kingdom of God using this text. In other words, the issue is whether the kingdom of God has already started "in this age" or will start in "the age to come."

> And whoever speaks a word against the Son of Man will be forgiven, but whoever speaks against the Holy Spirit will not be forgiven, either in this age or in the age to come. (Matt 12:32)

For example, in biblical theology, the coming of the kingdom of God is viewed as two ages, "this age" (already) and "the age to come" (not yet), coexisting (Matt 12:32).[16] But it is not easy to understand the interpretation that these two ages exist simultaneously. Applying the idea that the two ages of the kingdom of God coexist simultaneously to this analysis may make it even more confusing because, according to this analysis, the kingdom of God *already* exists, but it has *not yet* come into existence.[17]

How, then, should we interpret Matt 12:32?

The interpretation can be helpful when viewed alongside other passages like Luke 17:21 (cf. Matt 9:15; 11:11; 13:16–17; 23:13; Mark 10:15, 25–26).

> Nor will they say, "Look, here it is!" or "There!" for behold, the kingdom of God is in the midst of you [or within you]. (Luke 17:21)

---

16. Vos, *Pauline Eschatology*, 37–38; Frame, *Systematic Theology*, 88–91. Vos sees these two ages as "existing simultaneously," calling our present existence "semi-eschatological" (*Pauline Eschatology*, 37–41).

17. We may say that we live "in the tension of the already but not yet" (Frame, *Salvation Belongs to the Lord*, 311).

Some theologians argue that passages such as Matt 12:32; Mark 1:15; and Luke 17:21 connect the beginning of the kingdom with the second coming of Jesus, claiming that the kingdom of God has not yet begun. They argue that the kingdom of God already exists now, but the kingdom of God has not yet come. Their misinterpretation stems from the belief that the kingdom of God begins at the second coming of Jesus.[18]

What is the correct interpretation of these texts?

The kingdom of God has *already* begun, but the completion of the kingdom of God is *not yet* done. Considering that the eternal kingdom of God has already begun, it can be said that the end-times have already started. Therefore, the eschatological kingdom of God has already begun, but the completion of God's kingdom has not yet been achieved.[19] In other words, the kingdom of God, which Jesus initiated, will be completed when he returns. This kingdom of God is not a kingdom established by the achievement of human efforts, but a kingdom built solely by God's grace according to the purpose of his good will.[20]

Similarly, this correct analysis of the beginning of the kingdom of God can be applied to guilt (responsibility for sins) and pollution (sinful nature). That is, the redemptive work of Jesus Christ for our responsibility for sins (guilt) has "already" been completed on this earth, but the complete removal of our pollution of sin (sinful nature) will "not yet" be accomplished until Christ returns to complete the kingdom of God in the future.[21] If we focus on the eschatological view that the beginning of the kingdom of God is centered on Jesus' return, we might fall into a complacent faith life.

Therefore, if we focus on the eschatological view that the beginning of the kingdom of God is centered on Jesus' return, we might easily fall into a life of idleness. In other words, there is a higher likelihood that we will become overly focused or absorbed on the time or the moment of Jesus Christ's return.[22] One might fall into the misconception that Jesus

---

18. We will discuss more about the present nature of the kingdom of God as it relates to this in the future.

19. Vos, *Redemptive History*, 304–16; Hoekema, *Bible and the Future*, 48–53.

20. Hoekema, *Bible and the Future*, 45.

21. Vos, *Pauline Eschatology*, 1–41; Frame, *Systematic Theology*, 90, 1093–94; Bavinck, *Reformed Dogmatics*, 4:715; 3:248; Vos, *Pauline Eschatology*, 29, 47–61, 90, 301–2. We will discuss the issues of guilt and pollution more clearly in the last part of vol. 2, ch. 3.

22. Hoekema, *Bible and the Future*, 52. In eschatology, amillennialism and postmillennialism emphasize the "already," while premillennialism emphasizes the "not yet"

will return and give us another chance. This is a very dangerous thought. This is an unbiblical and incorrect eschatology. When Jesus returns, there will never be another chance for us to live a life of faith. The kingdom of God has already begun.

Regarding eschatology, I am disappointed by this excessive debate and focus on apocalyptic events related to the millennium, as mentioned in Rev 20. Consequently, I have only briefly addressed eschatology in this context. My main argument is not to encourage anticipation of a distant end-time, but to emphasize the importance of cultivating a life that bears fruit of eternal value through living in faith and obedience to the word in the present.

In biblical eschatology, three crucial points must be remembered: (1) the return of Jesus Christ, (2) the final judgment of Jesus Christ, and (3) the preparation of believers for the final judgment. Regarding preparation, and from the perspective of personal eschatology or judgment day, it's essential to acknowledge the four pivotal blessings bestowed upon the righteous in Jesus Christ: (1) the word, (2) prayer, (3) obedience, and (4) reward. Therefore, endowed with these four blessings, we must consciously choose to live by faith in Jesus daily, guided by the word of God, as every word spoken and deed done will be accounted for before God. We will explore these topics throughout these volumes.

If we focus solely on eschatology, it is easy to become absorbed on the "when" and overly focused on the signs or the timing of Jesus Christ's return. While waiting for the day when Jesus returns is good, instead of looking at eschatology separately, if we see it as "a part of soteriology" centered on the doctrine of justification, we can turn our eyes to the already-begun kingdom of God and find it easier to apply the word to our lives.[23]

As we saw earlier, the eternal kingdom of God has already begun and is moving toward completion as we wait for Jesus' return, and it also currently exists within us in a real way. The redemptive work of Jesus Christ, who initiated the eternal kingdom of God, connects justification

---

(Frame, *Systematic Theology*, 1094). There is a history of people falling into wrong heresies due to being overly absorbed in eschatology, focusing only on calculating the time or the date of Christ's return, asking, "When is Christ coming?" Thus, it is not desirable to focus solely on eschatology and emphasize it exclusively.

23. Bavinck, *Reformed Dogmatics*, 3:248; Vos, *Pauline Eschatology*, 29, 47–61, 90, 301–2. We should focus on how to imitate the image of Christ, instead of looking at the date of his return. Cf. Frame, *Systematic Theology*, 1095. We will look at guilt and pollution more clearly in the last part of vol 2, ch. 3.

with salvation, eternal life, sanctification, and glorification. Furthermore, the perfect obedience of Jesus also encompasses salvation, eternal life, sanctification, and glorification. All the things that the faithful Jesus has done for us are eternally unchanging. Therefore, the beginning and completion of the eternal kingdom of God can never be separated, and "this age" and "the age to come" are interconnected as one in Jesus Christ.

When we view the coming of the kingdom of God as Jesus' redemptive work for a single salvation, it becomes more fitting for Christians to apply the word to the present reality of their lives. This is because we become aware of the importance of the present reality of the kingdom of God. If we view the life of a Christian within the broader framework of soteriology centered on the doctrine of justification, we also realize that our faith response and obedience to the knowledge of Jesus Christ are absolutely necessary. As a citizen of the kingdom of God, my faith response and obedience now hold eternal value.[24]

As we will examine in *The Kingdom of Justification*, the doctrine of justification connects the issues of God's eternity and God's righteousness through the work of Christ. Therefore, the doctrine of justification connects the redemptive work of Jesus with the coming of the kingdom and helps us to properly see the starting point of our faith life. Jesus, by fully obeying the word according to God's righteousness, firmly established the foundation of the eternal kingdom of God (John 17:4–5).

D. Jesus Christ, the King of the Kingdom of God

Now let's take a look at Jesus, who is the King reigning over the kingdom of God. Jesus, the Representative of the new covenant, holds the offices of prophet, priest, and king.[25] Among these, the fact that Jesus actually became the King of the kingdom of God is a very important topic.[26] Jesus, who possesses both divinity and humanity, came to this earth in a human body and became the King of the world, Israel, and all nations.[27] However, Jesus, who possesses both divinity and humanity, began to reign over the kingdom of God after ascending to heaven and sitting on the

---

24. Hoekema, *Bible and the Future*, 52–53.

25. Frame, *Salvation Belongs to the Lord*, 146–51. Among the three offices, here, we will focus on the office of the king in order to examine the characteristics of the kingdom of God.

26. Frame, *Systematic Theology*, 91.

27. Frame, *Systematic Theology*, 92.

heavenly throne. Jesus has been ruling over the world since ascending to the heavenly throne (Matt 28:18-20).

The works that Jesus did before ascending to the throne as the King of the kingdom of God are astonishing. Jesus, who is God, came in a human body and saved the kingdom of God through an immense sacrifice. Jesus became the Redeemer and King by taking on all the sins of the people of the kingdom of God.[28] To be sure, the shocking news that the One who would ascend to the heavenly throne as the King of the kingdom of God laid down his own life is also the most blessed good news for us.

And Jesus, who possesses both divinity and humanity, ascended to the heavenly throne after his death on the cross and resurrection. He is now reigning as the King of the kingdom of God (Matt 25:31; 28:18-20; Heb 8:1; 12:2: Rev 21:5). This signifies the present reality of Jesus as the King of the kingdom of God. Recognizing and acknowledging the present reality of Jesus as the King of the kingdom of God can greatly benefit our faith journey as well. The Bible says in Heb 12:2 to fix our eyes on Jesus, who "is seated at the right hand of the throne of God."

> Looking to Jesus, the founder and perfecter of our faith, who for the joy that was set before him endured the cross, despising the shame, and is seated at the right hand of the throne of God. (Heb 12:2)

This passage encourages us to look to the Lord because Jesus became our Savior who loves us (Rom 8:35-39). Another reason we should look to Jesus is that he is the omniscient, omnipotent, omnipresent, and unchangeable Lord. Furthermore, we should look to Jesus because he has the supreme authority to determine what is right and wrong for all things in this world.[29] That is, God the Son has both the sufficient wisdom and the power to rule over all the things in the universe and the kingdom of God with this supreme authority.

Although Jesus is the Creator who created all things by his own power, now possessing both divinity and humanity, he governs the world. He also works with the Holy Spirit not only in carrying out his earthly ministry but also in advocating for us and ruling over the kingdom of God (1 John 2:1; John 14:16-17). Thus, as children of God, we must

---

28. Ridderbos, *Coming of the Kingdom*, 3-8, 27-36; Frame, *Systematic Theology*, 91-93.

29. Frame, *Doctrine of God*, 80. Only God has absolute authority in all areas of life. Through this supreme authority, he speaks his words of salvation. See also Frame, *Doctrine of God*, 80-102.

believe in not only Jesus' redemptive work but also in Jesus as the King who rules over the kingdom of God. Believing in Jesus as the King of the kingdom of God is also crucial to our life of faith. Therefore, Heb 12:2 encourages us to believe in and look to Jesus as both our Redeemer and the King of the kingdom of God.

In other words, Jesus, who possesses supreme "authority" and ruling "power," governs the kingdom of God and has the ability to "be present" (presence) with the people of God in a real and practical way. Jesus has the absolute "authority" and "power" to fulfill the promises of the covenant that God has made, as well as the power to be in a covenantal presence with the kingdom of God (Matt 28:18–20).[30] If we believe in this, we can trust that God will also keep all the promises he has made.

> And Jesus came and said to them, "All authority in heaven and on earth has been given to me. Go therefore and make disciples of all nations, baptizing them in the name of the Father and of the Son and of the Holy Spirit, teaching them to observe all that I have commanded you. And behold, I am with you always, to the end of the age." (Matt 28:18–20)

Jesus, the King of the kingdom of God, came to this earth to save his people and to initiate the eternal kingdom of God, and he will come again to complete it. Through the accomplishment of the new covenant by Jesus, a new way of life has been opened for the people of the eternal kingdom of God.[31] And the work of the Holy Spirit, who reveals that Jesus Christ is the King of the kingdom of God, has already begun.[32]

This is the meaning of the present reality of the kingdom of God. When Jesus Christ comes again, the kingdom of God will be completed.[33] Until he returns, the kingdom must appear on earth through the lives of God's children. The Holy Spirit enables us to manifest the kingdom of God through our lives on this earth as we proclaim the gospel, obey God's word, and live according to the word.

The life that manifests the kingdom of God is a life that reveals God's righteousness (the righteousness of Jesus) as it is presented in the gospel (Rom 1:17; 3:21–22), and a life that becomes the righteousness of God itself (2 Cor 2:15; 5:21; Eph 5:8–9). This is a life that seeks the kingdom of

---

30. Frame, *Doctrine of God*, 80–102.
31. Ridderbos, *Coming of the Kingdom*, 234–36.
32. Frame, *Systematic Theology*, 99.
33. Ridderbos, *Coming of the Kingdom*, 47–56.

God and his righteousness, and it is a life that brings glory to God (Matt 6:33; 1 Cor 6:20; 10:31).

> But seek first the kingdom of God and his righteousness, and all these things will be added to you. (Matt 6:33)

> So, whether you eat or drink, or whatever you do, do all to the glory of God. (1 Cor 10:31)

In conclusion, Scripture divides the ages into this present age and the age to come from the perspective of the kingdom of God and redemptive history.[34] However, Jesus' preaching about the kingdom of God binds these two ages into a single "unity" (Matt 12:32).[35] Jesus, who came into human history, unified these two ages by accomplishing the redemptive work for sinners. The kingdom of God is not divided into two separated parts based on the first and second comings of Jesus. As we have seen so far, the kingdom of God is available now to those who believe in Jesus Christ. And the eternal kingdom of God can be manifested in the world through the lives of God's children through the works of the Holy Spirit.

The gospel is the good news that through the perfect obedience of Jesus Christ, the Representative of the new covenant who came to this world according to the Father's will, the kingdom of God has been restored.[36] In other words, God worked dynamically through his own power by sending Jesus Christ to restore his kingdom.[37] Therefore, through Jesus Christ's redemptive work, the kingdom of God has appeared in the glory of God. Through the kingdom of God that Jesus Christ restored, the "glory of God" has been manifested in an absolute, transcendent, actual, and effective way.[38]

God continues to be glorified through Jesus. Jesus Christ saved the kingdom of God and rebuilt it, and through the work of the Holy Spirit, he continues to expand that kingdom even now. Jesus Christ spreads the kingdom of God through his children, who proclaim it to the world and expand it. God's children can manifest the kingdom of God in the world

---

34. Frame, *Systematic Theology*, 88–91. "For then he would have had to suffer repeatedly since the foundation of the world. But as it is, he has appeared once for all at the end of the ages to put away sin by the sacrifice of himself" (Heb 9:26).
35. Ridderbos, *Coming of the Kingdom*, 135.
36. Ridderbos, *Coming of the Kingdom*, 155–74.
37. Cf. Frame, *Systematic Theology*, 87; Ridderbos, *Coming of the Kingdom*, 24–27.
38. Ridderbos, *Coming of the Kingdom*, 24–25, 35.

when they listen to and keep God's word by faith, bearing its fruit with perseverance in their lives.

> As for that in the good soil, they are those who, hearing the word, hold it fast in an honest and good heart, and bear fruit with patience. (Luke 8:15)

The kingdom of God is the great divine work of God, which is "fulfilled" and "consummated" in Jesus Christ within human history.[39] In other words, the kingdom of God has been established through the redemptive work of Jesus Christ, who came as the Messiah.[40] So, the kingdom of God is a kingdom of those who believe in Jesus Christ and become the children of God. The kingdom of God is eternal.

2. THE KINGDOM OF GOD AND THE CHURCH

Let's look at the relationship between the kingdom of God and the church. From the perspective of redemptive history, the kingdom of God and the church in which God's children gather are "identical" in Jesus Christ.[41] So, on the one hand, the church is also the best place where the kingdom of God can be manifested to the world on this earth. On the other hand, the church must also become the place that offers the greatest hope and blessings to the world.

> That he worked in Christ when he raised him from the dead and seated him at his right hand in the heavenly places, far above all rule and authority and power and dominion, and above every name that is named, not only in this age but also in the one to come. And he put all things under his feet and gave him as head over all things to the church, which is his body, the fullness of him who fills all in all. (Eph 1:20–23)

God has established churches on this earth as a base for the kingdom of God. No one can deny the existence of these churches today. Jesus, the head of the church, is the foundation of the kingdom of God in the Old Testament and the church in the New Testament (Matt 16:18–19; Eph 1:20–23). And the foundation of the New Testament church was prepared through the nation of Israel, which was a foreshadowing of

---

39. Ridderbos, *Coming of the Kingdom*, 354; Frame, *Systematic Theology*, 87–91.
40. Ridderbos, *Coming of the Kingdom*, 352–56; Frame, *Systematic Theology*, 87.
41. Ridderbos, *Coming of the Kingdom*, 354–56.

the kingdom of God, and through God's covenants.[42] However, God has given Jesus Christ, the Messiah and covenant Representative, to the kingdom of God and the church by grace alone.[43] Thus, the people of God's kingdom and the church are all the people of God's covenant.[44] And the church, founded upon the fulfillment of the Old Testament covenants by Jesus and the foundation of the apostles and prophets, is "the people of God in all ages."[45]

> Built on the foundation of the apostles and prophets, Christ Jesus himself being the cornerstone. (Eph 2:20)

A. Is there a Relationship Between the Eternal Kingdom of God and the Church?

Without a doubt, God calls a new people of God through the Messiah into the church, continuing "the organized covenant relationship" that existed between God and the people of Israel through the church.[46] God has firmly united the kingdom of God and the Church through the same covenant relationship with one Messiah. Therefore, in terms of redemptive history, the kingdom of God and the church are one in Jesus Christ. The eternal kingdom of God has already appeared in history as "a present reality" under the name of the church.[47] Therefore, now on earth, the church can manifest the kingdom of God.

As we saw before, Jesus, who reigns as King of the kingdom of God, has already appeared "in this age" according to the word of the covenant, and the coming age has begun in Christ for the believers.[48] Through Jesus Christ, the eternal kingdom of God has been initiated in the New

---

42. Ridderbos, *Coming of the Kingdom*, 353–54.
43. Ridderbos, *Coming of the Kingdom*, 347–49, 351–54.
44. Ridderbos, *Coming of the Kingdom*, 341–42, 353–54. In Matt 18, Jesus changes his subject from the kingdom of God (Matt 18:1–14) to the church (Matt 18:15–20), connecting the kingdom and the church as one under the same heavenly Father. (363–69).
45. Frame, *Systematic Theology*, 1019. Cf. Ridderbos, *Coming of the Kingdom*, 353–58.
46. Ridderbos, *Coming of the Kingdom*, 353–54.
47. Ridderbos, *Coming of the Kingdom*, 355, 374–75.
48. Frame, *Systematic Theology*, 89; Ridderbos, *Coming of the Kingdom*, 81–97, 368.

Testament church. Therefore, the kingdom of God and the church were established directly by Jesus (Eph 1:20–23; 3:10–11; 5:26–27).

> And he put all things under his feet and gave him as head over all things to the church, which is his body, the fullness of him who fills all in all. (Eph 1:22–23)

In Christ, the kingdom of God has begun through Christ's redemptive work, and "the church has the keys to the kingdom of God" (Matt 16:19).[49] Indeed, the New Testament church, which is called to manifest the kingdom of God on earth, has not always walked an easy path. In the book of Revelation, the Bible teaches that the church of God in this world will go through many persecutions, tribulations, and hardships. In Rev 1:6, Scripture introduces us as "a kingdom, priests":

> And [to him who] made us a kingdom, priests to his God and Father, to him be glory and dominion forever and ever. Amen.

To be sure, to consider these passages (Rev 1:6, 9; 5:10) alongside the seven churches that represent the church in every age (Rev 2:1—3:22) can be helpful. Yes, that is correct. The book of Revelation equates God's children with the kingdom of God and the churches. All churches throughout the ages are a manifestation of the kingdom of God that has come to earth.

In Rev 12–19, five enemies of Christ who symbolically seek to destroy the church, which represent the kingdom of God in all ages, are presented.[50] These five enemies always fail in their attempts to destroy the church throughout the ages. In every era, the church triumphs according to the promise of Christ. The triune God is always with the churches purchased by the precious blood of Jesus, protecting them through the work of the Holy Spirit. As Christ promises, the churches in Jesus win battles in all ages.[51]

Jesus, King of love, continues to save his people and, even after his ascension, continues to expand the eternal kingdom of God through the church. God works through the Holy Spirit to manifest and expand the kingdom of God on earth, and Jesus will come again to complete this

---

49. Frame, *Systematic Theology*, 89.

50. Christ's five enemies are "the dragon, the sea-born beast, the earth-born beast or false prophet, the harlot Babylon, and the men who bear the mark of the beast" Hendriksen, *More Than Conquerors*, 166.

51. Hendriksen, *More Than Conquerors*, 166–210.

kingdom. Revelation 21–22 depicts the eternal kingdom of God as the victorious church in the image of the bride, resembling the likeness of Christ the Bridegroom.[52]

> Then I saw a new heaven and a new earth, for the first heaven and the first earth had passed away, and the sea was no more. And I saw the holy city, new Jerusalem, coming down out of heaven from God, prepared as a bride adorned for her husband. And I heard a loud voice from the throne saying, "Behold, the dwelling place of God is with man. He will dwell with them, and they will be his people, and God himself will be with them as their God. He will wipe away every tear from their eyes, and death shall be no more, neither shall there be mourning, nor crying, nor pain anymore, for the former things have passed away." (Rev 21:1–4)

Therefore, the gospel is the good news that announces the opening of the new era of God's kingdom through the church, which is the "great turning point in history" in every age.[53] In this respect, Matt 28:19–20 also announces that a new era has begun under the name of the church as the kingdom of God.[54] The eschatological kingdom of God has begun with the church. In this world and in heaven, the parousia (presence) of Jesus Christ, who embodies both divinity and humanity, is a manifestation as the eternal King of the kingdom of God.[55] The eternal kingdom of God, initiated by Jesus Christ, is governed by his word from the throne of heaven where he ascended after his resurrection. And Christ is leading the church to eternal victory (Heb 8:1–2; 12:1–2).

The Bible combines sixty-six pieces to draw one big picture, by putting a set of events together. The Bible connects numerous events in human history and presents one big picture of the kingdom of God.[56] In this regard, Acts 2 is also an amazing event in which the Holy Spirit came upon the church, which is the kingdom of God. This event demonstrates the relationship between eternal life and entering the kingdom of God. Therefore, the event of the coming of the Holy Spirit signifies the

52. Kline, *Images of the Spirit*, 49.

53. Ridderbos, *Coming of the Kingdom*, 465.

54. "Go therefore and make disciples of all nations, baptizing them in the name of the Father and of the Son and of the Holy Spirit, teaching them to observe all that I have commanded you. And behold, I am with you always, to the end of the age" (Matt 28:19–20).

55. Frame, *Systematic Theology*, 882–83, 889–913; Ridderbos, *Coming of the Kingdom*, 465–72, 505–27.

56. Ridderbos, *Coming of the Kingdom*, 520–27.

beginning of the entrance into the kingdom of God and the life of the kingdom of God through faith in Jesus Christ for sinners. The Holy Spirit continues to teach the church through the Bible, guiding it on the path of growth to become more like Jesus (2 Tim 3:16–17; Rev 2:1—3:22).

> And I assign to you, as my Father assigned to me, a kingdom. (Luke 22:29)

This passage says that Jesus entrusted the mission of representing the kingdom of God to his disciples. This mission is also given to the body of Christ, which is the church (Matt 28:19–20; Eph 1:20–23; 2:20). Therefore, from the perspective of the kingdom of God, the life of Christians within the church is very important.

Now, even when facing trials and temptations in their own lives, God's children have the responsibility to fight the good fight with faith to show the kingdom of God in the world. The Holy Spirit helps God's children who fulfill this responsibility. However, it is our responsibility. In other words, this responsibility is always to rely on the work of the Holy Spirit and live by faith regarding the gift of God's sovereign salvation and the gift of love. It is also our responsibility to live according to God's pleasing will, following the Holy Spirit who works within us.

> Therefore, my beloved, as you have always obeyed, so now, not only as in my presence but much more in my absence, work out your own salvation with fear and trembling, for it is God who works in you, both to will and to work for his good pleasure. (Phil 2:12–13)

B. Is Living in the Kingdom of God on Earth Possible?

We have seen so far that the present reality of God's kingdom is manifested in the world through God's children and the church. The life of God's kingdom practically begins with the work of the Holy Spirit at the moment of belief in this world (John 3:15–16; 17:3).[57] Now, God's children on earth can gather together in the church to worship God and receive nurturing for the life of God's kingdom. After Jesus ascended to the throne of heaven, he rules the world and leads the church to victory (Heb 8:1; 12:2; Phil 2:9–11; Matt 28:18–20; 1 Cor 15:24–28; Eph 1:20–23).[58]

---

57. Bavinck, *Reformed Dogmatics*, 3:340; 4:270, 701.
58. Vos, *Pauline Eschatology*, 246, 259–60; Frame, *Systematic Theology*, 93, 98.

Jesus helps God's children on this earth. Now, the life of the kingdom of God on earth is a life lived by faith in Jesus Christ. Therefore, whoever believes the truth of the gospel and has eternal life begins his or her life in the kingdom of God on this earth.

> And this is eternal life, that they know you, the only true God, and Jesus Christ whom you have sent. (John 17:3)

This verse says that eternal life is determined at the moment anyone believes and accepts Jesus Christ. This also means that the kingdom of God begins in their hearts as the Holy Spirit comes with the word of God when they accept him (John 14:20; 15:7; Rom 5:5; 2 Cor 1:22).[59]

Thus, the personal presence of God cannot be separated from his word and the work of the Holy Spirit (John 1:1–2; Heb 4:12).[60] The Holy Spirit coming upon our hearts is the coming of the King of kings, Jesus (John 14:20; 15:7; Eph 3:17). Moreover, the coming of Jesus, the King of the kingdom of God, is the coming of the kingdom of God (Matt 16:28; Luke 19:38; 1 Tim 6:15; Rev 11:15, 17; 15:3; 17:14; 19:16). Therefore, the life of faith of God's children is a life of living in the kingdom of God, a life of living with Jesus Christ, the King of kings (Matt 28:18–20). The Bible teaches that those who know the truth of the gospel need to be aware of living before God. We can summarize our earthly life in the kingdom of God into three aspects, connected with eternity.[61]

First, God's children are those who believe the present reality of the kingdom of God, as highlighted in Heb 12. The book of Hebrews reveals the direct relationship between the kingdom of God and the life of believers. Hebrews 12 highlights the present reality of the kingdom of God and introduces Jesus Christ as the author and perfecter of our faith. Hebrews 12:2 connects "such a great a cloud of witnesses" in Heb 12:1 with those who entered the kingdom of God by faith in Heb 11. The kingdom of God in Heb 12:22 ("the city of the living God, the heavenly Jerusalem")

---

59. "And who has also put his seal on us and given us his Spirit in our hearts as a guarantee" (2 Cor 1:22).

60. Scripture teaches us about "a speaking God," that "the word of God" is synonymous with "God" (Frame, *Doctrine of the Word*, 48–49). "Where the word of God is, there is God's Spirit." Therefore, "the personal presence of God" and "the word of God" cannot be separated (Frame, *Doctrine of the Word*, 137, 140).

61. In the third volume, *Kingdom of Faith*, we will examine our life in the kingdom of God on earth from the perspective of faith.

refers to the place that you, believers, have "come to" (*proserchomai*, προσέρχομαι) by faith.[62]

Further, this kingdom of God is "a kingdom that cannot be shaken" (Heb 12:28), which those who have believed in the Mediator of the new covenant have entered.[63] This kingdom is the eternal kingdom of God that has been restored through the perfect obedience of "Jesus, the mediator of a new covenant" (Heb 12:24). As we saw before, this kingdom can be entered by faith alone.

> But you have come to Mount Zion and to the city of the living God, the heavenly Jerusalem, and to innumerable angels in festal gathering, and to the assembly of the firstborn who are enrolled in heaven, and to God, the judge of all, and to the spirits of the righteous made perfect, and to Jesus, the mediator of a new covenant, and to the sprinkled blood that speaks a better word than the blood of Abel. (Heb 12:22-24)

In this passage, the righteous are those who are justified by faith in Jesus through his perfect obedience on the cross and to the word.[64] Moreover, the righteous who are justified only by the grace of God alone continuously "come to" (*proserchomai*, προσέρχομαι) God by faith and live before him (Heb 10:19-22, 38-39).[65] They live by faith in the word of God alone. Therefore, Heb 12:22-24 speaks of the present reality of the kingdom of God through the children of God who are justified in Jesus by grace alone.

In Matt 6:33, Jesus says, "But seek first the kingdom of God and his righteousness," urging us to make the kingdom of God the supreme goal in our lives.[66] As we saw before, this means that we can show God's king-

---

62. The verb "to come to" (*proserchomai*, προσέρχομαι) in Heb 1:18 and 22 is mainly used in the book of Hebrews in relation to God or Jesus Christ. This basically means "to come to God by faith": to come to God through Christ by faith (10:22); to come to God by faith (11:6); to come to God through Christ (7:25); to come to God (Mount Sinai and God [12:18]; Mount Zion and Jesus Christ [12:22-23]); the throne of grace (4:16); the sanctuary with sacrifice (10:1) (Bavinck, *Reformed Dogmatics*, 4:226, 701; *TDNT* 6:684; *EDNT* 3:164; BDAG 878).

63. "Therefore let us be grateful for receiving a kingdom that cannot be shaken, and thus let us offer to God acceptable worship, with reverence and awe, for our God is a consuming fire" (Heb 12:28-29).

64. For this, refer to vol. 2, ch. 2, "The Condition of Justification: The Perfect Obedience of Jesus Christ."

65. Bavinck, *Reformed Dogmatics*, 4:226, 701; *TDNT* 6:684; *EDNT* 3:164; BDAG 878.

66. Frame, *Systematic Theology*, 98. In Matt 5:1-11, Jesus teaches about Christian

dom to the world through our life of obedience to God's word. Therefore, the Great Commission is given to us to make disciples of all people in the world, teaching them to observe all that Jesus has commanded us, as he teaches in Matt 28:19-20. Those who know this Great Commission are those who recognize the present reality of this kingdom and live by faith in God's word alone.

Second, God's children have received the eternal word. The kingdom of God is established by an eternal word of God that no one can change.[67] This kingdom is established on the eternal word of the gospel, for Jesus performed the redemptive work for sinners according to the perfect and eternal word.

As we will see in volume 2, chapter 2, the gospel is based on the perfect obedience of Jesus Christ in accordance with the word of the covenant. In other words, the righteousness of sinners is based on the perfect righteousness that Jesus obtained through his perfect obedience.[68] This means that because Jesus achieved his perfect obedience according to the word of the covenant, his word becomes the assurance of our faith. God has given this word of the gospel to the children of God (Acts 8:4; 15:7; Eph 1:13; Col 1:5; 1 Pet 1:25).

> But the word of the Lord remains forever. And this word is the good news that was preached to you. (1 Pet 1:25)

As such, the word of the gospel that God has given to his children is the eternal word of promise. And this word of the gospel continuously defends God's children even if they commit sinful actions due to the pollution of sin while living on this earth.[69] Because Jesus fulfilled his redemptive work according to the word of God's covenant, this word of the gospel can continuously defend their sins on this earth and throughout eternity (Heb 10:19-22, 38-39). With the word of God, the Holy Spirit also continues to intercede for us with the eternal advocacy of our status as God's children.

---

life in the kingdom of God.

67. We will discuss more about the word of God in ch. 4 of this volume.

68. For the perfect obedience of Jesus, we will explore further in ch. 7 of this volume.

69. Bavinck, *Reformed Dogmatics*, 4:226. Here, the "sinful actions due to their pollution of sin" means the "actions of sinful nature" because of the pollution of sin. The sinful habits of God's children caused by sinful nature lead them to sin before God. However, we should always remember that God forgives our sins and pays the price for our guilt in Jesus. For the meaning of guilt and pollution, please refer to the last section of vol. 2, ch. 3.

With the knowledge of the word about justification, the Holy Spirit also removes "alienation, wrath and curse" caused by sin, and leads us into "a relation of peace with God."[70] The Holy Spirit enables believers to trust in God's grace through his word (Rom 8:26–30, 31–39), for the Spirit knows that the thoughts and actions of God's children are still "stained with sin," but he sees them as righteous only by grace through faith in Jesus Christ.[71] God's children can boldly go to Jesus through Christ's righteousness when they live on this earth (1 Pet 2:4–12).[72] They can boldly go to God because of their faith in God's word, even when their thoughts and works are still stained with sin.

> As you come to [*proserchomai*, προσέρχομαι] him, a living stone rejected by men but in the sight of God chosen and precious. (1 Pet 2:4)

After Jesus' ascension, the kingdom of God continues through God's children who live by faith in the living word of God. In other words, the work of God is still being continued through the citizens of the kingdom who live by faith in the living word of God.[73] In Jesus, God has justified sinners and given them the gift of the eternal word as their supreme guide in this life. Therefore, God giving his word to his children is an amazing grace of God.

Third, obeying the eternal word of God (1 Pet 1:23; Heb 4:12) is an eternal blessing for God's children. Obedience to God's word has eternal value because God has promised an eternal blessing for a life of obedience to his word on this earth. In fact, obedience to God's word is the responsibility, privilege, and blessing of God's children.[74]

It is truly amazing that the invisible God has given us the visible word, the Bible. We can make the word of God in Scripture the standard for all areas of our lives. In this way, the Bible enables us to be free from the wrong knowledge of the world.

In addition to giving us the Bible, the merciful God also delights in those who obey his word. In other words, when we encounter his word

---

70. Murray, *Collected Writings*, 2:220.

71. Bavinck, *Reformed Dogmatics*, 4:226. Here, "stained with sin" means "polluted by sin." For further details, please see the final part of vol. 2, ch. 3.

72. *TDNT* 6:684; *EDNT* 3:164; *BDAG* 878.

73. Frame, *Systematic Theology*, 93.

74. We will discuss in detail believing in and obeying God's word in vol. 3.

by faith, God encounters us. This is also a work of God's grace where the Holy Spirit helps us in our weaknesses.

> Likewise the Spirit helps us in our weakness. For we do not know what to pray for as we ought, but the Spirit himself intercedes for us with groanings too deep for words. And he who searches hearts knows what is the mind of the Spirit, because the Spirit intercedes for the saints according to the will of God. (Rom 8:26–27)

Even when we don't know what to do in our lives, the Holy Spirit helps us encounter the invisible God through the word of his promise. In other words, even when difficulties come our way, if we obey God's word, the Holy Spirit will make the word our strength and comfort, and it will become a breakthrough in our lives (Rom 8:26–27, 28–39; 2 Cor 5:14; 1 John 2:18–19). This is the gracious work of the Spirit. This is the blessed time when the Holy Spirit enables us to meet God by obeying his word. Once we meet the God of love through the work of the Holy Spirit, it becomes a blessed time to love Jesus and love his words through our obedience to the word.

And then, God's children who have received Jesus' love in the kingdom of God begin to obey his word because they love Jesus. In Jesus Christ, these children of God obey the word by faith even in things that the people of the world consider insignificant. And they gradually come to understand what the blessings of obeying the word are. These people who obey the word and pray with vigilance in the Spirit live their lives with the joy in the Lord and give glory to God (1 Cor 10:31; 2 Cor 5:14; Eph 5:22—6:9; 6:19–20; Rom 12:12; Phil 4:4). As they come to know the blessings of obedience to the word, they begin to work for the Lord with his love whatever they do, becoming more and more aware of his love.

> So, whether you eat or drink, or whatever you do, do all to the glory of God. (1 Cor 10:31)

> For the love of Christ controls us, because we have concluded this: that one has died for all, therefore all have died. (2 Cor 5:14)

> Rejoice in hope, be patient in tribulation, be constant in prayer. (Rom 12:12)

> Rejoice in the Lord always; again I will say, rejoice. (Phil 4:4)

> Whatever you do, work heartily, as for the Lord and not for men. (Col 3:23)

These passages speak about living in obedience to God's word. In other words, the Holy Spirit bestows various benefits and blessings upon the Christian life of obedience to God's word. When we obey the word, it becomes a source of thanksgiving, joy, and peace in our lives.[75] There are no greater blessings for us on earth than this. As we obey the word and pray, we become more and more like the holy image of God (1 Tim 4:5). God uses this blessed life to manifest his kingdom in the world and receive glory.

If we were to express the kingdom of God that will be presented in the *Justification and the Kingdom of God* volumes in a figure, it would be as figure 1-A below. In *The Kingdom of the Covenant*, volume 1, we will discuss the word of the covenant, the foundational law of the kingdom of God. In *The Kingdom of Justification*, we will explore the conditions for entering the kingdom of God. Finally, in *The Kingdom of Faith*, we will examine the lives of citizens within the kingdom of God. When discussing the kingdom of God, we cannot overlook the covenant, justification, and faith.

Figure 1-A The Kingdom of God

The Kingdom of the Covenant

The Kingdom of Justification   The Kingdom of Faith

---

75. Thanksgiving (Phil 4:6; Col 2:7; 3:15, 16; 1 Thess 5:18), joy (Rom 15:13; 2 Cor 7:4; Col 1:11; 1 John 1:4), peace (Rom 1:7; 2:10; 14:17; 15:13; 2 Cor 13:11; Phil 4:7, 9; 2 Thess 3:16; Heb 12:11; 2 Pet 3:14; Rev 1:5).

2

The Kingdom of the Covenant

IN THE PREVIOUS CHAPTER, we briefly looked at the characteristics of the kingdom of God and its relationship with the church. Now, here we will look at the kingdom of God from the perspective of the covenant.

1. GOD GIVES US HIS COVENANT

God's kingdom is the kingdom of the covenant. The kingdom of God is the kingdom established by God, who always keeps the covenant until the end. Therefore, the kingdom of God is a kingdom established in the covenantal relationship between God and humanity, and it is distinct from the kingdoms of the world. In this way, God's covenant becomes the foundation of the kingdom of God. The covenantal parties of the kingdom of God are established by God himself, and God, who is the covenantal party of the kingdom of God, directly establishes the kingdom and supplies everything necessary for his people according to the covenantal promise.

> So shall my word be that goes out from my mouth; it shall not return to me empty, but it shall accomplish that which I purpose, and shall succeed in the thing for which I sent it. (Isa 55:11)

God is the One who made the covenant according to his own will and keeps the covenant that he spoke, for he is the One who always fulfills his promises (Isa 55:11).[1] According to the covenant, God protects the people of the kingdom of God and saves them only by grace in accordance with the promise of the covenant.[2] We can summarize the kingdom of God from the perspective of the covenant into three brief points.

First, the kingdom of God is established by the word of the covenant.[3] God is the One who speaks. The speaking God speaks to us through the written word. Only the Bible speaks of God. The righteousness, or justice, of God as revealed in the Bible establishes the ultimate standard of judgment between good and evil.[4] God is the Lord in all areas of our lives. Therefore, God's word is the only supreme authority in every area of life. The word of God has the characteristics of God's sovereign attributes of control, authority, and presence. When we encounter God's word, we encounter God.

Second, the word of the covenant is God's law to govern his kingdom.[5] God's covenants set up the best structure for "the normative constitution" for the people of his kingdom throughout human history.[6] And the kingdom of God has been maintained by the laws and rules established by God through the covenantal word. Scripture shows how the kingdom of God has been governed and continuously developed through God's covenantal words with Adam, Noah, Abraham, Moses, David, and Jesus Christ.

Third, the word of the covenant is God's standard of life for words and deeds in his kingdom.[7] Without the word of the covenant, we cannot know how to live on this earth. God desires that those who enter into a covenant relationship with him believe and obey his word of the covenant by faith, living according to that covenant (Heb 11:6). The word, in this way, becomes the supreme standard of life for God's kingdom people. But the Ten Commandments or the law in the Old Testament cannot guarantee the salvation of sinner, but only guide them to the path of salvation to

---

1. Kline, *Structure of Biblical Authority*, 114–26.
2. Kline, *Structure of Biblical Authority*, 124–27.
3. Regarding the word of God, please refer to this vol., ch. 4, "The Word of God."
4. For the righteousness of God, please refer to this vol., ch. 3, "The Righteousness of the Eternal God."
5. Kline, *Structure of Biblical Authority*, 58–62, 64, 68–75, 80, 88–90, 101, 104–5, 150–51, 158–59, 192–93, 197.
6. Frame, *Systematic Theology*, 87.
7. Kline, *Structure of Biblical Authority*, 101–2, 109, 129–30, 168–71.

become the people of God's kingdom (Gal 3:24).[8] Scripture says that only those who have received God's grace can become those who love him and keep his commandments (Exod 20:6; John 14:15).[9] Those who accept and believe in the love of Jesus Christ obey the word of God by faith.

> If you love me, you will keep my commandments. (John 14:15)

A. God's Covenants

God established his kingdom through the word of the covenant. The stories in the Bible are stories of the covenant between God and humanity. The Bible develops a story centered on the word of God's covenant. As the Bible introduces the kingdom of God, it shows the story of "What has God done for us?" at the center. In chapter 1, the kingdom of God was introduced. Here, we will look at the kingdom of God from the perspective of the covenant.

The entire biblical narrative is deeply connected to historical events such as creation, fall, and redemption. The story of the Bible is the story of the restoration of the relationship between fallen humankind and God through the redemptive work of Jesus Christ. Understanding this story between God and humanity is very important in understanding the core of the Bible. Missing this core and viewing the Bible story as a collection of human theories can make one fall into a wrong interpretation of the Bible. The Bible is composed of one story that portrays the process of God establishing the eternal kingdom of God, centered on Jesus Christ. In fact, the Bible story is a covenantal story in which God establishes his eternal kingdom.[10]

Moreover, the covenants in the Bible provide great help in interpreting the whole Bible as one big picture. The covenants in the Bible also explain well the close relationship and mutual obligations between God and humans.[11] The covenants in the Bible play a crucial

---

8. Kline, *Structure of Biblical Authority*, 127.
9. Kline, *Structure of Biblical Authority*, 127–28.
10. Kline, *Structure of Biblical Authority*, 75.
11. The Hebrew noun for "covenant" (*berît*, בְּרִית) used in the Old Testament refers to "a contract based on bilateral blood covenant" (cutting a covenant) between two parties. It helps us look at the blood covenant of the Messiah Jesus Christ, the Representative of the new covenant. The New Testament term for "covenant" (*diathēkē*, διαθήκη) retains the meaning of the Old Testament's covenant but is also used at times to mean a will or testament left by a parent to their children (BDB 136–37; *TLOT* 256–66;

role in understanding the relationship between the kingdom of God and the redemptive work of Jesus Christ.

In other words, the covenants in the Bible play a crucial role in explaining how the triune God prepared and accomplished the redemption of sinners through Jesus Christ throughout human history. They serve as foundational pillars in understanding how God worked and brought about salvation. The covenants also serve as guides to understanding the fundamental purpose of God's creation.

Therefore, we need to understand that there are two covenant parties from a covenantal perspective in the Bible. They are "the Lord of the covenant" and "the covenant servant."[12] Now we can summarize the covenantal core of these two biblical parties into three main points.

First, the biblical covenants provide the essential legal structure that sustains the kingdom of God. For the kingdom to exist, there must be a covenant between the king (God) and the people.[13]

Second, the biblical covenants bind the "diversity" of God's promise messages throughout the whole Bible into the "unity" of God's "one economy of grace."[14]

Third, the Bible presents the redemptive work of Jesus Christ, manifested in human history, as an "interaction" between Jesus and "God the Father" within the context of the covenant.[15]

Through the biblical covenants, God has clearly revealed his will and plan for human salvation. In the Bible, therefore, "God's righteous salvation" is covenantal.[16] The beginning of the covenant, which reveals the purpose of human salvation, is not sought in Genesis in the Bible. In other words, the covenant of redemption for human salvation begins within the Trinity, one God in three persons. The "one economy of grace" of God, which is shown through the covenant of human salvation, flows throughout the entire Old and New Testaments.[17] Upon the basis of

---

BDAG 228–29; *EDNT* 1:299–301; Horton, *Covenant Theology*, 29–32, 62–73, 138, 146).

12. Horton, *Covenant and Salvation*, 255.

13. Frame, *Systematic Theology*, 58. Frame presents these three important themes of the Bible: the Lord's covenants, the kingdom of God and God's family.

14. Horton, *Covenant and Salvation*, 190.

15. Fesko, *Trinity and Covenant*, 177.

16. Frame, *Systematic Theology*, 266, 257–69. Cf. Frame, *Systematic Theology*, 59–60, 66–67, 72–75, 79–81; Horton, *Covenant and Salvation*, 109–14.

17. Horton, *Covenant and Salvation*, 190.

creation, the covenants presented in the Bible can be divided into the covenant of redemption and the covenant of grace.

B. The Covenant of Redemption

The covenant within the triune God, regarding human salvation before the creation of the world, is called the covenant of redemption, which refers to the internal covenant within the triune God as the internal work of the Trinity.[18] The covenant of redemption, therefore, leads all events in the Bible's story back to before the beginning of human history. And the covenant of redemption serves as the foundation and standard of all covenants throughout the whole Bible.

The covenant of redemption, in fact, is a covenant between God the Father and God the Son, in which God the Father, God the Son, and God the Holy Spirit (the triune God) participate together in the plan of redemption.[19] Through the covenant of redemption, the Son and the Spirit agreed to accept the office of servant for the salvation of humankind according to the plan of the Father. The Son as the Mediator executed the redemptive work as the Representative of the new covenant, and the Holy Spirit was appointed to apply the work of redemption accomplished by the Son.[20]

The covenant of redemption is distinct from other covenants between God and human beings in the Bible because it is a covenant agreed upon within the triune God. Ephesians points out that the covenant of redemption was established by the triune God before the creation of the world. In Eph 1:3–6, Scripture says that God actually had the plan of salvation before the creation, which had been hidden for a long time.

> Blessed be the God and Father of our Lord Jesus Christ, who has blessed us in Christ with every spiritual blessing in the heavenly places, even as he chose us in him before the foundation of the world, that we should be holy and blameless before him. In love he predestined us for adoption to himself as sons through Jesus

---

18. Vos, *Redemptive History*, 245; Frame, *Systematic Theology*, 59–60; Horton, *Covenant and Salvation*, 131; Bavinck, *Reformed Dogmatics*, 3:194. The covenant of redemption is also called the *pactum salutis* or the counsel of peace.

19. Frame, *Systematic Theology*, 59–60; Vos, *Redemptive History*, 245–46; Horton, *Covenant and Salvation*, 131–35; Bavinck, *Reformed Dogmatics*, 3:194.

20. Frame, *Systematic Theology*, 59–60; Frame, *Salvation Belongs to the Lord*, 34; Vos, *Redemptive History*, 247.

Christ, according to the purpose of his will, to the praise of his glorious grace, with which he has blessed us in the Beloved.

Scripture makes it clear that the pre-creation Trinitarian covenant of redemption is not something that began within humanity's fallen state as the plan and purpose of God's salvation for fallen humankind. Rather, it was initiated within the triune God (intra-Trinitarian), which is the internal work of the Trinity.[21] All the covenants in the Bible, however, are based on the covenant of redemption, and the covenant of redemption is directly connected to human history. All covenants in the Bible are grounded in the covenant of redemption, and they serve to firmly establish the connection between human history and the redemptive history of Jesus Christ.

In summary, the covenant of redemption is the *internal* work of the Trinity, while the covenant of grace is the *external* work of the Trinity.[22] The covenant of redemption has been accomplished through "the faithful obedience of the Son and the Spirit" to the sovereign decision of the Father.[23] Consequently, covenant theology can show throughout the Bible the "Christological unity" of the covenant of redemption through the law and the gospel.[24]

Further, the covenant of redemption also shows God has built his kingdom with his love. This covenant reveals that God had the plan of redemption for the people of the kingdom through Jesus Christ. Therefore, the importance of the covenant of redemption lies in showing that Jesus Christ is the Mediator of all the covenants (Rom 8:29–30; 2 Tim 1:9–10; Eph 3:9, 11–21; 1 Pet 1:20; 1 Cor 2:7; John 17:5, 24).

> [God] who saved us and called us to a holy calling, not because of our works but because of his own purpose and grace, which he gave us in Christ Jesus before the ages began, and which now has been manifested through the appearing of our Savior Christ Jesus, who abolished death and brought life and immortality to light through the gospel. (2 Tim 1:9–10)

The covenant of redemption is the covenant in which the Trinity had determined to give to sinners the benefits of Christ's accomplished

---

21. Cf. Vos, *Redemptive History*, 247–50; Horton, *Covenant and Salvation*, 135, 131, 148.

22. Vos, *Redemptive History*, 245–53; Horton, *Covenant and Salvation*, 131–35.

23. Frame, *Systematic Theology*, 60.

24. Kline, *Structure of Biblical Authority*, 74–75; Horton, *Covenant Theology*, 134.

righteousness and the gospel blessings within the covenant of grace.[25] The covenant of redemption, thus, is a covenant (pact) established within the Trinity. The redemptive covenant, which had been hidden in the Trinity, was revealed in human history through the covenant of grace—through the creation, the fall, and the redemptive work of Jesus Christ.

C. The Covenant of Grace

The covenant of grace demonstrated through the redemptive work of Jesus Christ that the covenant of redemption is entirely a covenant of God's grace. This covenant clearly demonstrates that salvation for sinners is possible only through God's grace. After the fall, fallen humankind had no ability to save themselves from sin.

What is the difference between the covenant of redemption and the covenant of grace?

As we saw, the covenant of redemption is an *internal* covenant within the Trinity before creation. But the covenant of grace is an *external* covenant, and was applied outside the Trinity and established between God and humanity on the basis of the redemptive history of the Mediator Jesus Christ. The covenant of grace also appears as the history of God's providence (economy) in human history. However, these two covenants are fundamentally related to human sin, and prove salvation and justification that are given by grace alone.

Furthermore, the covenant of grace is based on "God's eternal decree," the covenant of redemption.[26] That is, the purpose of salvation established in the covenant of redemption had been continuously revealed through human history after the fall of Adam, and it was ultimately fulfilled in the covenant of grace. God accomplished the fulfillment of the covenant of redemption and the covenant of grace through the Mediator of the new covenant, Jesus Christ.[27]

From a soteriological perspective, these two covenants demonstrate that, on the human side, (1) salvation is dependent solely on God's grace and (2) that salvation is unconditional. However, God, the Author of the covenants, has consistently fulfilled the purpose for which he established

---

25. Horton, *Covenant and Salvation*, 133.

26. Horton, *Covenant and Salvation*, 90.

27. Horton, *Covenant and Salvation*, 134–35, 182; Ridderbos, *Coming of the Kingdom*, 150.

these covenants on his own. Needless to say, this is undoubtedly a remarkable grace of God. God himself has fulfilled all the terms and conditions of the covenants, and accepted the covenant breakers who have violated the covenants. Therefore, since God executed the covenant of grace through the redemptive work of Jesus Christ, it can be said that it is "unconditional" on the human side.[28]

But just because it's called a grace covenant doesn't mean that God unconditionally accepts sinners. Of course, there are conditions for God to save sinners. There is a conditional aspect because one must meet the righteous standards of God. From the perspective of the new covenant Representative, Jesus, it is conditional due to the necessity of perfect obedience to save sinners.[29] The covenants in the Bible always have the underlying covenant of grace that requires satisfying the condition that human salvation is given through Jesus alone. In this regard, the covenants show that salvation is the work of the sovereign grace of God.[30] Only the Bible tells us the story that God the Creator saves us sinners, who have broken the covenant in Adam.

The covenant of grace also shows that there are basic conditions for God to accept sinners as righteous. This is also a matter of responsibility for all the sins that all human beings have. The covenant of grace does not mean that God unconditionally forgives and accepts all sinners through his grace.

The consequences of human sin, originating from Adam's fall, flow underneath all the covenants of the Bible. Although all people have become sinners in Adam, they still retain the obligation to obey all of God's covenant commands, just as Adam was required to before his sin. This establishes that all people are bound to obey God's word. Therefore, every sinner has a "conditional" responsibility to respond to each covenant with "living and active faith."[31] God, the Lord of the covenant, issues his commands through the covenant word, and in that regard, humans are conditionally obligated to the words in faith. However, it is crucial to remember that before being saved, all sinners lack the ability to obey God's commands (Rom 3:10–12; 7:12).

Previously, we examined that there was a salvation plan through the covenant of redemption, in which the triune God sent the Son as the

---

28. Frame, *Systematic Theology*, 66–67.
29. Horton, *Covenant and Salvation*, 148–59.
30. Horton, *Covenant and Salvation*, 150.
31. Frame, *Systematic Theology*, 67.

Redeemer.[32] As part of that plan, the fall of Adam through the events of the tree of knowledge of good and evil after human creation can be considered the beginning of the covenant of grace. Jesus Christ is also a party of this covenant of grace as the Mediator between God and his people.[33] Jesus satisfied all the conditions of the covenant of grace that the righteous God required of sinners. Jesus met the standards of the righteous God on behalf of sinners.

The covenant of grace shows why the salvation of sinners is the sovereign work of God. For this reason, this covenant plays a role like a pillar in soteriology. God, the Lord of the covenant, revealed already that the Messiah would come through the offspring of the woman (Gen 3:14–15). God's promise of salvation revealed in the covenant of grace was continuously delivered to the descendants of Adam in a new way throughout history.[34]

However, if we see the Old Testament covenants only in terms of their temporary historical situations and purposes, we cannot fully grasp God's grace as revealed in the whole Bible. As such, we may make the mistake of ignoring the context of the whole Bible. Focusing too much on just one covenant can cause us to overlook the continuity of the covenant of grace that the whole Bible reveals. Viewing the covenants in the Bible as part of one redemptive history helps us understand the Bible as a whole. The story of the covenants is the story of what God has done for us.

The covenants through Adam, Noah, Abraham, Moses, and David, as presented in the Bible, demonstrate the "continuity" of God's covenant of grace from the perspective of eternal blessings through the Messiah, Jesus Christ.[35] This continuity can also be seen as the "redemptive-historical continuity of promise and fulfillment" in Jesus Christ.[36] From the perspectives of human history, redemptive history, and covenantal justification, all covenants after Adam's fall share three common elements that flow underneath them:

1. Sin

---

32. Vos, *Redemptive History*, 252–67.
33. Frame, *Salvation Belongs to the Lord*, 121.
34. Horton, *Covenant and Salvation*, 134.
35. Horton, *Covenant Theology*, 102, 132–34.
36. Calvin also emphasizes the "unity of the covenant of grace" and the "redemptive-historical continuity of promise and fulfillment" (Horton, *Covenant and Salvation*, 99).

2. Blood covenant[37]

3. Obedience of faith

Throughout the Bible, from Adam's fall to the covenant with David, the issue of sin is involved in all covenants.

How can the issue of sin be resolved?

From the perspective of salvation from sin, all covenants have a redemptive continuity of the covenant of grace; however, there is no promise of salvation concerning the obedience to the words of these covenants. From Adam to David, each era's covenant given by God has different characteristics.[38] However, if we ignore the context of the whole Bible story and view each covenant separately, we will not be able to see each covenant as a part of the whole Bible story.[39] Such interpretation of the Bible is not desirable.

The next thing to focus on is the fact that the covenants with Adam, Noah, Abraham, Moses, and David all have the element of blood covenant, where animals are killed and offered as sacrifices to atone for human sins (Gen 3:15, 21; 17:11, 14; Exod 24:8; Ezek 44:7; Zech 9:11). In front of God, Israelites killed animals as sacrificial offerings in the altar, the tabernacle, or the temple in place of their own sins, and offered them

---

37. I think Gen 15:18 best illustrates the difference between the concept of covenants in the Bible and that of general worldly covenants (contracts). For "make a covenant," this text uses two Hebrew words (a verb, "cut," *karath*, כָּרַת; a noun, "covenant," *berith*, בְּרִית). Therefore, the meaning of "make a covenant" in the Hebrew original text is essentially "to cut a covenant." In this sense, Gen 15:18 shows that the covenant in the Bible is fundamentally based on "death" (animals [Gen 15:9–17]). In other words, this text represents the core of the blood covenant in the Bible well. This, of course, foreshadows the death of Jesus. We will discuss this further.

38. As Paul points out, to correctly recognize the difference between the law and the gospel, it is necessary to know the differences between the Abrahamic covenant and the Mosaic covenant. The Abrahamic covenant well demonstrates the meaning of the covenant of grace. We will discuss this further in the future.

39. Some would say that British Anglican hermeneutics scholar Thiselton's masterpiece, *The Hermeneutics of Doctrine*, well introduces the theology of many theologians from the perspective of Christian doctrine and hermeneutics, exposing their weaknesses as well as their fine points. However, there are some disappointments in Thiselton's book.

First, it does not present a keyword of hermeneutics, such as a covenantal perspective that can interpret the whole Bible.

Second, Thiselton's attempt to connect Christian doctrine and hermeneutics ultimately fails to present the unity or continuity of the Old and New Testaments, that is, the whole Bible.

Third, Thiselton does not regard God as the Author of the Bible and does not weave the whole Bible into a single story.

to God. In this way, the Old Testament blood covenant points to the blood of the eternal covenant through the death of Jesus Christ on the cross (Matt 26:28; Mark 14:24; Luke 22:20; 1 Cor 11:25; Heb 9:18, 20; 10:29; 12:24; 13:20–21).

Finally, the Old Testament covenants that point to the eternal blood covenant of Jesus Christ always require faithful obedience to the covenantal word from all people.

> Now may the God of peace who brought again from the dead our Lord Jesus, the great shepherd of the sheep, by the blood of the eternal covenant, equip you with everything good that you may do his will, working in us that which is pleasing in his sight, through Jesus Christ, to whom be glory forever and ever. Amen. (Heb 13:20–21)

Therefore, the entire Bible story tells us that after the fall of Adam, all people became slaves to sin. Through the covenants of the Old Testament, God made people look to the blood of the new covenant by faith and live. Salvation is promised only in the perfect obedience of the Messiah, Jesus Christ. So, all the Old Testament covenants with Adam, Noah, Abraham, Moses, and David have the role of making people look forward to the coming Messiah, Jesus Christ, through faith. In other words, through the covenants, God required all people to love him with all their heart and with all their soul and with all their might, and to seek obedience of faith to the word of God.[40]

> Hear, O Israel: The LORD our God, the LORD is one. You shall love the LORD your God with all your heart and with all your soul and with all your might. And these words that I command you today shall be on your heart. You shall teach them diligently to your children, and shall talk of them when you sit in your house, and when you walk by the way, and when you lie down, and when you rise. You shall bind them as a sign on your hand, and they shall be as frontlets between your eyes. You shall write them on the doorposts of your house and on your gates. (Deut 6:4–9)

In the New Testament, Paul's doctrine of justification by grace alone also helps clarify that the covenant of grace runs through the Old Testament covenants. The doctrine of justification reveals the unity of the

---

40. God's covenants do not require faithful obedience only from specific individuals or a single nation, but they equally demand faithful obedience from all people and all nations (Frame, *Systematic Theology*, 60–62, 70, 74, 77).

covenant of grace in the Old Testament covenants. It helps us see the message of the redemptive-historical continuity through the promise and fulfillment by Jesus Chris and the responsibility of our obedience of faith. At this point, the covenant of grace allows us to see the entire context of the Bible's story (historical events) as the building of the eternal kingdom of God. In summary, the covenant of grace shows that although there are differences in how each covenant in the Bible expects the Messiah, all covenants look to the same Messiah. Now, we will examine the covenants of the Bible for this purpose. There are two main reasons why this first covenant is called the covenant with Adam: (1) because it approaches the kingdom of God from the perspective of the doctrine of justification, and (2) because other covenants in these volumes are referred to by the names of Noah, Abraham, Moses, and David.

2. COVENANTS IN THE BIBLE

A. The Adamic Covenant

God's covenant with Adam, the representative of all humankind, is fundamentally a word of command for the building of God's kingdom.[41] While the covenant with Adam has been defined in various ways, its importance lies primarily in the fact that all humankind is in Adam. Adam is no ordinary man. He is the representative of all humanity. Therefore, God's children who believe in Jesus must first understand their union with Adam because knowing their union with Adam provides a foundation for understanding their union with Jesus (Rom 5:12–21).[42]

---

41. In fact, Hos 6:7 is the only place in the whole Bible that mentions Adam in connection with the Adamic covenant, where his sin is compared to the fall of Israelites. For this reason, theologians label this covenant in various ways. I call this covenant the Adamic covenant because of two reasons: (1) to approach God's kingdom from the perspective of the doctrine of justification; (2) to maintain consistency in naming (as other covenants in *Justification and the Kingdom of God* are named after Noah, Abraham, Moses, and David). Bavinck also calls this the Adamic covenant, citing Hos 6:7 while explaining the covenant with Adam (Bavinck, *Reformed Dogmatics*, 2:564–76).

"But like Adam they transgressed the covenant; there they dealt faithlessly with me" (Hos 6:7).

The Adamic covenant is also called: the covenant of works (Westminster Confession of Faith—traditional view), the covenant of nature, the covenant of life (Westminster Larger Catechism), the Edenic covenant, and covenant of the law (Bavinck, *Reformed Dogmatics*, 2:564–71; Frame, *Systematic Theology*, 62–66; Horton, *Covenant Theology*; Horton, *Covenant and Salvation*; Kline, *Structure of Biblical Authority*).

42. Kang, *Living Out the Gospel*, 170–93; Frame, *Salvation Belongs to the Lord*,

For as in Adam all die, so also in Christ shall all be made alive. (1 Cor 15:22)

The next important thing to focus is our understanding of Adam's actions in relation to the covenant with God. We refer to the Adamic covenant as the covenant of works, and when we use this term, the key point is to view Adam's actions in relation to God's covenant as the central point of obedience to the covenant.[43] That is, Adam is a covenant breaker in this

---

118–19. Please refer to "1. Union with Christ," in vol. 2, ch. 3. Of course, it is much more important for us to see our union with Jesus than that of our union with Adam since you may take a hint from the covenant of redemption before creation.

43. Some theologians call the covenant of works "the covenants made with Adam and given to Moses," speaking about Mosaic covenant at Sinai as republication of "the covenant of works" given to Adam. However, we must be cautious when using the term.

First, when referring to the Adamic covenant as the covenant of works, we must clarify the concept of the covenant of works and the doctrine of original sin. In other words, when referring to the Adamic covenant as the covenant of works, we must start from a clear foundation of the doctrine of original sin.

Second, it is necessary to establish a correct understanding of soteriology and justification in relation to the doctrine of original sin, because when the covenant of works is viewed independently, separate from Adam's sin and the rest of humanity, it can cause confusion in soteriology and justification. When we separate this covenant from the rest of the biblical covenants, it can also create problems.

In addition, there is no mention in the whole Bible, from Genesis to Revelation, of the promise of eternal life or entering the kingdom of God based on the perfect obedience of Adam. When emphasizing only the concept of obedience and disobedience based on the concept of the covenant of works, without a proper foundation on the correct biblical doctrine of original sin, there is a risk of misunderstanding that the Adamic covenant contains a promise of eternal life. Here we need to remember that each of the Old Testament covenants does not have a different way of salvation (Vos, *Redemptive History*, 242–45; Bavinck, *Reformed Dogmatics*, 2:564–71; Frame, *Systematic Theology*, 62–66, 72–75. Cf. Horton, *Covenant Theology*, 109–10; Kline, *Structure of Biblical Authority*; Horton, *Covenant and Salvation*). Please look at the Mosaic covenant below.

Bavinck rightly emphasizes that "the covenant of works and the covenant of grace do not differ" in looking at "their final goal" of salvation or eternal life. He also emphasizes that there is "only one mediator, only one mediator of union, only one mediator of reconciliation and only one faith." This means that there is only one Mediator, Jesus Christ, for salvation and eternal life (Bavinck, *Reformed Dogmatics*, 2:570).

From the perspective of the doctrine of justification, even when considering the entire context of the Bible, it is difficult to imagine that God, who is holy and righteous, immediately granted humans the qualification of righteousness (being justified) that allows them to be with him forever when he created them. The act of creating all things by God is completely different in nature from the attainment of eligibility for entering the kingdom of God. Obviously, at that time, Adam simply had to obey God's commandment completely. The promise and fulfillment of eternal life in all covenants is the work of God's grace planned within Jesus Christ, as demonstrated in the covenant of redemption and the covenant of grace. We will continue to discuss the Adamic covenant.

sense (Hos 6:7; Isa 24:5).[44] If we consider the Adamic covenant from these two aspects (union with Adam, disobedience), we can understand that we, too, are covenant breakers in Adam (Isa 24:5). Additionally, when we view ourselves in terms of our union with Jesus and the aspect of Jesus' obedience, we can also understand that we become covenant keepers in Jesus.[45] Now, let's examine the Adamic covenant by dividing it into the pre-fall covenant (Gen 1:26–30; 2:16–17) and the post-fall covenant (Gen 3:15–19).[46]

a. The Pre-Fall Covenant (Gen 1:26–30; 2:16–17)

THE IMAGE OF GOD

What is the image of God?

The most fundamental nature of humans lies in the image of God. The beautiful relationship between God and humans began when God gave humans his image. Before the fall of Adam, the image of God given to Adam was maintained (Gen 1:26–27).

The covenant representative of all humankind, Adam, was created in God's image in the most outstanding way among all creatures before the fall (Gen 1:26–27).[47] Since there are many theological views on the image of God, we will narrow it down to two aspects from the perspectives of God's kingdom and justification: the image of God in terms of Adam's office and the image of God in justification.

First and foremost, we can view the image of God given to Adam from the perspective of the threefold office bestowed upon him by God. Adam, the image bearer of God, had the "authority" of a king to rule over the earth ("presence" [Gen 1:26–28]) and the "power" to "subdue the earth" and to "rule over the fish of the sea, the birds of the air, and all living creatures on the earth" (Gen 1:28).[48] However, none of the things

---

44. Frame, *Salvation Belongs to the Lord*, 118–19.

45. For more information on Jesus' perfect obedience, please refer to vol. 2, ch. 2, "The Condition of Justification: The Perfect Obedience of Jus Christ."

46. Bavinck, *Reformed Dogmatics*, 2:564–76. If you want to view the Adamic covenant as a covenant of works, you can divide it into the pre-fall covenant of works and the post-fall covenant of grace (Frame, *Salvation Belongs to the Lord*, 122).

47. The discussion about the image of God in Adam is diverse. In this book, we will discuss the connection between the Adamic covenant and the image of God from the perspective of Paul's doctrine of justification.

48. It is also said that Adam had "the three anointed offices": kingly office (control), prophetic office (authority), and priestly office (presence) (Frame, *Systematic Theology*,

Adam possessed were obtained as a reward for his own efforts. God made Adam in his image, bestowed blessings, demanded obedience of faith to his word, and gave him the cultural mandate.[49]

God gave Adam his word, the highest authority, for the prophetic office, and enabled him to legitimately handle the office and work of a king who rules with the word.[50] And Adam's priestly office was given to do all things to the glory of God, to "pray and worship God in every place," and to "bring God's blessing upon the people" and "upon the earth" in order to fulfill God's purpose for creation.[51]

> Then God said, "Let us make man in our image, after our likeness. And let them have dominion over the fish of the sea and over the birds of the heavens and over the livestock and over all the earth and over every creeping thing that creeps on the earth." So God created man in his own image, in the image of God he created him; male and female he created them. And God blessed them. And God said to them, "Be fruitful and multiply and fill the earth and subdue it, and have dominion over the fish of the sea and over the birds of the heavens and over every living thing that moves on the earth." (Gen 1:26–28)

The next thing to focus on is the image of God with respect to the redemptive work of Jesus, that is, with the creation of Adam, the fall of Adam, and the salvation of sinners. In other words, we will seek an answer to the question "What did God do for us?" in finding the connection between the Old Testament and the New Testament through the image

---

786–91). Some theologians emphasize three elements regarding the image of God: physical, official, and ethical elements (88–89).

49. Frame, *Systematic Theology*, 63, 786–88, 1033–37; Frame, *Salvation Belongs to the Lord*, 97–99, 250–53. All the living environment and food that Adam enjoyed were the free gifts from God. God also gave him the cultural mandate as his responsibility.

50. Frame, *Systematic Theology*, 790.

51. Frame, *Systematic Theology*, 790–91; Kline, *Images of the Spirit*, 26–34, 35–96. In Luke's genealogy of Jesus, Adam is introduced as the son of God (Luke 3:38; 1 Pet 2:9). Those who believe in Jesus and become God's children have the "power, authority and presence within their domains" to manifest the glory of God (Ps 16:6; 1 Pet 2:9) (Frame, *Systematic Theology*, 791, 870).

"The lines have fallen for me in pleasant places; indeed, I have a beautiful inheritance" (Ps 16:6).

"But you are a chosen race, a royal priesthood, a holy nation, a people for his own possession, that you may proclaim the excellencies of him who called you out of darkness into his marvelous light" (1 Pet 2:9).

of God and the doctrine of justification so that we may understand the purpose of God's creation and salvation.

Notice that the image of God before the fall was not yet the "fully developed" image of God that God had planned, but it was merely the beginning as the "image bearer" of God that God desired.[52] Nevertheless, the creation of humans with the image of God demonstrates the greatness of God's infinite wisdom and grace.

The greatness of God's wisdom and power is manifested in the image of God that has been given only to humans among all creatures. In other words, it is clearly manifested in the highest intellectual moral abilities given to humans before the fall, such as wisdom, knowledge, righteousness, holiness, and goodness, which God gave only to humans as the image of God before the fall.[53] Of course, to better understand this image of God, we need to go back to the Bible.

Scripture helps us to see the image of God in us with the sense of the whole person, in a broad sense and a narrow sense. These three senses (diversity) of the image of God (unity) are simply for our logical and biblical understanding. These senses are important because they also help us interpret the epistles of the New Testament. Although each of these three senses helps our understanding of the image of God in humans, the image of God in the Bible is particularly inseparable from the perspective of the doctrine of justification.

First of all, Adam was created in the image bearer of God in terms of "the whole person," that is, "the whole human being" himself. This means that nothing within Adam was "excluded from the image of God."[54] And Adam, in the broad sense of the image of God, had intellectual and moral excellences.[55] Also, in the narrow sense (the biblical sense), this refers to

---

52. Hoekema, *Created in God's Image*, 63, 82.

53. Bavinck, *Reformed Dogmatics*, 2:557–58; Frame, *Systematic Theology*, 784–85; Hoekema, *Created in God's Image*, 70–71.

54. Scripture teaches the unity of human beings as a whole person in the image of God (Frame, *Doctrine of Christian Life*, 322, 355; Bavinck, *Reformed Dogmatics*, 2:554–57; Hoekema, *Created in God's Image*, 69, 71–72). From the perspective of "the whole human being," the "image and likeness of God" unique to humans includes not only "soul and body," but also "all human faculties, powers, and gifts." That is, everything in us is "from God's image" (Bavinck, *Reformed Dogmatics*, 2:561–62).

55. Bavinck, *Reformed Dogmatics*, 2:550; Kline, *Images of the Spirit*, 29–32; Hoekema, *Created in God's Image*, 71–72. Scripture teaches that Adam was created with rational and intellectual excellence in the area of wisdom and knowledge. However, this rational and intellectual excellence strictly excludes the concept of "moral and intellectual virtues" based on autonomous rationality in the philosophical sense, such as

the biblical virtues of wisdom, knowledge, righteousness, holiness, and goodness as explained by Paul in the perspective of restoration in Jesus Christ.[56]

However, whether we view the image of God in terms of the whole person, in its broad sense (intellectual and moral excellences) or in its narrow sense (wisdom, righteousness, holiness, and goodness), Adam's image of God cannot be separated from any of these aspects. The image of God is interdependent in nature, whether viewed as intellectual and moral excellences or as wisdom, righteousness, holiness, and goodness. In these senses, it is the sense of the whole person that makes it possible to see this interdependence. We need to examine these three senses of the image of God more closely.

As we saw earlier, God has given the greatest gift of the image of God exclusively to humans among all creatures. Among all creatures, humans have received the most precious gift from God. The beautiful relationship between God and humanity began with God giving the gift of his own image to humans. The God who created humans in his own image becomes the "highest standard" of all human wisdom, knowledge, righteousness, holiness, and goodness.[57] Accordingly, Paul introduces the "new self" and explains the goal of Adam's creation (Gen 1:26–27), following the image of God (Col 3:10; Eph 4:24). Paul's interpretation of Col 3:10 and Eph 4:24 becomes a very important link between the doctrine of justification and the image of God.[58]

> And have put on the new self, which is being renewed in knowledge after the image of its creator. (Col 3:10)

---

that of Aristotle (Frame, *Doctrine of Christian Life*, 94–95; Hoekema, *Created in God's Image*, 71–72).

56. Bavinck, *Reformed Dogmatics*, 2:557–62; Frame, *Doctrine of Christian Life*, 318–19, 321; Frame, *Doctrine of God*, 119–59, 394–401.

57. Frame, *Doctrine of Christian Life*, 318–19; Frame, *Systematic Theology*, 785, 790–91.

58. Understanding God's image in Adam as the whole person helps us understand the doctrine of justification "by grace alone" (*sola gratia*). For this, we consider all these three senses together, seeing the big picture of the image of God in Adam: the sense of the whole person, the broad sense and the narrow sense (biblical sense: wisdom, knowledge, righteousness, holiness, and goodness). Through the doctrine of justification, we can see that it's not just the restoration of marred righteousness, but also the restoration of marred wisdom, knowledge, and marred holiness and goodness (in the narrow biblical sense)—if we also consider it in the sense of the restoration of the marred whole person. For the restored image of God, refer to vol. 2, ch. 3, "4. Justification and the Restored Image of God."

> And to put on the new self, created after the likeness of God in true righteousness and holiness. (Eph 4:24)

These texts presuppose the fact that Adam, who bore the image of God, established a covenant with God based on the highest relationship. However, Adam, who made a covenant with God, had a responsibility towards this covenant as one who bore the image of God. This responsibility entails continually obeying, and maintaining and developing the knowledge, righteousness, holiness, and goodness given by God through one's actions in life.[59] When Adam was created in his own image, God also required his responsibility for it.[60] In other words, those who receive the word of God also have the responsibility to keep it. The demand for the responsibility of obeying God's word continues to appear in other covenants as well. This is the responsibility of obedience to God's word. Obedience to God's word is "our covenant faithfulness" to God's covenant with us.[61] However, Adam did not maintain faithfulness to the covenant with God. Unfortunately, Adam failed to pass his test of covenant responsibility to obey the word.

> And the LORD God commanded the man, saying, "You may surely eat of every tree of the garden, but of the tree of the knowledge of good and evil you shall not eat, for in the day that you eat of it you shall surely die." (Gen 2:16-17)

b. *The Post-Fall Covenant (Gen 3:15-19)*

God established Adam as the representative of all humankind and endowed him with the image of God for the building of God's kingdom. However, as a result of Adam's fall and the breaking of the covenant with God, the image of God in him was marred (Hos 6:7; Gen 9:6; Jas 3:9; Isa

---

59. Bavinck, *Reformed Dogmatics*, 2:558; Kline, *Images of the Spirit*, 29; Frame, *Doctrine of Christian Life*, 322-23, 355. Bavinck insists that humans were created "physically and ethically mature with knowledge in the mind, righteousness in the will, holiness in the heart" (Bavinck, *Reformed Dogmatics*, 2:557-58). But humans are not functionally separated into intellect, emotions, and will, but rather, there is a unity of human faculties as a whole person (Bavinck, *Reformed Dogmatics*, 2:554-62; Frame, *Doctrine of Christian Life*, 318-21; Frame, *Salvation Belongs to the Lord*, 92-94).

60. Frame, *Doctrine of Christian Life*, 319, 322-23, 355; Frame, *Systematic Theology*, 809-22.

61. Frame, *Systematic Theology*, 63.

24:5).[62] The Bible teaches the necessity of a redeemer due to Adam's sin because God's image of all humankind was marred within Adam's fall, and all humans have become covenant breakers in Adam.

> But like Adam they transgressed the covenant; there they dealt faithlessly with me. (Hos 6:7)

> The earth lies defiled under its inhabitants; for they have transgressed the laws, violated the statutes, broken the everlasting covenant. (Isa 24:5)

1. The Marred Image of God

What is sin?

Biblically, sin is always "lawlessness" (1 John 3:4) or "a transgression of the law of God."[63] As the representative, Adam disobeyed God's word and committed sin, leading to the fall. Consequently, all humans have had their image of God marred and become fallen people in Adam.[64] Adam violated the law of God's righteousness. There are three consequences of Adam's sin: guilt, pollution, and punishment.[65] We often forget that we are born with these three consequences. Sin, death, and curse came upon all humanity due to Adam's sin of disobedience. Lawlessness and injustice began to dominate the world. All humankind has become unable to escape God's judgment and punishment. We need to remember that the Adamic covenant clearly reveals the origin of sin to us.

After the fall of Adam, certainly, all human beings in Adam have been no longer recognized as righteous, holy, and good (moral excellence) by God. As previously mentioned, the fall of Adam was the fall of

---

62. It is much more biblical to say that the image of God was defaced or marred (Reformed) rather than lost (Lutheran) due to Adam's sin. This is because the loss of the image of God can be misunderstood as the loss of all intellectual and moral abilities (Frame, *Doctrine of Christian Life*, 320; Frame, *Systematic Theology*, 66; Frame, *Salvation Belongs to the Lord*, 119).

63. Frame, *Salvation Belongs to the Lord*, 100. The Mosaic law is also God's law, which represents God's righteousness and will. Violating the law and the Ten Commandments is also a breach of God's will and righteousness. Additionally, it is a transgression of God's law. In the Bible, sin encompasses both thoughts and actions of the heart.

64. Frame, *Systematic Theology*, 66. Please refer to vol. 2, ch. 3, "4. Justification, the Restored Image of God."

65. Frame, *Salvation Belongs to the Lord*, 102.

the whole person as a person.⁶⁶ Therefore, all humans in Adam have also lost their qualification as the people of God's kingdom. However, they cannot use Adam's fall as an excuse to escape from responsibility for their sins.⁶⁷ Paul emphasizes the necessity of the imputation of Christ's righteousness obtained through Jesus Christ's perfect obedience, as a result of Adam's disobedience (Rom 1:17; 3:21–22; 5:12–21).⁶⁸

Therefore, as a whole, the image of God was marred because of Adam's sin.⁶⁹ In the broad sense, the image of God in the intellectual and moral excellences was marred.⁷⁰ In the narrow sense, the image of God in the virtues of wisdom, knowledge, righteousness, holiness, and goodness was marred.⁷¹ As a result of Adam's sin, the beautiful image of God given to humans has been marred.

> Now the earth was corrupt in God's sight, and the earth was filled with violence. And God saw the earth, and behold, it was corrupt, for all flesh had corrupted their way on the earth. (Gen 6:11–12)

However, the image of God has been marred, not destroyed or entirely lost. God did not completely take away the image of God from Adam. In other words, under common grace given by God who rules all things in the universe ("non-saving grace"), human ability still exists in

---

66. Frame, *Doctrine of Christian Life*, 320–22, 355; Bavinck, *Reformed Dogmatics*, 2:554–57, 561–62.

67. Frame, *Doctrine of Christian Life*, 320.

68. Note here that in the covenant of redemption, union with Christ precedes union with Adam.

69. To see the image of God in the sense of the whole person as one person helps us to understand the marred image of God as the result of sin in the doctrine of original sin. Human corruption was the corruption of the whole person as one person, not a partial corruption. That is, it was not a partial corruption in one aspect of intellectual and moral excellences (the broad sense). It was the corruption of the whole person.

The result of human corruption is also not just a partial corruption in wisdom, knowledge, righteousness, holiness, or goodness (the narrow sense). It is also not a partial corruption in just one part of intellect, emotion, or will. It is a corruption of the whole person. For example, New England theology, influenced by the American Great Awakening movement, argued that the result of Adam's fall was "a partial corruption" (a corruption of the will). However, Adam's fall is a corruption of the whole person (Kang, *Justification*, 126, 177).

70. Bavinck, *Reformed Dogmatics*, 2:550; Kline, *Images of the Spirit*, 29–32; Frame, *Doctrine of Christian Life*, 94–95, 321.

71. Bavinck, *Reformed Dogmatics*, 2:557–62; Frame, *Doctrine of Christian Life*, 318–19, 321; Frame, *Doctrine of God*, 119–59, 394–401.

humans.[72] The image of God in humans for cultural development and scientific development (human rational ability) has not been completely destroyed. Similarly, a moral ability for common goodness (ethical goodness) in the world has not been completely destroyed.[73]

However, Scripture clearly shows that after Adam's fall, "every intention of the thoughts of his heart" in the world has been "only evil continually" (Gen 6:5). Therefore, due to Adam's fall, if the Mediator of the new covenant, Jesus Christ, had not come to this world, there would have been no hope for this world.

> The LORD saw that the wickedness of man was great in the earth, and that every intention of the thoughts of his heart was only evil continually. (Gen 6:5)

> But if our unrighteousness serves to show the righteousness of God, what shall we say? That God is unrighteous to inflict wrath on us? (I speak in a human way.) (Rom 3:5)

> For Christ also suffered once for sins, the righteous for the unrighteous, that he might bring us to God, being put to death in the flesh but made alive in the spirit. (1 Pet 3:18)

As a result of the marred image of God caused by Adam's fall, all human beings constantly behave like "irrational animals" and do transgression and wrongdoing from their hearts, walking only in the way of sins throughout their lives (2 Pet 2:12–16; Jude 1:5–16).[74]

> But these, like irrational animals, creatures of instinct, born to be caught and destroyed, blaspheming about matters of which they are ignorant, will also be destroyed in their destruction, suffering wrong as the wage for their wrongdoing. They count it pleasure to revel in the daytime. They are blots and blemishes, reveling in their deceptions, while they feast with you. They have eyes full of adultery, insatiable for sin. They entice unsteady souls. They have hearts trained in greed. Accursed children! Forsaking the right way, they have gone astray. They have followed the way of Balaam, the son of Beor, who loved gain

---

72. Frame, *Doctrine of Christian Life*, 860.

73. Frame, *Doctrine of God*, 429–47; Frame, *Doctrine of Christian Life*, 318–21, 860–62; Frame, *Systematic Theology*, 855–71.

74. Through the sin of Adam, the representative of all humankind, guilt and pollution of sin have been transferred to Adam's descendants. For guilt and pollution of sin, please refer to vol. 2, ch. 3, "4. Justification and the Restored Image of God."

from wrongdoing, but was rebuked for his own transgression; a speechless donkey spoke with human voice and restrained the prophet's madness. (2 Pet 2:12–16)

In summary, after Adam's fall, all human beings are evil and unrighteous before God (Isa 26:10; 55:7). Therefore, the only way for the unrighteous, who cannot escape from God's judgment because of sin, to be saved is by repenting of their sins and turning back to God (Isa 55:7; 2 Thess 2:12; 1 John 1:9).[75]

Without the grace of God given only through Jesus Christ, sinners live their lives following the desires of the flesh (the mind of sinful nature) and live as enemies of God (Rom 8:5–7). After Adam's fall, no human beings can any longer please God on their own (Rom 8:8). Sinners in Adam cannot absolutely do good before God. The unrighteous in Adam cannot come before the righteous God by their own strength.[76]

Those in Adam have no ability to obey the word of God, the law of the kingdom of God, on their own (Rom 7:12). The Adamic covenant clearly tells us that without God's grace, we have no ability to save ourselves from the wrath of God against our sins. Matthew 13:14–15 clearly says this:

> Indeed, in their case the prophecy of Isaiah is fulfilled that says: "You will indeed hear but never understand, and you will indeed see but never perceive." For this people's heart has grown dull, and with their ears they can barely hear, and their eyes they have closed, lest they should see with their eyes and hear with their ears and understand with their heart and turn, and I would heal them.[77]

II. The First Gospel

So far, we have compared the pre-fall covenant and the post-fall covenant through the Adamic covenant in the created image of God and have seen the need for the restoration of righteousness in the marred image of

---

75. "Let the wicked forsake his way, and the unrighteous man his thoughts; let him return to the Lord, that he may have compassion on him, and to our God, for he will abundantly pardon" (Isa 55:7).

76. Frame, *Systematic Theology*, 863.

77. Mark 4:12 calls "forgive" (Matt 13:15) "heal." These two words are synonymously used. "So that 'they may indeed see but not perceive, and may indeed hear but not understand, lest they should turn and be forgiven'" (Mark 4:12).

God, which satisfies God's righteousness. The fall of Adam, the covenant representative of all humankind, led to the marring of God's image in all humans united with Adam. The marred image of God highlights the problem that sinners must satisfy God's righteousness. Therefore, the restoration of marred righteousness became necessary for all sinners.

> I will put enmity between you and the woman, and between your offspring and her offspring; he shall bruise your head, and you shall bruise his heel. (Gen 3:15)

How can we restore the marred image of God in sinners that occurred after Adam's fall?

In order for us sinners to restore the damaged image of God, we need "justification" through the perfect obedience of Jesus Christ (justification by Christ alone), who can satisfy God's righteousness. In this way, salvation from the sins of sinners also includes justification for the restoration of marred righteousness. After Adam's fall, God gave Adam the amazing promise of grace called the "first gospel" (Gen 3:15), which announced the coming of the Messiah. In the Adamic covenant, the "first gospel" leads us to hope for and anticipate Jesus Christ, the Messiah, who is both the Judge and Redeemer, solely by grace.

B. The Noahic Covenant

After the Adamic covenant, God governed redemptive history and led human history by giving covenants to humans until the coming of Jesus Christ. And the covenant of grace continued in the Noahic covenant, following the redemptive history of Jesus. Of course, the results of the Adamic covenant flowed underneath the Noahic covenant. The beginning of the Noahic covenant was when the descendants of Adam multiplied on the earth (Gen 6:1–4), but the sinful actions that began in human society did not stop and continued to worsen and develop. Eventually, the world was filled with the wickedness of humans, reaching an extreme situation.

> The LORD saw that the wickedness of man was great in the earth, and that every intention of the thoughts of his heart was only evil continually. And the LORD regretted that he had made man on the earth, and it grieved him to his heart. So the LORD said, "I will blot out man whom I have created from the face of the land,

man and animals and creeping things and birds of the heavens, for I am sorry that I have made them." (Gen 6:5-7)

This passage proves through the Noahic covenant that salvation comes from God's grace alone, apart from human works (cf. Gen 6:8-9). Through covenants like the Noahic covenant, God communicated with humans and always required them to have an "alive and active" obedience of faith (Gen 6:22; 7:1, 5).[78] However, the people of Noah's time engaged only in evil deeds in the sight of God. Therefore, the continuity of the covenant of grace is well demonstrated in God's grace already given to Noah before the judgment of the world through the flood.[79] The Noahic covenant clearly shows that God controls the world.

> But Noah found favor in the eyes of the LORD. These are the generations of Noah. Noah was a righteous man, blameless in his generation. Noah walked with God. (Gen 6:8-9)

Noah and his family were saved from the flood judgment by God's grace alone (Gen 7:6—8:19). In the New Testament, Noah's flood is a "type of God's final judgment on sin" (Matt 24:37-39; Luke 17:26-27; Heb 11:7; 1 Pet 3:20-22; 2 Pet 2:5; 3:5-6).[80] Moreover, in the New Testament, the flood judgment is connected to Jesus' baptism and his redemptive work, and the baptism of believers is connected to Jesus' death and resurrection.[81] The New Testament views the judgment of the flood and baptism as the "sign and seal" of the covenant of grace, and interprets them as believers' union with the death and resurrection of Jesus.[82]

> Having been buried with him in baptism, in which you were also raised with him through faith in the powerful working of God, who raised him from the dead. (Col 2:12)

---

78. Frame, *Systematic Theology*, 67-8.

79. For the first time, a Hebrew word (*hen*, חֵן) that means "the grace of God" is used here. This word, "grace," shown to Noah here can be understood in connection with the concept of grace in the context of the doctrine of justification, as seen in God's counting the faith of Abraham "righteous" (Gen 15:5-7). Cf. Gen 6:8; 18:3; 19:19; Exod 33:12-13, 16-17; Exod 34:9; Num 11:11, 15. BDB 336. Cf. Kline, *Kingdom Prologue*, 235-36.

80. Frame, *Systematic Theology*, 68.

81. Frame, *Systematic Theology*, 68; Horton, *Covenant Theology*, 150.

82. Ridderbos, *Coming of the Kingdom*, 166, 384-86, 388; Crowe, *Last Adam*, 68-70; Frame, *Systematic Theology*, 68; Horton, *Justification*, 2:397, 485; Horton, *Covenant Theology*, 144-55.

Because they formerly did not obey, when God's patience waited in the days of Noah, while the ark was being prepared, in which a few, that is, eight persons, were brought safely through water. Baptism, which corresponds to this, now saves you, not as a removal of dirt from the body but as an appeal to God for a good conscience, through the resurrection of Jesus Christ, who has gone into heaven and is at the right hand of God, with angels, authorities, and powers having been subjected to him. (1 Pet 3:20–22)

In fact, interpreting the flood of Noah with the baptism and union with Christ is an amazing interpretation that is impossible for human wisdom alone. This is a good example that shows how the sixty-six books of the Bible are closely connected to the work of the Holy Spirit. In Rom 6:1–11, Paul explains that baptism for believers is a union with Jesus Christ's death and resurrection, and teaches that this results in the "justification of sinners."[83] Peter also teaches that we must live a Christian life worthy of the righteous "by the righteousness of Jesus Christ" (2 Pet 1:1), focusing on justification by Christ alone (1 Pet 2:24; 2 Pet 1:1; 2:5; 3:13).[84] When Peter speaks of the flood judgment, it is clear that he already has in mind the imputation (transferring) of Jesus Christ's righteousness through union with him (1 Pet 3:12, 18; 4:18; 2 Pet 2:5, 7–8).[85] We need to pay attention to and remember biblical texts like this where Scripture clearly interprets itself.

After the fall, God saw that the wickedness of people was so great in the world, and that every intention of the thoughts in their hearts was continually only evil. When God judged the evil world with the flood and made a covenant with Noah, he mentioned the cultural mandate of the Adamic covenant and promised to preserve all living creatures by his grace alone (Gen 9:1–3).[86] Because the preservation of humanity is the

---

83. "For if we have been united with him in a death like his, we shall certainly be united with him in a resurrection like his. We know that our old self was crucified with him in order that the body of sin might be brought to nothing, so that we would no longer be enslaved to sin. For one who has died has been set free from sin" (Rom 6:5–7).

84. BDAG 247–49.

85. "And 'If the righteous is scarcely saved, what will become of the ungodly and the sinner?'" (1 Pet 4:18).

86. "And God blessed Noah and his sons and said to them, 'Be fruitful and multiply and fill the earth. The fear of you and the dread of you shall be upon every beast of the earth and upon every bird of the heavens, upon everything that creeps on the ground and all the fish of the sea. Into your hand they are delivered. Every moving thing that lives shall be food for you. And as I gave you the green plants, I give you everything'"

only way for the coming of the Messiah, Jesus Christ, God promised it through the Noahic covenant:

> "Behold, I establish my covenant with you and your offspring after you, and with every living creature that is with you, the birds, the livestock, and every beast of the earth with you, as many as came out of the ark; it is for every beast of the earth. I establish my covenant with you, that never again shall all flesh be cut off by the waters of the flood, and never again shall there be a flood to destroy the earth." And God said, "This is the sign of the covenant that I make between me and you and every living creature that is with you, for all future generations: I have set my bow in the cloud, and it shall be a sign of the covenant between me and the earth." (Gen 9:9–13)

Therefore, the judgment of Noah's flood in the New Testament is a "type of God's final judgment on human sin."[87] Also, remember that the Noahic covenant is a covenant of nature preservation, a covenant of nature protection to preserve humanity. Through the Noahic covenant, God made a promise to Noah to preserve the genealogy of the Messiah, who is a descendant of a woman (Gen 9:7, 9–11, 26–28). Noah's son Shem is Abraham's ancestor (Gen 6:10; 9:26–28; 11:10–21; Matt 1:1). As an eternal covenant, this covenant of nature preservation and human multiplication makes it clear that God will keep his promise to protect nature and humanity until the first and second comings of Jesus Christ (2 Pet 3:4–7).[88]

In 2 Pet 3:1–7, Peter introduces the creation by the word of God and the Noahic covenant. Therefore, the Noahic covenant is a covenant of a promise of preserving the world until the day of judgment and the promise of the coming of Jesus Christ, the covenant Representative of all.

> And that by means of these the world that then existed was deluged with water and perished. But by the same word the heavens and earth that now exist are stored up for fire, being kept until the day of judgment and destruction of the ungodly. (2 Pet 3:6–7)

(Gen 9:1–3).

87. Frame, *Systematic Theology*, 68–69.

88. "They will say, 'Where is the promise of his coming? For ever since the fathers fell asleep, all things are continuing as they were from the beginning of creation.' For they deliberately overlook this fact, that the heavens existed long ago, and the earth was formed out of water and through water by the word of God" (2 Pet 3:4–5).

> And he who sat there had the appearance of jasper and carnelian, and around the throne was a rainbow that had the appearance of an emerald. (Rev 4:3)

In summary, the Adamic covenant and the covenant of grace run through the Noahic covenant. Through the preservation of humanity, God gave Noah the word of covenant that promised the coming of the Messiah who would restore the people of God. Because Noah obeyed God's word to build the ark (Gen 6:13–22), the genealogy of the Messiah could be continuously preserved. The Adamic covenant and the Noahic covenant testify that God continued to build his kingdom in human history without giving up. Through the Noahic covenant, God continued to keep and execute the covenant of grace in human history.

C. The Abrahamic Covenant

The Abrahamic covenant shows a more advanced development of God's revelation about the kingdom of God. This covenant moves the flow of the redemptive-historical story from Adam and all humankind to Abraham and his descendants. After the tower of Babel story of the fallen people (Gen 11:1–9), the Abrahamic covenant is a covenant to promise to establish a people of God's kingdom, who believe in him from all nations. In Gen 12:1–2, God promised to make Abraham and his descendants into "a great nation" and demanded obedience of faith.[89] This promise to this great nation refers to the people of God's kingdom who are born again in Jesus Christ.

> Now the LORD said to Abram, "Go from your country and your kindred and your father's house to the land that I will show you. And I will make of you a great nation, and I will bless you and make your name great, so that you will be a blessing." (Gen 12:1–2)

In the Old Testament, the Abrahamic covenant best exemplifies salvation "by grace alone."[90] In other words, salvation is by God's grace alone, apart from human works. Both Noah and Abraham were recipients of God's grace. In Gen 15, it is especially evident that the foundation of righteousness is God's grace alone. Through the Abrahamic covenant,

---

89. Cf. Frame, *Systematic Theology*, 70–71.

90. Frame, *Systematic Theology*, 71. For further discussion, please refer to "2-B. Jesus' Perfect Obedience in the Broad Sense," in vol. 2, ch. 2.

God shifts the focus from the lineage of Adam, the covenant representative of all humankind, to the lineage of faith in Jesus Christ, the covenant Representative of all believers.[91]

In Matt 1:1–17, Scripture connects Abraham to the lineage of Jesus Christ. The Abrahamic covenant clearly demonstrates the lineage of faith through justification by faith in Jesus Christ alone, even before the calling of the people of Israel (Gen 15:5–7; 17:4–7; 22:17–18).

> And he brought him outside and said, "Look toward heaven, and number the stars, if you are able to number them." Then he said to him, "So shall your offspring be." And he believed the Lord, and he counted it to him as righteousness. And he said to him, "I am the Lord who brought you out from Ur of the Chaldeans to give you this land to possess." (Gen 15:5–7)

The New Testament explains in more detail that Abraham is the father of all who believe in God (Rom 3:21–31; 4:1–25; Gal 4:21–31; Heb 10:38–39; 11:1–2, 6, 8–12, 17–19). The Abrahamic covenant, looked at it with the New Testament, shows that the coming Messiah, Jesus Christ, is the true object of faith. God had already foretold his plan to elevate Abraham's faith to "faith in the coming Messiah." In other words, God had already bestowed the grace of faith upon Abraham before Jesus was incarnated and paid the full price for sins.

In this way, salvation always takes place through the covenant of God's grace.[92] Abraham was also saved by faith alone in the word of God's promise by grace alone. Therefore, the elevation of Abraham's faith to faith in Jesus signifies that it is solely the work of God's grace.

> That is why his faith was "counted to him as righteousness." But the words "it was counted to him" were not written for his sake alone, but for ours also. It will be counted to us who believe in him who raised from the dead Jesus our Lord. (Rom 4:22–24)

As Paul says, the faith of sinful Abraham in the Old Testament was "counted to him as righteousness" because God had the purpose to make

---

91. Jacob remembers the covenant between God and Abraham.
"But you said, 'I will surely do you good, and make your offspring as the sand of the sea, which cannot be numbered for multitude'" (Gen 32:12).

92. Horton, *Covenant Theology*, 36. Paul, in Gal 4:21–31, compares the free woman Sarah and the slave woman Hagar, revealing that the Abrahamic covenant is a covenant of grace. He also says that all believers, like Isaac, are "children of promise" (Gal 4:28). Salvation is entirely by God's sovereign grace through his promise, apart from human merits (Horton, *Covenant Theology*, 35–44).

him "the father of faith in God" (Rom 4:11) by grace alone. This presupposes that neither Noah, a descendant of Adam, nor Abraham had any qualification to be justified by works. On the one hand, the Adamic covenant runs through the Abrahamic covenant. Even if people kept these covenants, there was no promise of forgiveness of their sins or being justified by their works. On the other hand, they could be saved or declared righteous by grace alone.

Before believing in Jesus, Paul himself did not understand "justification by God's grace alone," shown in Gen 15:5–7. Later, having realized this, he quotes this passage in Rom 4:3, and explains the true purpose of God calling Abraham from Ur of Chaldean. The call of Abraham was to be the father of faith for justification "by Jesus Christ alone" (Rom 3:22).[93] So, Abraham is to be the father of faith for all who believe in only Jesus Christ, including both Israelites and all gentiles.[94]

> That is why it depends on faith, in order that the promise may rest on grace and be guaranteed to all his offspring—not only to the adherent of the law but also to the one who shares the faith of Abraham, who is the father of us all. (Rom 4:16)

God further revealed his purpose for calling Abraham when Abraham was ninety-nine years old (Gen 17:4–7). Israelites, the descendants of Abraham, Isaac, and Jacob, became the people of God according to the Abrahamic covenant. This is the word of the covenant of grace, stating that God will be the God of Abraham and his descendants of faith, and make the descendants of faith the people of God's kingdom. God fulfills this word of promise only by grace.

> Behold, my covenant is with you, and you shall be the father of a multitude of nations. No longer shall your name be called Abram, but your name shall be Abraham, for I have made you the father of a multitude of nations. I will make you exceedingly fruitful, and I will make you into nations, and kings shall come from you. And I will establish my covenant between me and you and your offspring after you throughout their generations for an everlasting covenant, to be God to you and to your offspring after you. (Gen 17:4–7)

---

93. "The righteousness of God through faith in Jesus Christ for all who believe. For there is no distinction" (Rom 3:22).

94. We will discuss this in more detail in "2-B. Jesus' Perfect Obedience in the Broad Sense," in vol. 2, ch. 2.

In Gen 17, God once again promises to make a great nation through Abraham and make them his people. It is evident that the people of the eternal kingdom of God are the descendants of all who believe in Jesus Christ alone. God thus establishes an eternal covenant with these descendants of faith, promising to be their God. Therefore, this faith believes in God and trusts in the word of God's promises. Abraham is the father of this faith.

God made a unilateral promise to Abraham, just as he did with the Noahic covenant. However, according to the promise with Abraham, he used all necessary means to carry out his plan and kept the covenant to the end. Of course, the essential core of the covenant of grace lies in the fact that God himself has surely kept the covenant he has promised. However, we must not forget that while the Abrahamic covenant is a covenant of grace, it demands a responsibility of obedience of faith to the covenant's word like all other covenants (Gen 15:6; 26:4–5; Heb 11:8–12, 17–19; Jas 2:21–23).[95]

> I will surely bless you, and I will surely multiply your offspring as the stars of heaven and as the sand that is on the seashore. And your offspring shall possess the gate of his enemies, and in your offspring shall all the nations of the earth be blessed, because you have obeyed my voice. (Gen 22:17–18)[96]

Finally, God calls the coming Messiah "your offspring" to Abraham. Through Abraham's offspring, Abraham's sin would be forgiven. This offspring would come to this earth to accomplish the salvation of sinners and would eventually sit on the heavenly throne as the eternal King, ruling the kingdom of God. Likewise, the important concept of the offspring as the eternal King appears not only in the Adamic covenant (Gen 3:15) but also in the Abrahamic and Davidic covenants.[97]

In summary, not only Abraham but all of us are saved and declared righteous *only* by faith, *only* through the perfect obedience of Jesus Christ alone, *only* by grace, *only* through our union with Christ and the

---

95. Frame, *Systematic Theology*, 70–72. "I will multiply your offspring as the stars of heaven and will give to your offspring all these lands. And in your offspring all the nations of the earth shall be blessed, because Abraham obeyed my voice and kept my charge, my commandments, my statutes, and my laws" (Gen 26:4–5).

96. This text reminds us of the first gospel, saying of "her offspring," "he shall bruise your head, and you shall bruise his heel" (Gen 3:15).

97. Cf. Horton, *Covenant Theology*, 43–47.

imputation of the perfect righteousness of this eternal King alone.[98] In this way, this concept of the offspring in the Adamic, Abrahamic, and Davidic covenants is founded upon the perfect sacrifice of Jesus Christ, the Mediator of the covenant of grace.

As God reveals to Abraham the eternal King, the offspring, God makes him experience the pain of sacrificing his only son Isaac.[99] This signifies that through the sacrifice of Jesus Christ, Abraham's descendant, all the sins of the people of the eternal kingdom of God would be forgiven, and the qualifications of the people of God's kingdom would be restored.

Therefore, the Abrahamic covenant shows what the only way is for the sinful descendants (sinners) of Adam to become the descendants of faith who believe in the Redeemer. Our salvation is only through Jesus Christ by the grace of God (*sola gratia*), and there is no other way. The requirement of the Adamic covenant also runs through the Abrahamic covenant. Additionally, the Abrahamic covenant requires obedience to the word of God's covenant. The best place to see the meaning of the covenant of grace in the Old Testament is the Abrahamic covenant.

D. The Mosaic Covenant

The Mosaic covenant is a covenant to become the people of God's kingdom. To set the Israelites free from being the slaves of Egypt was to make them "a holy people" of God's kingdom (Exod 19). For this reason, as the law to rule Israel, the Mosaic covenant shows a difference from the Adamic, Noahic, and Abrahamic covenants. However, like all other covenants, the Mosaic covenant also shows the "necessity of God's grace" and has the same requirement for "human obedience" to the covenant.[100] The Mosaic covenant also has underlying requirements for sin and obedience, as seen in the Adamic covenant.

The most important lesson the Mosaic covenant teaches is that God, who rules over the kingdom of God through the word, requires obedience of faith. The Mosaic covenant promises blessings for those who keep the word and curses for those who disobey it. So, the people of the eternal

---

98. See vol. 2.

99. The Abrahamic covenant shows the elements of a blood covenant: the animal sacrifice in Gen 15:9–21, circumcision in Gen 17, and the offering of Isaac as a sacrifice in Gen 22. Cf. Horton, *Covenant Theology*, 146–48.

100. Frame, *Systematic Theology*, 73.

kingdom of God are those who accept and believe in the word of God as it is. In other words, the people of God's kingdom are those who live by making God's word the standard for judgment and action. Obeying God's word is an act of acknowledging God's rule through faith (Deut 8:3; Matt 4:4).

> And he humbled you and let you hunger and fed you with manna, which you did not know, nor did your fathers know, that he might make you know that man does not live by bread alone, but man lives by every word that comes from the mouth of the LORD. (Deut 8:3)

1. The Mosaic Covenant and the History of Israel in the Old Testament

The Old Testament is mainly composed of historical stories. In the Old Testament, the story of the Pentateuch of Moses shows the legal framework along with the covenant between God and Israel. In the Pentateuch of Moses, the Ten Commandments and the Mosaic law describe the legal obligations in detail within the covenant relationship between God and Israel.[101] In other words, the Ten Commandments and the Mosaic law served as the framework for the covenantal relationship between God and Israel that guided the history of Israel in the Old Testament. They served as the framework for the covenant relationship between God and Israel, leading the story of Israel's history up until the incarnation of Jesus Christ.[102] Therefore, understanding the Mosaic covenant is very important for comprehending the Old Testament.

As we have seen so far, God made covenants with humans, as in the case of the Israelites. When the Bible describes the obligations of the covenant between God and Israel, it appears to show the relationship between agreements of kings, a king of a suzerain state and a king of a vassal state. In particular, the covenant relationship between God and Israel through the Ten Commandments and the Mosaic law is sometimes seen as the relationship between the suzerain and the vassal.[103] This relation-

---

101. Kline, *Structure of Biblical Authority*, 53–54.
102. Kline, *Structure of Biblical Authority*, 56–57.
103. Frame, *Systematic Theology*, 18–19.

ship is also viewed as a covenant relationship between the suzerain who gives the covenant and the vassal who takes an oath of loyalty to him.[104]

However, the covenantal relationship between God and Israel shows a striking difference from the relationships between the kings of the world. Remember that there is a very significant connection between the biblical covenants. Why is this connection important?

First of all, we should view this covenant in relation to the Abrahamic covenant. On the one hand, God, who remembered the Abrahamic covenant, freed the Israelites who were living as slaves in Egypt.

> And God heard their groaning, and God remembered his covenant with Abraham, with Isaac, and with Jacob. God saw the people of Israel—and God knew. (Exod 2:24-25)

That is, the Mosaic covenant took place in connection with the previous covenants. God connected it to the previous covenants such as Adamic, Noahic, and Abrahamic covenants. On the other hand, God's legal administration through the Mosaic covenant continued through the Davidic covenant and up to the new covenant.

While it may not be easy to accept, the Mosaic covenant is also a covenant relationship between God the Creator and the Israelites, the creatures. God is the King and the Lord, while the Israelites, the descendants of Adam, are sinners and servants of God. Remember that God would surely keep the covenant he made with Israel. The Mosaic covenant includes the elements of "grace and law," with the Lord God requiring obedience of faith to the covenant word.[105]

---

104. Kline, *Structure of Biblical Authority*, 114–30, 131–53; Frame, *Systematic Theology*, 18–19, 83–84. M. G. Kline finds this relationship between the suzerain and the vassal from the suzerainty treaty of the ancient Hittite culture. Kline also views the book of Deuteronomy in the form of a suzerainty treaty.

According to him, this pattern of the suzerainty treaty can be summarized into five parts in relation to the covenants: (1) the name of the great king, (2) the historical prologue, (3) the stipulations, (4) the sanctions (the blessings for obedience and curses for disobedience), and (5) future administration of the covenant.

When looking at the structure of this treaty, we must not forget that the God of the Mosaic covenant is the one who remembers the previous covenants. Through the Mosaic covenant, God, the Author of the biblical covenants, continually maintains the "legal administration" of God throughout the history of Israel in the Old Testament. Of course, God maintained the continuity between the Mosaic covenant and other covenants by using his wisdom and power. In other words, as we saw in the Adamic covenant, it means that we need to view the Mosaic covenant in relation to other covenants. Focusing too much on one covenant can cause us to miss God's overall purpose as shown in the whole Bible.

105. Please refer to "2-A. Jesus' Perfect Obedience in the Narrow Sense (Centered

The Mosaic law contains expectations and hope for the judging righteousness of God on sinners and the saving righteousness of the coming Messiah. In fact, the Mosaic covenant is introduced as a model of the legal framework for the eternal kingdom of God, not only for Israel but for all humanity. We will now take a brief look at the Mosaic law.

II. The Mosaic Law

After making a covenant with God through the Mosaic covenant, the people of Israel had to now live according to the law of the righteous God. Through this covenant, Israel, a type of the eternal kingdom of God, became God's people, and God became their God. The Mosaic covenant is distinguished from other covenants due to its legal function in governing Israel. We can summarize the essential characteristics of the Mosaic law in four aspects.

First, God gave the Ten Commandments and the Mosaic law as the "social and moral judgment standard" and "guidelines for life" to Israel, God's covenant people. The Ten Commandments given on Mount Sinai (Exod 20:1–17) and the Mosaic law given beyond the Jordan, in the land of Moab (forty years later [Deut 1:6]) are the legal covenant by which God governed Israel (Exod 19:4—20:20).[106] Therefore, the covenant people had an obligation to fully obey the Mosaic covenant, which was the law of Israel.[107] The Ten Commandments (the Decalogue) and the Mosaic law are a type of the law of the eternal kingdom of God for the holy people of the covenantal kingdom.[108]

> "You yourselves have seen what I did to the Egyptians, and how I bore you on eagles' wings and brought you to myself. Now therefore, if you will indeed obey my voice and keep my covenant, you shall be my treasured possession among all peoples, for all the earth is mine; and you shall be to me a kingdom of priests and a holy nation." These are the words that you shall speak to the people of Israel. (Exod 19:4–5)

---

on the Mosaic Law)," in vol. 2, ch. 2.

106. The Ten Commandments in Exodus (20:1–7) is the summary of the Mosaic law in Deuteronomy. Cf. Horton, *Covenant Theology*, 39.

107. Frame, *Systematic Theology*, 72–75.

108. Israel is the shadow and type of the eternal kingdom of God. Cf. Kline, *Structure of Biblical Authority*, 105; Frame, *Systematic Theology*, 72–75.

Second, God basically gives the Decalogue and the Mosaic law "to rule the nation of Israel."[109] The Decalogue and the Mosaic law can be broadly divided into three major categories: (1) social law (judicial law [Exod 21:1—23:13]), (2) sacrificial law (ceremonial law [Exod 25:1—30:38; Lev 1:1—8:36; Num 15:1–31]), and (3) moral law (Exod 20:1–17; Matt 22:34–40; Mark 12:28–31; Luke 13:9–10; Gal 5:14), which can be summarized as "love for your God and love for neighbors."[110]

> "Teacher, which is the great commandment in the Law?" And he said to him, "You shall love the Lord your God with all your heart and with all your soul and with all your mind. This is the great and first commandment. And a second is like it: You shall love your neighbor as yourself. On these two commandments depend all the Law and the Prophets." (Matt 22:36–40)

God promised blessings for obedience to the word of the Mosaic law and curses for disobedience (Deut 27:26; 28:1–6, 15–19). Like other covenants, the Mosaic law also required the perfect obedience of faith.[111] However, there was no promise of salvation for obedience to the Mosaic law.

Third, God gave the Mosaic law as "our guardian" (Gal 3:24) that led to the coming of the Messiah, Jesus Christ. Obedience to the Mosaic law should be viewed in terms of both external actions (social law and sacrificial law) and internal actions (moral law: love God and neighbor). God demanded obedience in both external and internal actions. If one looks at obedience to the Mosaic law only in terms of external actions (social laws and ceremonial laws), one may fall into the trap of recognizing human merits in the doctrine of justification.[112] Therefore, when we

---

109. Kang, *Living Out the Gospel*, 239.

110. Kang, *Living Out the Gospel*, 239. Calvin and Luther view the Mosaic law given to Israel as moral law, ceremonial law, and judicial law (*Institutes* 4.20.14–15; Luther, *Commentary on Galatians*, 90).

111. Horton, *Covenant Theology*, 38, 130.

112. As we saw, the Adamic covenant (post-fall of Adam) and the Mosaic covenant (Mosaic law) are sometimes viewed in the concept of the covenant of works. In this case, the blessings for obedience as well as curses for disobedience to the covenant of works are seen from the perspective of the covenant of law. We should be cautious when connecting the concept of the covenant of works with the doctrine of justification (Horton, *Covenant Theology*, 32–39, 40–57, 83–94, 105–10, 130, 174–82; Horton, *Covenant and Salvation*, 11–36, 87–91; Horton, *Justification*, 2:414–15; Kline, *Structure of Biblical Authority*). We need to examine this more to make it clear.

God gave these two covenants in the Old Testament to fit the temporary and historical characteristics of their times, so the "works principle" from the perspective of the

look at the Mosaic law, we should be able to see the necessity of Jesus' perfect obedience for sinners.

Jesus points out the internal aspect of obedience to the Mosaic law as a matter of the heart. He proves that without the gracious work of God through the Holy Spirit, it is impossible to love God and love one's neighbor.[113] Romans and Galatians correctly teach that sinners have neither the ability to obey God's word nor the ability to love God without the work of the Holy Spirit.

The Mosaic law, as shown in the New Testament, reveals the sins of all people through the demand for perfect obedience (Rom 2:12; 3:10, 20; 5:19). The Mosaic law clearly shows that sinful humans can never overcome sin by their own abilities and have no capacity to obey God's word. This is because it is impossible for all sinners to obey the holy, righteous, and good law of Moses.[114]

---

covenant of law can help us see the difference from other covenants. We must be careful when talking about the *meritorious* obedience of the Mosaic covenant using this works principle from a justification standpoint. For example, Meredith G. Kline says that Israel failed to "maintain the necessary *meritorious* obedience" to Mosaic covenant using this works principle (Kline, *Kingdom Prologue*, 109; emphasis added) Kline's theology, however, does not mean the meritorious human actions that can be justified by God here. To him, the perfect obedience of Jesus is the only "meritorious obedience" for sinners to be justified by God (109). In fact, Kline applies this "works principle" only to "the typological kingdom in Canaan," not to "inheriting the eternal kingdom" (237). Cf. Horton, *Covenant and Salvation*, 97–101; Horton, *Covenant Theology*; Horton, *Justification*, vol. 2; Kline, *Structure of Biblical Authority*; Irons, "Kline on Works Principle." Kline uses the term "meritorious obedience" with this "works principle" when speaking of the reward for faithful obedience to the Mosaic covenant. He never uses the term "meritorious" in the sense of the merit of human works, like the medieval theologians.

Salvation is entirely the work of God. We need to remember that the Reformers severely criticized the concept of "indwelling grace" in medieval theology when medieval theologians used the term "meritorious" in the sense of meritorious works in the doctrine of justification (works righteousness). We know that most theologians generally try to avoid words that can cause confusion or be misunderstood in a way that they do not intend. It would be better, therefore, if theologians use words that are likely to cause less confusion in the future. We will discuss the concept of indwelling grace in more detail in vol. 2, ch. 1.

113. Please refer to "2-A. Jesus' Perfect Obedience in the Narrow Sense (Centered on the Mosaic Law)," in vol. 2, ch. 2.

114. As we saw earlier, Scripture teaches that sins and the curses entered the world due to the disobedience of Adam, the covenant breaker (Rom 1:18—3:20; 5:12–21). It reveals the necessity of the perfect obedience and righteousness of Jesus Christ because of the unrighteousness of Adam, the representative of all humanity. Because of Adam's sin, Scripture (especially Jesus and Paul) strongly criticizes those who view the gospel in the sense of human meritorious works (works righteousness) of the Mosaic law. Scripture strongly rejects any attempt to graft the doctrine of justification onto the

> So the law is holy, and the commandment is holy and righteous and good. (Rom 7:12)

> For by works of the law no human being will be justified in his sight, since through the law comes knowledge of sin. (Rom 3:20)

> As it is written: None is righteous, no, not one. (Rom 3:10)

God gave us the Mosaic law so that it could expose the inability of sinners to achieve salvation by their own efforts and to instead turn our eyes to the Messiah Jesus Christ. Therefore, the Mosaic law points to the coming Messiah.[115] Jesus restored the eternal kingdom of God through his life and death of perfect obedience. He abolished the social and sacrificial laws related to external actions, and fulfilled the moral law (love God and love neighbor) related to internal actions.[116]

Fourth, the Mosaic law best demonstrates the structure of "the righteousness of God." The righteousness of God shown in the Mosaic law is the standard that judges sins and the unrighteousness of sinners. Lawlessness and unrighteousness resulting from sin called forth the judging righteousness of God. However, no means of salvation through human effort could satisfy God's righteousness. No one could pay the price for the penalty of sin, bear the punishment that came as a consequence of sin against God's word, or achieve the perfect obedience that God demanded. Thus, the Mosaic law shows that the salvation of all humanity, who are all sinners, is impossible without God's grace. There is no way for those who commit lawlessness and unrighteousness to satisfy the standard of the judging righteousness of God. The Mosaic law clearly reveals

---

works principle of the wrong covenantal perspective of the law. In other words, when approaching the doctrine of justification with the concept of obedience in the works principle—like the meritorious reward concept of medieval theology—all interpretations that view it in terms of human merit-based rewards are rejected. God declares us righteous in justification, and makes us righteous in sanctification by his grace alone. Therefore, anyone who tries to view the doctrines of justification and sanctification under the new covenant of the New Testament through this works principle must be very careful. For the concept of human merit in the doctrine of justification, please refer to "2. Gospel and Jesus Christ," in vol. 2, ch. 1.

115. Cf. Horton, *Covenant Theology*, 32, 38.

116. There is no one who does not sin from the heart. Jesus also uses the Mosaic law to point out the problem of sin that originates from the heart. "For out of the heart come evil thoughts, murder, adultery, sexual immorality, theft, false witness, slander" (Matt 15:19).

that God has the only solution to satisfy the judging righteousness of God for sinners.

In conclusion, on the one hand, the Mosaic law serves both as the law to rule Israel and as a summary of the list of all possible sins that modern humans can commit. It clearly shows the judging righteousness of God. On the other hand, the summary of the Mosaic law is the Decalogue, and the summary of the Decalogue is "love for God and love for neighbors." A life of obedience to all the word of the law is a life of "loving God and loving neighbor." Therefore, a life without "love for God and love for neighbor" is in violation of the words of the Mosaic law. The Mosaic law also shows the necessity of the saving righteousness of God because there is no one who can escape "the law of God's love" that the Mosaic law speaks of (Rom 1:18—3:20). Thus, the Mosaic law poses the question to not only the people of Israel but also to all of us living in modern times: "Do you have the ability to love God and love your neighbors?"[117]

III. The Messiah

What is the relationship between the Mosaic law and the Messiah?

As we saw, the Israelites became a holy nation, but they were not free from the status of sinners who commit evil sins from the heart.

On the one hand, the judging righteousness of God revealed in the Mosaic law clearly shows that all human beings are sinners and cannot obtain salvation through human merits by works.

On the other hand, the Mosaic law tells us about the necessity of the saving righteousness of God through Jesus. Therefore, the Mosaic law in the Old Testament demonstrates the clear necessity of the gospel that shows the saving righteousness of God more than any other covenants (Rom 1:17; 3:21–22). Thus, we can find two key elements from the Mosaic law centered on the Messiah in redemptive history.

First, the Israelites who received the Mosaic law are connected not only to the Mosaic covenant but also to the Abrahamic covenant—through Abraham, their ancestor. Although the Mosaic covenant is distinguished as the national law of Israel from the Abrahamic covenant, it is rooted in the Abrahamic covenant as well. Throughout the history of

---

117. An answer to this question will be discussed in detail in vol. 2, ch. 1, "The Gospel and Jesus Christ"; and vol. 2, ch. 2, "The Conditions of Justification: The Perfect Obedience of Jesus Christ."

Israel, the relationship with the Abrahamic covenant continued for the Israelites.

> And God heard their groaning, and God remembered his covenant with Abraham, with Isaac, and with Jacob. (Exod 2:24)

As we saw in the covenant of grace, the Mosaic covenant also has the elements of blood covenant, involving the sacrifice of animals killed as substitutes for human sin, as seen in the covenants with Adam, Noah, Abraham, and David (Gen 3:15, 21; 17:11, 14; Exod 24:8; Ezek 44:7; Zech 9:11). The Israelites pledged with the "blood of the covenant" as a covenant people through the Mosaic covenant with God.

> Then he took the Book of the Covenant and read it in the hearing of the people. And they said, "All that the Lord has spoken we will do, and we will be obedient." And Moses took the blood and threw it on the people and said, "Behold the blood of the covenant that the Lord has made with you in accordance with all these words." (Exod 24:7–8)

God pledged with the blood of the covenant with the Israelites, but the Israelites did not change from a sinful to a righteous status. The establishment of the blood covenant between God and the Israelites foreshadows the blood that Jesus Christ, the coming Messiah, will shed for the forgiveness of sins. God made a vow to the Israelites by "God's grace alone" and "through Jesus Christ alone." This means that, like the blood covenant established for the forgiveness of "committed sin" in the Adamic covenant by the blood of the offspring of the woman, the Mosaic covenant is also a covenant established by the blood of Jesus Christ (Gen 3:15; Heb 9:15).

> For this is my blood of the covenant, which is poured out for many for the forgiveness of sins (Matt 26:28).[118]

Second, the Mosaic law leads to the expectation of the Messiah who will satisfy the righteousness of God. The Mosaic law demanded perfect obedience to the word of God from the Israelites. To obey the word of God by faith is an act of acknowledging the reign of God. But there is the issue that no sinner can meet the standard of the righteousness of God shown in the Mosaic law. Therefore, on the basis of the covenant

---

118. See also Mark 14:24; Luke 22:20; Heb 9:18, 20; 10:29; 12:24; 13:20. "In the same way also he took the cup, after supper, saying, 'This cup is the new covenant in my blood. Do this, as often as you drink it, in remembrance of me'" (1 Cor 11:25).

of redemption, there is a "common unity," the necessity of the redemptive work of Jesus Christ in the relationship between the Old Testament and the New Testament, as well as the relationship between the Mosaic law and the gospel.[119] God gave the Mosaic law for the purpose to make people realize their inability to obey the word of God and to lead them to expect the Messiah, Jesus Christ.

Jesus Christ, the Representative of the new covenant, is the Achiever who fulfilled all the conditions of righteousness for sinners. Jesus Christ took on all the necessary conditions to satisfy God, as well as all the curses for sin, on behalf of all believers through his life and death of perfect obedience.[120] So, the life of perfect obedience by Jesus becomes the foundation for declaring sinners righteous.[121]

All humans, including the Israelites who received the Mosaic law, are justified "by grace alone," "in Christ alone," and "by faith alone" apart from works. That is, when you believe in Jesus only by God's grace, God considers "the perfect righteousness achieved by Jesus" yours and declares you righteous.[122] Therefore, it is very significant to see that salvation is entirely the work of God "by God's grace alone," apart from works, even to the Israelites who received the Mosaic covenant. Obviously, the Adamic covenant and the covenant of grace also run through the Mosaic covenant. Additionally, the Mosaic law also has requirements for obedience to the word of God's covenant.

E. The Davidic Covenant

When God made a covenant with David the king, God made a promise that his throne would be eternal. Through David, the greatest king of Israel, we can see that the revelation of the Messiah, the King of kings, is becoming more specific. The Messiah of the Davidic covenant is the Mediator of the covenant of redemption and the covenant of grace, the Fulfiller of all covenants. God's promise that the Davidic throne will be eternal is not just a promise given to David and the people of Israel, but a

---

119. Cf. Frame, *Systematic Theology*, 76–77.

120. Cf. Horton, *Covenant Theology*, 41–42, 57, 59, 69, 71–72, 91, 101–2, 105, 108–9.

121. For the perfect obedience of Jesus' life, please refer to "2-B. Jesus' Perfect Obedience in the Broad Sense," in vol. 2, ch. 2.

122. For the perfect righteousness, please see vol. 2, ch. 3, "The Fulfillment of All Covenants: The Transmission of the Perfect Righteousness of Jesus Christ."

promise made to all the people of God's kingdom. The eternal kingdom through David's lineage will be the eternal kingdom of God.[123] Therefore, the Davidic covenant is God's promise that the Messiah, the eternal King, will come from among the descendants of David the king.

> When your days are fulfilled to walk with your fathers, I will raise up your offspring after you, one of your own sons, and I will establish his kingdom. He shall build a house for me, and I will establish his throne forever. I will be to him a father, and he shall be to me a son. I will not take my steadfast love from him, as I took it from him who was before you, but I will confirm him in my house and in my kingdom forever, and his throne shall be established forever. (2 Chr 17:11–14)

In this promise of God, Jesus, the offspring of David the king, becomes the King of the eternal kingdom of God.[124] In the Davidic covenant, the offspring of the Davidic covenant reminds us of "the offspring of the woman" in the Adamic covenant (Gen 3:15) and "the offspring of Abraham" (Gen 10:32; 11:10–32; 22:17–18). Like the Adamic covenant and the Abrahamic covenant, the root of the messianic promise in the Davidic covenant is also the covenant of redemption.[125] Thus, the mediator of both the Adamic covenant and the Davidic covenant is Jesus Christ who came as the Messiah. This Messiah is also the Mediator of the covenants of redemption and grace.

> Therefore he is the mediator of a new covenant, so that those who are called may receive the promised eternal inheritance, since a death has occurred that redeems them from the transgressions committed under the first covenant. (Heb 9:15)

In looking forward to the coming Messiah, the Davidic covenant shares a common connection with the Adamic covenant, the Noahic covenant, the Abrahamic covenant, and the Mosaic covenant. The promises

---

123. Cf. Frame, *Systematic Theology*, 76–77; Horton, *Covenant Theology*, 56.

124. In 2 Sam 7:12–16, the Davidic covenant is also mentioned.
"When your days are fulfilled and you lie down with your fathers, I will raise up your offspring after you, who shall come from your body, and I will establish his kingdom. He shall build a house for my name, and I will establish the throne of his kingdom forever. I will be to him a father, and he shall be to me a son. When he commits iniquity, I will discipline him with the rod of men, with the stripes of the sons of men, but my steadfast love will not depart from him, as I took it from Saul, whom I put away from before you. And your house and your kingdom shall be made sure forever before me. Your throne shall be established forever" (2 Sam 7:12–16).

125. Cf. Horton, *Covenant Theology*, 78–83, 109–10.

of God in the Adamic covenant, the Noahic covenant, the Abrahamic covenant, and the Mosaic covenant continued in the Davidic covenant as well. There is also continuity of the Adamic covenant and the covenant of grace in the Davidic covenant.[126]

However, there is a difference between the Messiah of the Davidic covenant and the Messiah of other covenants. The difference lies in the fact that the Messiah of the Davidic covenant is the offspring that brings the eternal blessings to us as the King of the eternal kingdom of God. The Messiah of Davidic covenant is Jesus Christ, "the King of the eternal kingdom of God." All the promises of the Davidic covenant were fulfilled in Jesus Christ, the eternal King.[127]

> And the crowds that went before him and that followed him were shouting, "Hosanna to the Son of David! Blessed is he who comes in the name of the Lord! Hosanna in the highest!" (Matt 21:9)

Moreover, the Davidic covenant is God's everlasting promise established on God's sure grace, which is based on the redemptive work of the coming Messiah, Jesus Christ. Isaiah the prophet also proclaims that the Davidic covenant is the "everlasting covenant" of God given only by grace, which will save sinners through the coming Messiah.[128]

In Rom 4:6–8, Scripture says that David spoke of the blessing of forgiveness of sins given by the coming Messiah. This is "the blessing of the one to whom God counts (credits, NIV) righteousness apart from works" (Rom 4:6) only by grace.

> Just as David also speaks of the blessing of the one to whom God counts righteousness apart from works: "Blessed are those whose lawless deeds are forgiven, and whose sins are covered; blessed is the man against whom the Lord will not count his sin." (Rom 4:6–8)[129]

---

126. Horton, *Covenant and Salvation*, 134; Horton, *Covenant Theology*, 102, 131, 134.

127. Matthew reveals that Jesus Christ, as a descendant of David, came from human genealogy according to God's promises. Matthew 1:1–17 shows the genealogy of Jesus Christ, who came into the world as a descendant of David. See also Matt 9:27; 12:23; 20:30–31; 21:9, 15; 22:42 (Frame, *Systematic Theology*, 78; Ridderbos, *Coming of the Kingdom*, 34–36). Cf. Jer 23:5; 30:9; Isa 9:6–7; Luke 1:32, 69.

128. "Incline your ear, and come to me; hear, that your soul may live; and I will make with you an everlasting covenant, my steadfast, sure love for David" (Isa 55:3).

129. Actually, Paul in Rom 4:6–8 quotes David's Ps 32:1–2:
"Blessed is the one whose transgression is forgiven, whose sin is covered. Blessed is the man against whom the Lord counts no iniquity, and in whose spirit there is no

Before Jesus came to the earth, David had sung of the day when sinners would be forgiven of their sins and justified by God's grace alone, by the merit of the Messiah Jesus alone, by faith alone. For this reason, the covenant of grace is the ground of the Davidic covenant like other covenants. Likewise, the Davidic covenant indicates that David anticipated the era of the new covenant through the Messiah.[130]

Therefore, God revealed and worked by his will to restore the broken relationship with humanity through the Davidic covenant. God also had consistently demanded continuous obedience of faith to the word of God's covenant throughout human history. Thus, the Davidic covenant, just as other covenants, shows the grace of God and obedience of faith, which are the two major themes of God's sovereignty and human responsibility in the Bible.[131] In addition, there are two things that serve as the foundation of the Davidic covenant: (1) the Adamic covenant and the Mosaic covenant and (2) the demand for obedience to the word of the covenant. Remember that God demands obedience of faith to God's gifts even though he gives salvation and faith as gifts only by God's grace through the Representative of the new covenant, Jesus Christ.

God has fulfilled all his promises given to David through Jesus Christ, who is both David's descendant and the true King (Matt 9:27; 12:23; 20:30–31; 21:9, 15; 22:42), and given us what he has achieved through him.[132] This is the magnificent and amazing grace of God.

Jesus, who came for us, is not only the descendant of David in the flesh, but also "David's Lord and Root" (Rev 5:5; 22:16).[133] Jesus as "the offspring of the woman who rules the earth" is the King of all creatures who delivers the blessings of God to his own people by grace alone.[134]

As the Davidic covenant tells us, we should remember that God has been continuously working and accomplishing all the covenants, even in times when humans have been completely unaware of the fact. The story of salvation in Jesus, through the redemptive work of Jesus Christ, which is at the core of the covenant of grace, also serves as the foundation of the Davidic covenant. Although it seemed like God was silent for a long time

---

deceit."

130. Kline, *Structure of Biblical Authority*, 84.

131. Frame, *Systematic Theology*, 77; Kline, *Structure of Biblical Authority*, 146.

132. Frame, *Systematic Theology*, 78–79; Frame, *Doctrine of God*, 296; Horton, *Covenant Theology*, 132–34.

133. Frame, *Doctrine of God*, 655.

134. Frame, *Systematic Theology*, 79.

for the salvation of sinners, in reality, he made an enormous sacrifice to save sinners according to his promise. God has been diligently carrying out every preparation without fail to accept sinful humans as his children throughout human history.

As such, the Old Testament covenants continually tell the story of sinners becoming part of God's family in the Messiah Jesus Christ. The "story of the Bible" transforms into the narrative of us becoming the family of the eternal King in him through Jesus Christ, the Representative of the new covenant. The Old Testament covenants point to this new covenant.

F. The New Covenant

> Behold, the days are coming, declares the LORD, when I will make a new covenant with the house of Israel and the house of Judah, not like the covenant that I made with their fathers on the day when I took them by the hand to bring them out of the land of Egypt, my covenant that they broke, though I was their husband, declares the LORD. For this is the covenant that I will make with the house of Israel after those days, declares the LORD: I will put my law within them, and I will write it on their hearts. And I will be their God, and they shall be my people. (Jer 31:31–33)

Through the new covenant, the purpose of God's creation hidden throughout human history since Adam was evidently revealed. Not only the purpose of the creation, but also the secret of the kingdom of God has been revealed to the world. Also, the continuity of God's will for the kingdom of God shown in the Old Testament covenants has been culminated in salvation through the Messiah Jesus Christ. As we saw, sin that was begun in the Adamic covenant and God's grace that was shown in the Abrahamic covenant ran through all the Old Testament covenants. The secret of God's covenant of redemption and the promise of God's covenant of grace, which had continued for a long time, were fulfilled in the new covenant through the Messiah.

The Adamic covenant shows that sinners under the fall of Adam do not have the ability to obey the word of God. Since all the descendants of Adam are sinners in Adam, the Mosaic law of the Mosaic covenant—holy and righteous and good (Rom 7:12)—also reveals that all humankind have no ability to save themselves or to be justified apart from God's grace (Rom 1:18–3:20, 3:9–12, 3:19–20, 5:12–21). So, after the fall of

Adam, all the covenants have directly or indirectly demonstrated a fact that salvation or justification is entirely the work of God by grace alone, apart from human works. Only the Messiah, the Representative of the new covenant, can save sinners. Finally, God, who had appointed Jesus Christ as the Representative of the new covenant, fulfilled all the Old Testament covenants through him. To save sinners through Jesus is the fulfillment of the promised covenant of grace.[135]

As we saw earlier, God prophesized that he would establish the people of God's kingdom through all the covenants. Therefore, the fulfillment of the new covenant can be seen in two ways: the fulfillment of the covenant with Israel (the old covenant) and the fulfillment of all the covenants, including the Adamic covenant, within Jesus Christ in redemptive history.[136] The Adamic covenant, the Noahic covenant, the Abrahamic covenant, the Mosaic covenant, and the Davidic covenant—all these covenants were fulfilled in Jesus Christ.[137] This is a covenantal fulfillment by which God has established a new relationship between God and his people.

> And he said to them, "O foolish ones, and slow of heart to believe all that the prophets have spoken! Was it not necessary that the Christ should suffer these things and enter into his glory?" And beginning with Moses and all the Prophets, he interpreted to them in all the Scriptures the things concerning himself. (Luke 24:25-27)[138]

THE FULFILLMENT OF THE NEW COVENANT

To take a closer look at "What is the fulfillment of the new covenant?," we need more perspective of the Old Testament covenants. The penalty of sin for disobedience in the Adamic covenant was paid in full through the obedience to the new covenant. God's judgment on sin shown in the Noahic covenant was carried out on the cross in the new covenant. The grace of justification revealed in the Abrahamic covenant was fulfilled in the new covenant. The demands of loving God and loving neighbor in the Mosaic

---

135. Frame, *Systematic Theology*, 79-80; Frame, *Doctrine of God*, 450.

136. Ridderbos, *Coming of the Kingdom*, 192-202, 253-55; Frame, *Systematic Theology*, 79.

137. Matthew 1:1-17 is famous for connecting Abraham and David with Jesus Christ.

138. Frame, *Systematic Theology*, 79.

covenant were all fulfilled in the new covenant. The prophecy of the eternal King in the Davidic covenant was also fulfilled in the new covenant.

Furthermore, the prophecies of the offspring in the Adamic, Abrahamic, and Davidic covenants were also fulfilled in the new covenant. The blood covenant in the Adamic, Noahic, Abrahamic, Mosaic, and Davidic covenants was accomplished in the new covenant. God made something clear for sinners when the blood covenant was fulfilled; the blood of the new covenant, the blood of Jesus (Matt 26:28; 1 Cor 11:25; Heb 10:29; 12:24), does two things for Christians in terms of *guilt* and *pollution of sin*. First, the blood of Jesus pays the price for the punishment of all sins (past, present, future) and sets us free from *guilt* (to cleanse us from all our sins: Matt 26:28; Eph 1:7; Rom 3:25; 5:9; Heb 9:12, 14, 22; 10:29; 13:12; Rev 7:14).[139] Second, the blood of Jesus cleanses Christians from the filth of sins committed throughout their lives (*pollution of sin*: Heb 9:12–14; 1 Pet 1:2; 1 John 1:7; Rev 7:14).[140]

> For this is my blood of the covenant, which is poured out for many for the forgiveness of sins. (Matt 26:28)

> In the same way also he took the cup, after supper, saying, "This cup is the new covenant in my blood. Do this, as often as you drink it, in remembrance of me." (1 Cor 11:25)

The fulfillment of the new covenant has also had a decisive impact on the establishment of the kingdom of God. Adam, Noah, Abraham, Moses, David and "all of God's people in every age" receive salvation from sin through the redemptive work of Jesus Christ. So, the work of Christ who is the Representative of the new covenant is "the source of all human salvation for sin."[141] God had continuously made the covenants with humans, consistently demonstrating the fulfillment of the purpose of building the kingdom of God and the salvation of humanity. In this way, as we saw, the Old Testament covenants foreshadow the coming of the Messiah who would save sinners.

The next thing to keep in mind is that the fulfillment of the new covenant has proved an important fact that God always keeps his covenant promises. All the covenants, including the new covenant, demonstrate

---

139. Kang, *Living Out the Gospel*, 130–36, 177, 198.

140. Kang, *Living Out the Gospel*, 158, 167, 177, 198, 274–76. For guilt and pollution of sin, please see "4. Justification and the Restored Image of God," in vol. 2, ch. 3.

141. Frame, *Systematic Theology*, 80.

the unchanging faithfulness of God. Moreover, the covenants in the Bible show that God always keeps his promises. God has once again shown that he is unchanging in keeping his promises through the Messiah who fulfilled the new covenant. Furthermore, this new covenant confirms God's faithfulness, righteousness, and great grace. In other words, this proves God's faithfulness to the words of the covenant.

The fulfillment of the new covenant not only proves the faithfulness of God, but also affirms the attributes of God's righteousness, eternity, and immutability (unchanging nature). That is, the fulfillment of the new covenant achieves the message of God's grace and love proclaimed in the Old Testament covenants, thus confirming these attributes of God. The diversity of messages shown in the Old Testament covenants is unified in the fulfillment of the new covenant, demonstrating God's righteousness, faithfulness, and eternal immutability. In other words, the covenants maintain the continuity of the expectation of the Messiah while showing the unity of the gospel "by grace alone," which is the core message of the messianic covenants.

The fulfillment of the new covenant has brought about changes in the way of looking at the law of the kingdom of God and Christian life.

On the one hand, this means that Christians who are in Jesus Christ should have a different perspective on the Mosaic law than the Israelites in the Old Testament. To Christians, the Mosaic law is no longer a guardian leading them to Christ, but instead a teacher guiding them "to the love for God and the love for their neighbors" (Jesus' commandment).[142]

> For you were called to freedom, brothers. Only do not use your freedom as an opportunity for the flesh, but through love serve one another. For the whole law is fulfilled in one word: "You shall love your neighbor as yourself." (Gal 5:13–14)

On the other hand, the fulfillment of the new covenant has changed not only the perspective on the Mosaic law, but also the way Christians live in relation to the law. It is helpful for us to view this as a difference in

---

142. For Christians in the new covenant, the concepts of obedience (blessings) or disobedience (curses) spoken of in the Mosaic law no longer exist. In other words, the purpose of the Mosaic law for Christians under the new covenant has changed. That is, for Christians, the Mosaic law serves the purpose of guiding and encouraging the Christian life (the third purpose of the moral law as found in the Mosaic law). Calvin insists on the three functions (purposes) of the Mosaic law: (1) to reveal our sins and pursue grace in Christ, (2) to restrain sins under common grace (general society and unbelievers), and (3) to provide moral teaching and encouragement for believers (*Institutes* 2.7.6–15).

life resulting from a change in status through Jesus Christ; the fulfillment of the new covenant has brought about a change in status for sinners, who are righteous in Jesus Christ.[143]

Therefore, the fulfillment of the new covenant not only clearly shows the significant difference between the lives of sinners (who are in Adam) and the lives of the righteous (who are justified in Jesus), but also has drawn a line between them. That is, it has brought about a difference in the way of living in obedience to God's word. This is also the difference between the obedience to the Mosaic law of sinners who are in Adam and the obedience to the Mosaic law of believers who are in Jesus Christ. The former is the obedience of the unrighteous who are enslaved to sin and not accepted by God (Rom 3:10, 20; 7:12), while the latter is the obedience of the righteous who are freed from sin and accepted by God (Rom 8:4; 13:8–10; Gal 5:13–14). Therefore, the obedience recognized by God is the obedience of the righteous who are justified "by God's grace alone" and "by faith alone" through "union with Jesus Christ."[144]

After being justified by God's grace, the sanctification of Christians under the new covenant is also an extension of the gift of God's grace, resulting from the help of the Holy Spirit. That is, the Lord Jesus Christ continues to work through the Spirit until he comes back, regardless of sin, to complete what he has begun. Now, Jesus Christ is with us through the Holy Spirit, but when the Lord comes again, we will see him face to face. And from that moment on, we will be with the Lord forever and ever, regardless of sin (Rev 22:3–4; 1 Cor 13:12; 2 Cor 3:18).[145] The fulfillment of the new covenant has opened this path.

> No longer will there be anything accursed, but the throne of God and of the Lamb will be in it, and his servants will worship him. They will see his face, and his name will be on their foreheads. And night will be no more. They will need no light of lamp or sun, for the Lord God will be their light, and they will reign forever and ever. (Rev 22:3–4)

In conclusion, God has fulfilled the new covenant through the sacrifice of the perfect obedience of Jesus Christ with God's free and saving grace and love. The freedom of sin given through the fulfillment of the

---

143. For justification in Jesus Christ, please refer to vol. 2, ch. 2.

144. Kang, *Living Out the Gospel*, 239, 250–54.

145. "For now we see in a mirror dimly, but then face to face. Now I know in part; then I shall know fully, even as I have been fully known" (1 Cor 13:12).

new covenant that he kept his promises has opened the way for establishing the eternal kingdom of God anew. And the fulfillment of the new covenant helps us clearly see all the purposes for which God created humanity. God now makes humanity, who will be the glory and praise of God (Phil 1:9–11), into the eternal people of God in Jesus Christ.

> And I heard a loud voice from the throne saying, "Behold, the dwelling place of God is with man. He will dwell with them, and they will be his people, and God himself will be with them as their God." (Rev 21:3)

We should remember, as we saw, that all the covenants of the Bible have come only from the triune God. Simply put, God is the Author of all the covenants in the Bible. And the fulfillment of all God's promises through the covenants and the new covenant demonstrates God's thorough preparation and completion for the eternal kingdom of God and God's children. The grace of God, hidden for a long time, has been revealed to the world through Jesus, the Fulfiller of the new covenant. Jesus Christ, the Representative of the new covenant, has shown God's infinite grace and love through his tremendous sacrifice, perfect sacrifice and perfect obedience. We, as created beings, could never comprehend this infinite grace and love.

We must also not forget that God, through the fulfillment of the new covenant, invites us, who are both creatures and sinners, to join the family of God the King. God continues to carry out his plan for the kingdom of God towards humanity through the fulfillment of the new covenant. Thus, the core of the biblical story is that God still invites us today to be a part of the family of the new covenant. And this is the secret of the kingdom of God that Jesus speaks of (Luke 8:10–15; 14:15–24). However, the new covenant also emphasizes God's sovereign grace in salvation and human responsibility in the life of faith for the regenerate.[146]

God requires obedience to the word of the new covenant, just as he required obedience of faith to the other covenants. This obedience of faith is to the holy, righteous, and good word of God (Rom 7:12). If we want to fundamentally understand God's word, we first need to examine God's righteousness.

---

146. Frame, *Systematic Theology*, 81.

3

The Righteousness of the Eternal God

God is holy, righteous, and good. God has given us his word according to his attributes. In particular, God's righteousness is an important measure for understanding his holy and good attributes. And we can know the righteous attribute of God especially through the Bible. God's righteousness forms the foundation of the law of God's kingdom, which sets the basic structure of the whole Bible and is directly related to soteriology. God's covenants are also directly related to God's righteousness. In Scripture, the criterion for viewing the redemptive work of Jesus Christ also comes from the standard of God's righteousness. Thus, God's righteousness is the most important concept when looking at the relationship between God and human beings.

Undoubtedly, the righteousness of God revealed in the Bible is a very important measure for us to understand the attributes of God. If we do not understand the concept of God's righteousness in Scripture, we cannot glimpse God's heart in looking at human sins.

Therefore, the righteousness of God in the Bible fundamentally shows the criteria for "How does God deal with human beings who are created in his image?" It is hard to imagine that when God created humans, he did so without any thoughts or standards.

However, the present age has either ignored this Creator God or turned him into someone who deals with humans without any thought. The Bible treats God's righteousness as very important in the role of God governing his kingdom, protecting his people, and providing salvation.

Why is the righteousness of God important for us today?

Why do we need to know about God's righteousness?

How we answer these questions will determine the direction of our faith journey.

Throughout the Bible, God's righteousness (justice) fundamentally provides God's standard of right and wrong (good and evil). The Bible clearly indicates that God acts according to "a perfect internal standard of right and wrong."[1] If we do not understand the concept of divine righteousness in the Bible, it is difficult to know God and to understand God's righteousness revealed in salvation (Rom 1:17; 3:21). Therefore, we need to carefully examine the concept of God's righteousness as shown in the Bible. Among the concepts of God's righteousness in relation to humans, we can see three key meanings: (1) the legal standard of governance, (2) the standard of salvation, and (3) the standard of a good life.

1. GOD'S RIGHTEOUSNESS AS THE LEGAL STANDARD FOR GOVERNANCE

First, the righteousness of God in the Bible shows the legal standard by which God governs the world (Ps 9:7–8).[2] God is the King who governs all things in the world, and it is God who established the law governing the world. God's law that governs the world is based on God's righteousness. In the Old Testament, the representative Hebrew word that contains the fundamental concept of God's standard of judgment is *righteousness* (*tsedeq*, צֶדֶק; *tsedaqah*, צְדָקָה). The concept of *righteousness* in the Bible fundamentally assumes that God is the Lawmaker, the Judge, and the Executor of the law.[3]

---

1. Frame, *Doctrine of God*, 446, 458; Frame, *Systematic Theology*, 257.

2. Frame, *Doctrine of God*, 451–52; Frame, *Systematic Theology*, 262.

3. In the OT, the Hebrew words for "righteousness" (*tsedeq*, צֶדֶק; *tsedaqah*, צְדָקָה) are used 275 times. These two words represent the concept of God's righteousness in the OT. Upon examining these two words, it becomes clear that they are used both complementarily and fundamentally to convey the same meaning. Other words belonging to this word group (nouns, adjectives, verbs) are not significantly different in this regard.

The representative meaning of the first word (*tsedeq*, צֶדֶק): God's eternal righteousness (Dan 9:24), paths of righteousness (Ps 23:3), Israel's justice (Deut 16:20), law (God's righteousness) keeper (Isa 51:7), king's righteousness (Isa 32:1), saving righteousness (Isa 51:5; Ps 65:6). This mainly refers to the concept of God's righteousness as the law that governs God's kingdom, Israel, and human beings (*DCH* 80–85; cf. BDB 841–42; *TLOT* 1046–62).

The representative meaning of the second word (*tsedaqah*, צְדָקָה): justice of earthly

God clearly establishes the law and proclaims himself as the King who governs all things, nations, and human beings according to that law in both the Old Testament and the New Testament.[4] It is important to remember that God's righteousness also serves to protect innocent human beings.[5] In Ps 9:7–8, Scripture introduces God as the Judge who judges the world.

> The LORD reigns forever; he has established his throne for judgment. He rules the world in righteousness and judges the peoples with equity. (Ps 9:7–8)

In Scripture, God is the One who rules over the world (Ps 9:7–8), Israel (Deut 16:18, 20; Isa 51:7) and human beings (Ps 9:7–8).[6] As we explore the concept of Old Testament righteousness, we should remember that even the Mosaic law given to Israel was also based on God's righteousness. That is, the righteousness of God is the foundation of the Mosaic law used by the judges of Israel.

> You shall appoint judges and officers in all your towns that the LORD your God is giving you, according to your tribes, and they shall judge the people with righteous judgment. (Deut 16:18)

> Justice, and only justice, you shall follow, that you may live and inherit the land that the LORD your God is giving you. (Deut 16:20)

In the Old Testament, God's righteousness is the foundation of not only the Mosaic law, but also all the covenants. God's covenants that we

---

ruler (king) and judge (Amos 5:7, 24; 6:12; Isa 32:16), saving righteousness (Isa 48:18; 51:8; 56:1b; 61:10–11), God's righteous will (Deut 33:21), good deeds of a human being (Ezek 3:20; 18:24; 33:13), God's righteous act (acts of salvation: Judg 5:11, 11; 1 Sam 12:7; Mic 6:5). Mainly, this is used as the concept of justice and righteousness in relation to the following areas: (1) all creatures, nations, societies, and human relationships; (2) God's work of salvation (*DCH* 85–88; cf. BDB 842–43; Swanson, *Dictionary of Biblical Languages (OT)*, §7406; *TLOT* 1046–62).

4. The Greek word for *righteousness* (*dikaiosune*, δικαιοσύνη) in the New Testament has deep roots in the Hebrew word, *righteousness*, and is used with a very similar meaning. However, there is a difference in that the concept of God's saving righteousness in the New Testament specifically refers to Jesus Christ (Rom 1:17, 3:21–22). For the New Testament righteousness, refer to "4. Justification," in vol. 2, ch. 1. Cf. the NT righteousness: BDAG 247–49. The OT righteousness: *DCH* 80–88; BDB 841–43; Swanson, *Dictionary of Biblical Languages (OT)*, §7406; *TLOT* 1046–62.

5. Frame, *Doctrine of God*, 454.

6. In these texts (Ps 9:7–8; Deut 16:18, 20; Isa 51:7), the Hebrew word "righteousness" (*tsedeq*, צֶדֶק) is used (*DCH* 80–85).

examined in chapter 2 are also based on God's unchanging righteousness. Accordingly, all the words of God's covenants do not deviate from the standard of God's righteousness. Therefore, you can never overemphasize the covenantal and legal significance of the standard of God's righteousness from the aspect of the relationship between God and human beings. In the Bible, "all his commands" are God's law and are fundamentally based on God's righteousness.[7]

Among the words of God's righteousness in the Old Testament, particularly Isa 32:1 catches our attention. Isaiah 32:1 introduces the Messiah as the King who rules the world, nations, and people with the righteousness of God. In other words, the Messiah, the Judge who will judge the world, is also the King who rules with God's righteousness revealed in the Old Testament.[8] Of course, this King in the Old Testament is the Messiah Jesus Christ in the New Testament. King Jesus also rules the kingdom of God with God's righteousness.[9]

> Behold, a king will reign in righteousness, and princes will rule in justice. (Isa 32:1)

What we need to remember here is that the representative Hebrew words for "righteousness" used in the Old Testament are fundamentally based on God's righteousness. This means that God, as the King, rules the world with his righteousness and bestows salvation according to the standard of his righteousness.[10]

We can learn God's righteous attributes through the word "righteousness in the Bible." The one and only righteous God, who is both the Legislator and Judge, has given his law not only to Israel but to the entire world. In Jas 4:11–12, Scripture emphasizes that humans are neither lawgivers nor judges, but only doers who keep God's law.

---

7. Cf. Ridderbos, *Coming of the Kingdom*, 312–21.

8. Isaiah 32:1 also uses the Hebrew word for "righteousness" (*tsedeq*, צֶדֶק) (*DCH* 80–85). See also what we discussed earlier, "1-D. Jesus Christ, the King of the Kingdom of God," in this vol., ch. 2.

9. Cf. *DCH* 82.

10. As mentioned earlier, these two words for righteousness (*tsedeq*, צֶדֶק [Isa 51:5; Ps 65:6]; *tsedaqah*, צְדָקָה [Isa 48:18; 51:8; 56:1b; 61:10–11]) are used complementarily and interchangeably in the Old Testament. Therefore, I will not repeat the examples of the second representative Hebrew word for righteousness (*tsedaqah*, צְדָקָה) here. Please refer to the explanation above. Words derived from the words of righteousness used in the Old Testament are no different. Words with legal meanings in the Bible also fundamentally come from the concept of God's righteousness.

> Do not speak evil against one another, brothers. The one who speaks against a brother or judges his brother, speaks evil against the law and judges the law. But if you judge the law, you are not a doer of the law but a judge. There is only one lawgiver and judge, he who is able to save and to destroy. But who are you to judge your neighbor? (Jas 4:11–12)

God alone is self-existent and works according to the law of his righteous nature. God acts according to his own "a perfect internal standard of right and wrong."[11] God acting according to his own law is righteousness.[12] His holiness also is another aspect of God's righteousness, just like his goodness. Just as God's holiness includes righteousness, his goodness is also accompanied by righteousness.[13] Scripture teaches that we can see the structure of both God's holiness and God's goodness through God's righteousness since they are not separable but very deeply interrelated. This is a *tremendously* important fact. Therefore, no one can deny that God's righteousness is the most important thing in relation to human beings. God saves us and rules us according to the standard of his righteousness.

God acts faithfully according to his own law, separates himself from sin and creatures, and acts in holiness and goodness (Rom 6:19, 22).[14] God's righteousness can be considered the "structure" of his goodness.[15] Hence, in the Bible, the righteousness of God also helps us see the standards of God's fundamental holiness and goodness. God has given his righteousness to Israel as the foundation of Israel's justice and desired Israel to live in obedience to God's righteous law.

> Justice, and only justice, you shall follow, that you may live and inherit the land that the LORD your God is giving you. (Deut 16:20)

---

11. Frame, *Doctrine of God*, 448; Frame, *Systematic Theology*, 257.

12. Frame, *Doctrine of God*, 448, 298; Frame, *Systematic Theology*, 257.

13. Frame, *Salvation Belongs to the Lord*, 211; Frame, *Systematic Theology*, 257. Frame also says that God's righteousness is "the form, the structure of God's goodness" (*Systematic Theology*, 257). Moreover, from the perspective of judgment and salvation, "God's holiness is very similar to his righteousness" (279; see also 262–63, 278). For Israel, holiness also was "both a fact and a norm" (Frame, *Salvation Belongs to the Lord*, 213). Therefore, these attributes of God, righteousness, holiness and goodness, cannot be separated from each other. They are "just different ways of describing a *person*" (Frame, *Systematic Theology*, 257).

14. Frame, *Systematic Theology*, 233–35, 257–68, 276–79.

15. Frame, *Systematic Theology*, 257.

> Listen to me, you who know righteousness, the people in whose heart is my law; fear not the reproach of man, nor be dismayed at their revealing. (Isa 51:7)

In summary, God has given the righteous law of God to all humans created in his own image. He has given his word, the law of the kingdom of God, because he desires us to live lives that are obedient, holy, righteous, and good. Therefore, on the one hand, the holy, just, and good Mosaic law in the Bible teaches about the righteousness of the holy God (Rom 7:12). On the other hand, the Mosaic law also demonstrates that the standard of God's righteousness is the highest standard of righteousness in all areas of life.[16]

Jesus Christ also presents the norms of God's righteousness. The righteousness spoken by Jesus Christ is "always traced back to God's own words."[17] In fact, God's words are God's commands that reveal the will of the righteous God. God's righteousness is revealed in the words of the commandments in the Bible.[18] And God's authoritative demands through the words of God governs "all areas of life."[19] If we can see the standard of God's righteousness that governs the world, we can also have confidence in our faith in Jesus Christ, the King of God's kingdom.

2. GOD'S RIGHTEOUSNESS AS THE STANDARD OF SALVATION

The next thing to explore is God's righteousness as the standard of salvation. In Scripture, righteousness is not only God's legal standard of governance, but also God's standard of salvation. In other words, God's righteousness in the Bible serves the standard of both a judging righteousness and a saving righteousness.[20]

---

16. Frame, *Doctrine of God*, 451.
17. Ridderbos, *Coming of the Kingdom*, 290.
18. Ridderbos, *Coming of the Kingdom*, 290–91.
19. Frame, *Doctrine of God*, 89; Frame, *Doctrine of the Word*, 50–53.
20. Frame, *Doctrine of God*, 451–58. The Hebrew words for "righteousness" (*tsedeq*, צֶדֶק; *tsedaqah*, צְדָקָה) in the Old Testament and the Greek word for "righteousness" (*dikaiosune*, δικαιοσύνη) in the New Testament show the concept of "saving righteousness" (*DCH* 84, 87; BDAG 247–48). Schreiner briefly discusses "the judging and saving righteousness" centered on the cross but does not explain it in relation to the Old Testament (Schreiner, *Faith Alone*, 171–72). Therefore, we need to explore the concepts of the "judging righteousness" and "saving righteousness" further. We will examine God's righteousness particularly in relation to justification in more detail in vol. 2, ch. 2. Here,

To Adam, righteousness is a judging righteousness that judges lawlessness and unrighteousness resulting from Adam's fall, disobedience, and sin.[21] Also, God's judging righteousness, as manifested in the Mosaic law of Israel, demands perfect obedience and the payment from sinners. However, throughout the Bible, God's righteousness is also "a means of salvation."[22] Now let's briefly explore judging righteousness and saving righteousness in the Bible.

A. Old Testament: God's Judging Righteousness and Saving Righteousness

Let's look at the meaning of God's judging righteousness and saving righteousness in the Old Testament.

On the one hand, God's judging righteousness in the Old Testament, which judges sin, calls for God's saving righteousness revealed in the gospel (Rom 1:17; 3:21–22).[23]

On the other hand, the requirement of God's saving righteousness in the Old Testament was fulfilled in Jesus Christ. In fact, surprisingly, not only the New Testament but also the Old Testament teach that God's righteousness and salvation go hand in hand (Pss 40:10; 85:9–10; 98:2–3; Isa 45:8).[24]

> My righteousness draws near, my salvation has gone out, and my arms will judge the peoples; the coastlands hope for me, and for my arm they wait. (Isa 51:5)

Then why do we need God's saving righteousness?
Where can we find the origin of God's judging righteousness?

---

in connection to the gospel, we will briefly review the concepts of the judging righteousness and saving righteousness. I hope that the discussion serves as a foundational guide to the justification that will be explored in vol. 2.

21. Adam's sin was a violation of God's law. The Bible teaches that "we can violate God's law by our acts, by our attitudes"—by our thoughts, by our words—"or just by being sinful persons, having a sinful nature" (Frame, *Salvation Belongs to the Lord*, 101).

22. Frame, *Doctrine of God*, 451; Frame, *Systematic Theology*, 262–68.

23. Bavinck, *Our Reasonable Faith*, 451–53, 457–58; Schreiner, *Faith Alone*, 144–45, 171–72.

24. Frame, *Doctrine of God*, 452.

a. God's Judgment and Salvation

Now we will take a look at why people need God's saving righteousness.

When did God begin to judge humans?

To Adam, the first covenant breaker, God declared death as the punishment for the sin of breaking the law of God's word (Rom 5:12). As a result of the sin of Adam, the covenant representative of all humanity, every human is born with guilt (responsibility for sins) and pollution of sin.[25] And God judges all thoughts of human hearts and all actions of humans according to God's righteousness, which is the standard of right and wrong (Ps 50:6; Eccl. 3:17; 11:9; 12:14). The result of God's judgment on sinners is that they must pay the price for their sins.

Therefore, all humankind who are in Adam must receive the punishment of death due to their responsibility for their sins.

> As it is written: "None is righteous, no, not one; no one understands; no one seeks for God. All have turned aside; together they have become worthless; no one does good, not even one." (Rom 3:10–12)

> Therefore, just as sin came into the world through one man, and death through sin, and so death spread to all men because all sinned. (Rom 5:12)

> For God will bring every deed into judgment, with every secret thing, whether good or evil. (Eccl 12:14).

These texts say that sin entered the world according to the standard of God's righteousness that judges the sins of sinners.[26] However,

---

25. Note that God's judging righteousness and saving righteousness are very closely related to the marred image of God in sinners who are in Adam. In other words, the righteousness of Jesus Christ, the Messiah who comes for the restoration of the marred image of God and covenant relationship, is absolutely necessary for sinners. Through the perfect obedience of Jesus, God has restored the marred image of God.

We will briefly discuss the importance of wisdom and knowledge in "2. The Importance of the Word of God," in this volume, ch. 4. Please also refer to "2-A. The Adamic Covenant," in this volume, ch. 2; and "4. Justification, the Recovered Image of God," in vol. 2, ch. 3. For guilt and pollution, please refer again to "4. Justification and the Recovered Image of God," in vol. 2, ch. 3.

26. Romans 1:29–32 provides a brief list of those who practice unrighteousness.

"They were filled with all manner of unrighteousness, evil, covetousness, malice. They are full of envy, murder, strife, deceit, maliciousness. They are gossips, slanderers, haters of God, insolent, haughty, boastful, inventors of evil, disobedient to parents, foolish, faithless, heartless, ruthless. Though they know God's righteous decree that

the Adamic covenant reveals not only God's judging righteousness. The animal skins (Gen 3:21) and the offspring of the woman of the first gospel in the Adamic covenant (Gen 3:15) also foreshadow God's judging righteousness against the sins of Adam and Eve and God's saving righteousness of the Messiah. After the flood, Noah also offered animal sacrifice, which symbolizes the punishment of sins (Gen 8:20). In fact, the Noahic covenant already implies both God's judging righteousness, as seen in the flood (Gen 7:6—8:19), and God's saving righteousness, as demonstrated by the ark (Gen 6:13—7:6). The Abrahamic covenant also foreshadows God's judging righteousness through animal sacrifices (Gen 15:9-21) and God's saving righteousness through the event of offering Isaac (Gen 22:1-9).

In the Mosaic covenant, we can see that God put forth his righteousness even when he saved the disobedient Israelites from Egypt. The Israelites "did not deserve to be saved."[27] The exodus, the liberation of the people of Israel from slavery in Egypt, serves as a type of Jesus saving sinners from their sins, showing God's saving grace according to the standard of God's perfect righteousness.[28] God's work of salvation is not only the work of his righteousness but also the work of his love and grace.[29] In the Old Testament, when God carried out the work of salvation, he acted according to the standard of his righteousness (Ps 111).

> Listen to me, you stubborn of heart, you who are far from righteousness: I bring near my righteousness; it is not far off, and my salvation will not delay; I will put salvation in Zion, for Israel my glory. (Isa 46:12-13)

One of the reasons the Mosaic covenant in the Old Testament catches our attention is that the elements of God's judging and saving righteousness, which appeared directly and indirectly in other covenants, were

---

those who practice such things deserve to die, they not only do them but give approval to those who practice them" (Rom 1:29-32).

27. Frame, *Doctrine of God*, 451.

28. God, in his righteousness, has saved the afflicted, the weak, the oppressed, or the needy from their sufferings or "their powerful oppressors" (Pss 72:1-4; 82) (Frame, *Doctrine of God*, 453-56). Psalm 72 is a prayer to the messianic King. Cf. Pss 10:14; 35:10; 68:5; 82:3; 113:7; 140:12; 146:7-9; Jer 22:16.

Michael Sandel, a professor of government at Harvard University, highlights the "three approaches to justice" to understand the goal of modern political philosophy, as human "welfare, freedom, and virtue." These concepts remind us of the biblical concept of God's righteousness (Sandel, *Justice*, 6-30).

29. Cf. Frame, *Doctrine of God*, 452.

legalized through the Mosaic law. The animal sacrifices symbolizing God's judging righteousness, which continued even after Noah's flood, were also legalized as sacrificial laws (ceremonial law: Exod 25:1—30:38; Lev 1:1—8:36; 16:1–34; Deut 15:1–31). As a result, from the Mosaic law, the people of Israel could continually learn about the severity and cruelty of their sins, the strict punishment of God for sin, and the coming Messiah.

Under the influence of God's judging righteousness and God's saving righteousness shown in the Mosaic law, the Davidic covenant (1 Chr 17:11–14) also contained a promise concerning the King of God's kingdom and the Messiah as the Redeemer. The Messiah of the Davidic covenant is Jesus, the eternal King of God's kingdom. As we saw earlier, the Mosaic law played the role of governing God's people, including during the time of the Davidic covenant, until Jesus came to earth.

What was the reason God gave the Mosaic law, which legalized God's judging righteousness and saving righteousness found in other covenants?

Was it to instill fear of God in the Israelites?

Or was it to create a sense of fear among the Israelites by threatening curses for disobedience?

Not at all. God gave the Mosaic law to the Israelites to draw them closer to him. Through the Mosaic law, God wanted the Israelites to come before him who loves them and say, "I cannot do this. Please help me, a sinner." This is the reason God legalized the covenants that had existed before the Mosaic law into the Mosaic law.

b. The Necessity of the Messiah's Perfect Obedience

All the Old Testament covenants, as we saw, contain God's desire for created humans to look forward to the coming of the Messiah. God especially wanted them to see their unrighteousness through the mirror of the Mosaic law and have hope in the coming Messiah. God also wanted them to come to him through repentance of sin and obedience to his word.

Who knew what the coming Messiah had to do for them?

Only God knew. The Messiah had to come and perfectly obey the word of God on behalf of them. In this way, the Mosaic law of the Old Testament points out the necessity of the Messiah's perfect obedience for sinners.

In the Old Testament, people of faith were able to look forward to the coming Messiah with firm faith and hope in God's saving righteousness through the Mosaic law (Heb 11). And whenever they kept the words of the Mosaic law by faith, God increased their faith and blessed them according to his promises. Just like them, if we keep the Lord's words by faith, he will bless us according to his promises.

In conclusion, the necessity of the Messiah's perfect obedience was for the purpose of declaring unrighteous sinners as righteous. The New Testament does not separate God's judging righteousness and saving righteousness that appeared in the Mosaic law. This is because God's judging and saving righteousness revealed in the Mosaic law were fulfilled by the Messiah in the New Testament. Next, we need to examine the necessity of the Messiah's obedience and righteousness as spoken of in the New Testament.

B. God's Judging and Saving Righteousness in the New Testament

In the Bible, the Old Testament serves as the foundation for understanding God's judging and saving righteousness in the New Testament. In this sense, the Old and New Testaments have complementary meanings. Just as the meaning of the Messiah in the Old Testament becomes clear in the New Testament, the meaning of the saving righteousness in the Old Testament becomes clear through Jesus in the New Testament. The same goes for the Old Testament Mosaic law and the New Testament gospel.

When we look at the Mosaic law through the gospel, it becomes easy to understand what it means for the judging and saving righteousness to be simultaneously accomplished for sinners. In other words, the redemptive work of Jesus has solved the issues of both the judging and saving righteousness for sinners. Now we need to examine whether this refers only to God's judging and saving righteousness centered on the cross.[30]

In the New Testament, the most explicit statements about the nature of God's righteousness in the gospel and the law can be found in Rom

---

30. Later, when we study the perfect righteousness of Jesus Christ, we will examine whether this refers only to God's judging and saving righteousness centered on the cross. For this, please refer to vol. 2, ch. 2, "The Condition of Justification: The Perfect Obedience of Jesus Christ." Schreiner insists that "both the judging and saving righteousness are revealed" in the cross of Jesus (Schreiner, *Faith Alone*, 171–72).

1:17 and 3:21–22.[31] In particular, Paul clearly states in Romans that both the gospel and the law are related to God's righteousness.

> For in it the righteousness of God is revealed from faith for faith, as it is written, "The righteous shall live by faith." (Rom 1:17)

> But now the righteousness of God has been manifested apart from the law, although the Law and the Prophets bear witness to it—the righteousness of God through faith in Jesus Christ for all who believe. For there is no distinction. (Rom 3:21–22)

What is the reason Paul mentions God's righteousness in these passages?

What does it mean that our salvation is related to God's righteousness?

Paul emphasizes in these passages that it is not just a matter of forgiveness of sins for sinners to become God's children legally. In particular, Romans also emphasizes that in order to become children of the holy, righteous, and good God, one must be justified by God (justification). By using the term "justification," Paul clearly explains how, based on the standard of God's judging and saving righteousness, God can save us sinners to be justified through his grace alone in Jesus Christ. Therefore, the New Testament *justification* fundamentally and legally best explains the gospel.

GOD'S JUSTICE AND GOD'S GRACE

In Romans, Paul intentionally connects God's righteousness (justice) and God's grace in Jesus Christ. In other words, Romans teaches that the gospel includes both God's judging righteousness and saving righteousness. The gospel contains both God's *legal* judgment with punitive righteousness and God's *legal* grace according to God's righteousness.[32]

> For Christ is the end of the law for righteousness to everyone who believes. (Rom 10:4)

---

31. Paul strongly presupposes that believing in Jesus Christ leads to salvation (Acts 16:31; Eph 2:8), eternal life (John 3:16; 5:24), and being justified (Rom 3:26; Phil 3:9). For this, please refer to the definition of the gospel in vol. 2, ch. 1,"The Gospel, Justification, and Jesus."

32. Cf. Bavinck, *Our Reasonable Faith*, 457–58. Galatians 2:16 also speaks of the same meaning concerning the law and the gospel.

> Yet we know that a person is not justified by works of the law but through faith in Jesus Christ, so we also have believed in Christ Jesus, in order to be justified by faith in Christ and not by works of the law, because by works of the law no one will be justified. (Gal 2:16)

Why is Paul so interested in justification (being justified)?

He is interested in connecting justification to the gospel, the Mosaic law, and God's judging and saving righteousness to explore the redemptive work of Jesus throughout the Bible. In other words, he focuses on how sinners can legally satisfy God's righteousness and discusses God's judging and saving righteousness in Jesus. From the perspective of justification, we can summarize the reason God has given the Mosaic law in two ways.

First, the Mosaic law makes people realize their sin (Rom 3:9–10, 20).

> For by works of the law no human being will be justified in his sight, since through the law comes knowledge of sin. (Rom 3:20)

Second, the Mosaic law makes people realize their inability to obey the holy, righteous, and good word of God.

> So the law is holy, and the commandment is holy and righteous and good. (Rom 7:12)

The Mosaic law makes all people realize their sin (Rom 3:20) and their inability to obey the holy, righteous, and good word (Rom 7:12). As mentioned earlier, the event of the tree of the knowledge of good and evil (the Adamic covenant) and the Mosaic law clearly reveal God's judging righteousness for sinners. Also Romans effectively summarizes the list of human sinful deeds related to the event of the tree of the knowledge of good and evil through the Mosaic law (Rom 2:12—3:20; 5:13).[33] According to Romans, no humans have a way to escape God's judgment (Rom 2:13; 3:19–20; 5:13).

> For it is not the hearers of the law who are righteous before God, but the doers of the law who will be justified. (Rom 2:13)

For Paul, the Mosaic law also speaks of the necessity of the Messiah for the justification of sinners (Rom 2:13; 3:9–10, 19–20; 5:13; 7:12),

---

33. After the fall of Adam, all humankind, under the Adamic and Mosaic covenants, are sinners before God. The Mosaic law serves as a "judging law" that defines and enforces the punishment of sinners (Horton, *Covenant and Salvation*, 265).

coming from the fact that all human deeds are unrighteous before God. In other words, the Mosaic law exposes that because of the sinful action in Adam, we sinners neither can be justified by God nor can obey the righteous word of the law (Rom 3:9–12; 7:12).

> So then, the law was our guardian until Christ came, in order that we might be justified by faith. But now that faith has come, we are no longer under a guardian. (Gal 3:24–25)

The Messiah Jesus Christ has solved both the issue of remission of sins and the issue of righteousness through his perfect obedience for the justification of sinners. Therefore, it is entirely by God's grace that all the requirements of the Mosaic law have been fulfilled for sinners through the Messiah. The Messiah obeyed all the words according to the commands of God the Father and suffered God's righteous judgment for our sins on the cross. Paul remarkably explains that God's righteousness and God's grace are simultaneously accomplished in Jesus, using both the gospel and the Mosaic law.

C. Jesus and God's Righteousness

Did Jesus ever speak directly about the righteousness of God, which is the standard of salvation?

Jesus does mention in Matt 6:33, "But seek first the kingdom of God and his righteousness." However, this is about the goal of God's children who are already saved, not about God's righteousness, which is the standard of salvation.

Jesus speaks of *righteousness* related to the justification of sinners in Matt 5:20—God's righteousness, which is the standard of salvation—pointing out that we need a greater righteousness than that of the Pharisees and the scribes to enter the kingdom of God. This is because their righteousness relied on human works, representing "the righteousness of human meritorious works," that is, "legalistic righteousness" (Phil 3:6). But they can never enter the kingdom of God with this human righteousness.

> For I tell you, unless your righteousness exceeds that of the scribes and Pharisees, you will never enter the kingdom of heaven. (Matt 5:20)[34]

---

34. The righteousness of the Pharisees and the scribes is a righteousness that seeks

In Matt 5:20, Jesus has in mind his own righteousness that he will accomplish on behalf of sinners. Remember that the righteousness of human works cannot be a sufficient condition to enter the kingdom of God because they are unrighteous sinners who are in Adam. According to Jesus Christ, unrighteous sinners in Adam cannot be justified by the righteous God through their works. Only Jesus Christ, who is sinless, can be justified by the righteous God through his perfect obedience to all the words of God.[35] Only Jesus' perfect obedience can satisfy the righteousness of God, which is the standard for salvation.

We will explore the perfect obedience of Jesus Christ later in chapter 2 of *The Kingdom of Justification*. But first, we need to briefly look at what his righteousness means.

a. The Justification of Jesus Christ

To better understand Jesus' righteousness, we need to interpret Matt 5:20 and 3:15 together. In these passages, Jesus' righteousness is the fruit of fulfilling all righteousness. In this respect, Jesus tells John the Baptist that it is necessary for him to fulfill all righteousness.

> But Jesus answered him, "Let it be so now, for thus it is fitting for us to fulfill all righteousness." Then he consented. (Matt 3:15)

What does he mean "to fulfill all righteousness"?

Jesus means that he must fulfill "all righteousness" for sinners (Matt 3:15).

Then comes the next question, "How can he fulfill all righteousness?" Jesus must fulfill all righteousness for sinners through his perfect obedience to all the words of God.

Why did the sinless Jesus need to be justified?

This question may connect to our study on God's judging and saving righteousness. We need to pay attention to what Paul explains about

---

"to establish their own righteousness" rather than obeying God's righteousness (Rom 10:3).

"For, being ignorant of the righteousness of God, and seeking to establish their own, they did not submit to God's righteousness" (Rom 10:3).

35. Only Jesus Christ, who was born of the virgin Mary without sin and has divinity and humanity, has the ability to obey all the words of God (Kang, *Living Out the Gospel*, 55–70). As such, Jesus is the only One whose deeds are perfect before God. Only Jesus lived in accordance with God's law (the word) (Crowe, *Last Adam* 86, 88; Kang, *Living Out the Gospel*, 87, 90–93, 213–14).

the redemptive work of Jesus, which is related to justification. Paul says that Jesus "was just" or "is the justifier" or "was justified" (Rom 3:4; 6:7).[36]

> It was to show his righteousness at the present time, so that he might be just and the justifier of the one who has faith in Jesus. (Rom 3:26)[37]

> Great indeed, we confess, is the mystery of godliness: He was manifested in the flesh, vindicated [or justified] by the Spirit, seen by angels, proclaimed among the nations, believed on in the world, taken up in glory. (1 Tim 3:16)[38]

Jesus must be justified according to God's righteousness, which is the standard of salvation, so that he can justify those who believe in Jesus (Rom 3:26). In other words, he was justified by God for the justification of sinners through his perfect obedience to all the words of God in the sinners' place. For the justification of sinners, Jesus, as the Representative of believers, had to fulfill both God's judging righteousness and saving righteousness simultaneously in order to satisfy God's standard of salvation. Paul refers to this as the "righteousness bestowed by God" for the justification of sinners (Rom 3:21–22, 24, 26, 28; 5:1, 9; 1 Cor 6:11; Titus 3:7), apart from the works of the law.[39]

> And be found in him, not having a righteousness of my own that comes from the law, but that which comes through faith in Christ, the righteousness from God that depends on faith. (Phil 3:9)

This righteousness is "the righteousness from God" fulfilled by Christ, which is credited to sinners and given to us by God's grace alone by faith (Gal 3:8–9; Phil 3:9) when we believe in Jesus Christ.[40] It is the righteousness of Jesus that satisfied the sufficient conditions of justification to

---

36. Bavinck, *Our Reasonable Faith*, 453, 459.

37. Isaiah 42:6 also calls the Messiah "righteousness," prophesying that he will be "a covenant for the people, a light for the nations."
"I am the Lord; I have called you in righteousness [*tsedaqah*, צְדָקָה]; I will take you by the hand and keep you; I will give you as a covenant for the people, a light for the nations" (Isa 42:6).

38. In Rom 3:26 and 1 Tim 3:16, Paul uses two Greek words, "righteous" (just, *dikaios*, δίκαιος [Rom 3:26]) and "justify" (*dikaioo*, δικαιόω [1 Tim 3:16]), which are translated as "just" and "be justified" (or "vindicated").

39. BDAG 247.

40. Please refer to vol. 2, ch. 2.

declare sinners righteous according to the standard of God's righteousness as well as God's standard of salvation. In this sense, salvation is only God's act that turns human unrighteousness into the perfect righteousness obtained by Jesus, transferring his righteousness to believers by God's grace alone. This is entirely the gift of God's grace (Rom 5:17; 1 Cor 1:30; Eph 2:8–9). This perfect righteousness connects the judging righteousness and the saving righteousness of the Old Testament to Jesus' perfect righteousness in the New Testament.

> But now the righteousness of God has been manifested apart from the law, although the Law and the Prophets bear witness to it—the righteousness of God through faith in Jesus Christ for all who believe. For there is no distinction. (Rom 3:21–22)

Therefore, it is more helpful to see "God's judging and saving righteousness" in the whole picture of the Bible through the lens of Jesus' perfect obedience that accomplished "all righteousness," rather than seeing it only through Jesus' obedience on the cross. In other words, we should remember that Jesus' perfect obedience simultaneously satisfied the conditions of both God's judging righteousness and saving righteousness for the justification of sinners. We will discuss the broader and narrower senses of Jesus' perfect obedience in more detail in chapter 2 of volume 2.

b. Perfect Obedience, Perfect Righteousness

Now, we need to briefly look at the perfect righteousness achieved through Jesus' perfect obedience, which satisfies the standard of salvation set by God's righteousness. This understanding is crucial for comprehending the concept of God's righteousness presented in the Bible and our justification.

Jesus accomplished the perfect obedience for the remission of sinners' sins and their justification. Jesus' perfect obedience consists of his obedience on the cross and obedience to all the words of God for the justification of sinners. This perfect obedience also fulfills all the requirements of the Mosaic law, which are summarized as loving God and loving one's neighbor in Luke 10:25–27.[41] And this perfect obedience accomplished "the perfect righteousness of Jesus," which satisfies the standard of salvation set by God's righteousness.

---

41. For the perfect obedience, please see vol. 2, ch. 2.

The righteousness obtained by the perfect obedience of Jesus is a perfect righteousness by which God declares sinners righteous in Jesus Christ alone, by faith alone.[42] As we saw, this righteousness of Jesus Christ also satisfies all the demands of God's righteousness for the justification of sinners. In other words, it is the righteousness for the salvation and justification (being declared righteous) of sinful human beings as created beings, which meets all the conditions of God's standard of salvation. It is achieved only through Jesus for sinners by God's grace alone (*sola gratia*).[43]

> And the Scripture, foreseeing that God would justify the Gentiles by faith, preached the gospel beforehand to Abraham, saying, "In you shall all the nations be blessed." So then, those who are of faith are blessed along with Abraham, the man of faith. (Gal 3:8–9)

The righteousness in this passage is the righteousness required by unrighteous sinners, who are unable to solve the problem of sin and righteousness on their own. For the justification of sinners, Jesus' righteousness meets the demands of both God's judging righteousness and God's saving righteousness, as revealed together in the Old Testament (Rom 1:17; 3:21–22). Moreover, this "alien righteousness" comes solely from outside of us (*extra nos*), from the righteousness of Jesus that comes by God's grace alone (*sola gratia*).

However, this passage might be too shocking to some people because it has two significant elements:

1. God preached the gospel to Abraham.
2. God justified the gentiles by faith.

Some people might ask, "How did God preach the gospel to Abraham and the gentiles and justify them?"

God regards the faith of the gentiles in Jesus Christ as righteousness, just as he regarded Abraham's faith in God as faith in the Messiah, Jesus Christ. So, Jesus is the Justifier who has justified sinners in all ages by his own righteousness obtained through his perfect obedience. What amazing good news! Notice, however, that the righteousness of Jesus is neither

---

42. Calvin, *Commentary on Romans*, 185 (Rom 4:25).
43. Kang, *Living Out the Gospel*, 94.

the righteousness of God's attribute nor the righteousness of the divine nature of God the Son, who possesses both divinity and humanity.[44]

This is the perfect righteousness of Christ that is credited to all the believers when they place their faith in Jesus Christ. This is the reason Paul says, "Rejoice always in the Lord" (Phil 4:4).[45] It is because the righteousness of Jesus becomes ours *solely by grace and only through faith in Jesus*. There is no other way. In Phil 3:9, Paul boasts that the perfect righteousness of Jesus has become his own "through faith in Christ" alone.

> And be found in him, not having a righteousness of my own that comes from the law, but that which comes through faith in Christ, the righteousness from God that depends on faith. (Phil 3:9)

This perfect righteousness of Jesus, which satisfies the standard of God's righteousness for salvation and justification, becomes ours in Jesus Christ through union with Christ and the imputation (being transferred or being credited) of Christ's righteousness by God's grace alone, only by faith in Jesus alone.[46] Thus, salvation and justification are entirely the work of God, a gift given to sinners in Jesus through the work of the Holy Spirit.[47]

> For if, because of one man's trespass, death reigned through that one man, much more will those who receive the abundance of grace and the free gift of righteousness reign in life through the one man Jesus Christ. (Rom 5:17)

In summary, the righteousness of God in the Bible reveals the greatness of God's salvation through the execution of his severe punishment for sin upon Jesus Christ. We must not forget this incredible act of God's grace. Although God hates sin, he has placed the responsibility for the sin

---

44. Calvin the Reformer rightly criticizes that "Osiander replaces Christ's righteousness with the divine nature of Christ in justification" (Kang, *Justification*, 75). See also Kang, *Justification*, 76–77; *Institutes* 3.11.5–10; Kang, *Living Out the Gospel*, 216–18, 220.

45. How can Jesus' righteousness be credited to us? The perfect righteousness of Jesus becomes ours through the union and imputation (transfer, regard) in Jesus. This concept is discussed in detail in vol. 2, ch. 3. Our justification is entirely a gift of God's grace (Kang, *Living Out the Gospel*, 88–94, 216–18, 220).

46. For more details, refer to vol. 2, ch. 3.

47. Kang, *Living Out the Gospel*, 88–94. Paul specifically explains "the righteousness bestowed by God" in Rom 1 and 2 Corinthians (BDAG 247; Swanson, *Dictionary of Biblical Languages [NT]*, §1466).

he hates on Jesus, in accordance with the standard of God's righteousness for salvation and justification. Therefore, God not only saves but also justifies sinners, according to the standard of God's righteousness, through the remission of sins and the imputation of Christ's righteousness in Jesus (1 John 1:9; Rom 3:21–22).[48] Note that the work of God's great love and grace in saving and justifying sinners always accompanies his righteous actions (Ps 34:15–22).[49]

Therefore, the righteousness of God revealed in the Bible is the essence of our faith in Jesus, demonstrating the great grace of God through Jesus. The standard of salvation that satisfies God's righteousness for unrighteous sinners is neither obscure nor abstract. On the contrary, the righteousness of God found in the Bible is the clear assurance of our salvation, justification, God's love, and God's grace. God saves unrighteous sinners according to his own righteousness and declares them righteous (justified) in Jesus Christ. The Bible shows that God has governed the world and sent Jesus to save sinners according to this standard. God's righteousness, which is the standard of salvation, is the foundation of the blessings of faith in Jesus.

3. GOD'S RIGHTEOUSNESS AS THE STANDARD OF A GOOD LIFE

So far, we have seen that God uses God's righteousness as the highest legal standard for governing the world and as the highest legal authority in the work of salvation. Finally, we will examine how the righteousness of God in the Bible shows the standard for a good life for humans.

How can we live a good life that satisfies God's standard of a good life?

We must first remember that there is a gate that must be passed in order to live a good life, as all humans are sinners before God after the fall of Adam (Matt 19:16–17; John 10:7–9).[50] To live a good life as described in the Bible, one must first qualify as a child of God who can enter the kingdom of God. This is because all actions of those who do not believe

---

48. Cf. Frame, *Doctrine of God*, 452.

49. Frame, *Doctrine of God*, 452–53, 455.

50. Notice that Jesus connects "good deeds" to eternal life in Matt 19:16–17. No one does good before God since we all are unrighteous sinners (Rom 3:12). We will continue to discuss this more.

in Jesus are neither righteous nor good before God (Rom 1:17; 3:21–26; Ezek 3:20; 18:24; 33:13).[51]

> As it is written: "None is righteous, no, not one; no one understands; no one seeks for God. All have turned aside; together they have become worthless; no one does good, not even one." (Rom 3:10–12)

> And to the one who does not work but believes in him who justifies the ungodly, his faith is counted as righteousness. (Rom 4:5)

Romans 3:10–12 clearly presupposes that only the righteous can be regarded as those who perform good deeds before God. As we saw, justification is the act of God declaring us righteous in Jesus Christ. Our faith in Jesus Christ is considered righteous only by God's grace (Rom 4:5).

What is the standard of our righteousness? Of course, it is the righteousness of God.

What is the standard of our goodness? It is the goodness of God.[52]

And so where can we find the structure of our goodness? We can find it only in the righteousness of God.

Therefore, the righteousness of God is not only the standard of our righteousness but also the standard of our goodness.[53] Note that righteousness, holiness, and goodness are all attributes of the same God, and therefore cannot be separated from each other. Now, let's hear what Paul has to say about our good deeds.

> So do not let what you regard as good be spoken of as evil. (Rom 14:16)

> To the pure, all things are pure, but to the defiled and unbelieving, nothing is pure; but both their minds and their consciences are defiled. They profess to know God, but they deny him by their works. They are detestable, disobedient, unfit for any good work. (Titus 1:15–16)

---

51. Vols. 2 and 3 are written on the premise that for those who believe in Jesus, the marred goodness within them is restored. Please refer to "4. Justification and the Restored Image of God," in vol. 2, ch. 2; and "4. The Growth of the Image of God," in vol. 3, ch. 2.

52. As we saw, righteousness can be called the "structure of God's goodness" (Frame, *Systematic Theology*, 257).

53. Frame, *Systematic Theology*, 257.

Titus 1:15–16 is also the key passage to state that the unregenerate can never do good works before God. Since God's righteousness is the standard of our goodness, it reveals the standard for any and all good deeds. Because righteousness, holiness, and goodness cannot be separated from each other, these passages (Rom 3:10–12; 14:16; Titus 1:15–16) present two important facts concerning a good life: (1) justification is God declaring us righteous in Jesus Christ; (2) justification (righteousness) connects holiness and goodness in Jesus.[54]

Only God's children can be considered righteous, holy, and good in Jesus Christ. And only believers can live a righteous, holy, and good life and grow in Jesus Christ as God's children (Col 1:10; Eph 4:13; 1 Pet 3:18; 2 Tim 3:16–17; Rom 14:15; 1 Cor 1:30). So, "the righteousness that God expects from us is essentially to image" his goodness, his holiness, his righteousness.[55] This is our responsibility.

Furthermore, God's righteous laws in Scripture teach us to "imitate" God's ethical "character and conduct."[56] Therefore, the laws of God's righteous words are the highest standards of righteousness, holiness and goodness for human life.[57] The Ten Commandments and the Mosaic law given by God to Israel were also given as the ultimate goals for a good life. After setting the Israelites free from the life of slavery in Egypt, God gave them the Mosaic law to live a life befitting God's people.

Therefore, we must not forget that the standards of God's righteousness, holiness, and goodness serve as the standards for a good human life, and come from the same attributes of God.[58] Scripture often teaches that the standards of holiness and goodness come from God's righteousness.[59] In this way, the righteousness of God is the standard of God's goodness as well as the standards of human goodness.[60] In the Bible, God's words are the laws of the kingdom of God that represent God's righteousness.

It is remarkable that God's righteousness not only exposes human sin but also becomes the standard for atoning for sin in Jesus Christ. Additionally, the standards for punishment for sins in human life and

---

54. Later, we will explore this connection between justification (righteousness) and holiness and goodness in "4. Justification and the Restored Image of God," in vol. 2, ch. 2.
55. Frame, *Doctrine of God*, 449; Frame, *Systematic Theology*, 260.
56. Frame, *Doctrine of God*, 449; Frame, *Systematic Theology*, 233–35.
57. Frame, *Doctrine of God*, 451.
58. Frame, *Systematic Theology*, 257.
59. Frame, *Systematic Theology*, 233–35, 257–68, 276–79.
60. Frame, *Systematic Theology*, 257.

rewards for a life of faith also originate from God's righteous words (Rom 7:12).[61] Second Timothy 3:16–17 is one of the most significant passages to present that God's righteousness is the standards for the most blessed life and the best life. According to this passage, the Bible is the only textbook capable of training God's people to live a good life within God's righteousness.

> All Scripture is breathed out by God and profitable for teaching, for reproof, for correction, and for training in righteousness, that the man of God may be complete, equipped for every good work. (2 Tim 3:16–17)

God's righteousness in the Bible, therefore, becomes the foundation for a good life of God's children who desire to imitate the character and conduct of Jesus (John 13:34–35; 15:12; Eph 5:2; 1 John 4:10–11; 2 Tim 3:16–17). In this way, God's righteousness in Scripture guides us to imitate God's ethical character, which includes God's love, God's holiness, God's righteousness, God's goodness.[62] This righteousness of God is well shown in the words of God, "the laws of God" revealed in the Bible.[63] As we saw earlier, on the one hand, the Mosaic law also teaches us who is considered lawless in the eyes of God. On the other hand, the Mosaic law, shown God's righteousness, serves to protect the hearts of the righteous, who have become righteous in Jesus, from the lawless.[64]

> Now we know that the law is good, if one uses it lawfully, understanding this, that the law is not laid down for the just but for the lawless and disobedient, for the ungodly and sinners, for the unholy and profane, for those who strike their fathers and mothers, for murderers, the sexually immoral, men who practice homosexuality, enslavers, liars, perjurers, and whatever else is contrary to sound doctrine, in accordance with the gospel of the glory of the blessed God with which I have been entrusted. (1 Tim 1:8–11)

In conclusion, God's righteousness shows humans the way to live the life of the highest goodness through Jesus Christ (Rom 8:1–4; Gal 5:13–14). God's righteousness, as revealed in the words of the Bible, is

---

61. Frame, *Doctrine of God*, 448–51.
62. Frame, *Doctrine of God*, 449.
63. Frame, *Doctrine of God*, 448–49.
64. Earlier, we saw that Calvin suggested "to teach believers and exhort" was one of three functions of the Mosaic law (*Institutes* 2.7.6–15).

the highest standard of righteousness and the highest standard of the good life in this world.⁶⁵ We now should remember that God has justified sinners through the redemptive work of the perfect obedience of Jesus and enabled them to live the most blessed life according to the standards of God's righteousness. Jesus Christ will judge our deeds with this righteousness (Rev 19:11; 22:11–12). This best life of goodness is also a life that fulfills the requirements of the law, according to the work of the Holy Spirit.

> There is therefore now no condemnation for those who are in Christ Jesus. For the law of the Spirit of life has set you free in Christ Jesus from the law of sin and death. For God has done what the law, weakened by the flesh, could not do. By sending his own Son in the likeness of sinful flesh and for sin, he condemned sin in the flesh, in order that the righteous requirement of the law might be fulfilled in us, who walk not according to the flesh but according to the Spirit. (Rom 8:1–4)

> Owe no one anything, except to love each other, for the one who loves another has fulfilled the law. For the commandments, "You shall not commit adultery, You shall not murder, You shall not steal, You shall not covet," and any other commandment, are summed up in this word: "You shall love your neighbor as yourself." Love does no wrong to a neighbor; therefore love is the fulfilling of the law. (Rom 13:8–10)

> For you were called to freedom, brothers. Only do not use your freedom as an opportunity for the flesh, but through love serve one another. For the whole law is fulfilled in one word: "You shall love your neighbor as yourself." (Gal 5:13–14)

Therefore, the words of the Bible alone present the blueprint for the highest good life for humans. In other words, the highest standard of goodness for our lives is God's righteousness revealed in his word. Further, the standards of the highest good life pursued in general philosophy and worldly politics can be found only in the Bible.⁶⁶

---

65. Frame, *Doctrine of God*, 451.

66. For "justice and good life" in politics, Harvard University professor of government Michael Sandel points out that "justice is not only about the right way to distribute things. It is also about the right way to value things" (Sandel, *Justice*, 261). In his book, Sandel discusses moral and political issues of Aristotle and Kant, along with moral philosophy and the purpose of politics, related to the good life. In the conclusion of the book, he argues that "a politics of moral engagement" would be "a more promising basis

The highest good life shown by God's righteousness is a life believing in Jesus Christ, living according to the word of God, and receiving the guidance of the Holy Spirit through the prayers of faith (Mark 16:16; Acts 16:31; John 3:15–16; Rom 1:16–17; Col 3:16; 1 Tim 4:5; 2 Tim 3:16–17; 1 Pet 2:2; Col 4:2; 1 Thess 5:17; Phil 4:6; John 14:26; 15:26; Gal 6:16–24; Rom 8:26–27). This is a life of believing in the word of God in Jesus, doing every good work (Eph 2:10; Prov 7:18; 15:17; John 13:34; 15:17; Rom 12:10; 1 Thess 4:9; 2 Thess 1:3; Heb 10:24; 1 Pet 4:8; 1 John 3:23; 4:7, 11–12; 2 John 1:5, 11), loving one another, supporting each other, and helping each other (John 13:35; Rom 12:10, 17; Gal 5:13; 1 John 3:23; Jas 5:13; Col 1:10; 2 Thess 2:17; 1 Tim 5:10; 2 Tim 2:21; 3:17; Titus 3:1; Heb 13:18, 21).

---

for a just society," seeking "the connection between distributive justice and the common good," respecting others' "moral and religious convictions," in relation to the good life (Sandel, *Justice*, 268–69).

4

The Word of God

IN THE STUDY OF God's covenant and God's righteousness, we have examined that the kingdom of God is a kingdom established by God's covenant and God's righteousness. Now, in the last chapter of this first volume, we will consider what the word of God is. As we have seen so far, the covenant of God is the words of God's promises, and the righteousness of God is the foundation of the word of God. Notice that the covenant, the righteousness, and the word have *legal* elements in them as a common ground. The Bible that contains the word of God is not an ordinary book.

Interestingly, the Bible contains many stories to convey the word of God. The whole Bible introduces the kingdom of God through stories centered on the relationship between God and humans. Throughout Scripture, God speaks through the human authors of the Bible to humans, whom he created in his own image. The main point of the Bible lies in the redemptive history of Jesus Christ, using the events of creation, fall, and redemption to show how God has established our relationship with him.

The redemptive history revealed in the Bible is "that series of events by which God redeems his people from sin, a narrative fulfilled in Christ."[1] In the Bible, this redemptive history cannot be separated from the faith that God has demanded from humans.[2] God has spoken in the Bible about the kingdom of God, which is the kingdom of the

---

1. Frame, *Systematic Theology*, 540.
2. Cf. Frame, *Systematic Theology*, 541–42. Please refer to vol. 3.

covenant, the kingdom of justification, and the kingdom of faith, along with redemptive history. The important themes mentioned in the Bible share the commonality of being the word of God: God's covenant, God's knowledge, God's righteousness, God's wisdom, God's law, the Mosaic law, and the gospel. These topics all share the same foundation as the word of God. God desires obedience of faith to the word of God from humans.

Next, it is important to focus on that fact all the stories in the Bible lead us to a life with eternal value. The stories of the Bible teach a life with eternal value centered on the lives of important people. Through these stories, God leads us to a life of eternal value, focusing on the events that occurred in the relationship between God and people. In fact, the Author of the stories in the Bible is God himself.

God wrote his words in the Bible to reveal himself to humans.[3] God has conveyed his will and thoughts through the words of the Bible. To this end, God used prophets, apostles, and other biblical writers, employing various forms such as poetry, prose, stories, prophecies, and letters. God also used numerous historical events, people, and words in order to convey his message to us.[4]

Just as food is of the utmost importance to our bodies, the word of God is of the utmost importance to our lives. We should never take away the word of God from our lives. The goal of biblical interpretation is to apply the word of God to all areas of our lives. For this reason, *Justification and the Kingdom of God* continuously emphasizes the importance of the word of God and the importance of application in biblical interpretation.

God reveals himself through Scripture and unveils the works he has done for us. He reaches out to us through his word. In fact, God encounters us through his word. For this reason, we now look at the three key aspects of the word of the Bible: (1) the characteristics of the word of God, (2) the importance of the word of God, and (3) the purpose of the word of God.

---

3. Natural revelation through nature that God has prepared for humans becomes a stage to show God's kindness, God's wisdom, human corruption, and God's grace of salvation (Acts 14:17; Gen 3:17–19; 9:6; Rom 1:18–21; 3:21–22). To God's children, nature and this world can serve as tools to apply the grace they have received from God in their lives. Cf. Frame, *Systematic Theology*, 537–39.

4. Frame, *Systematic Theology*, 535–36; Frame, *Doctrine of God*, 469–94.

1. THE CHARACTERISTICS OF THE WORD OF GOD

First, the characteristics of God's word. There are various characteristics of the word of God that the Bible describes. We, however, will explore the most important ones centered on the relationship between God and humans since we cannot cover all the characteristics in this book. We will examine the speaking God; move on to the lordship attributes of God's word; and finally, look at the power of life, work, and judgment of God's word.

A. The Speaking God

One thing we should never forget is that God is "a speaking God."[5] God made the universe, all things, and humans with his word (John 1:1–2). There is something even more important for us: the Creator God loves humans and "speaks to us" through his word.[6] The fact that God speaks to us through the written word is an incredibly important point. Additionally, the word of God in the Bible has a fundamental characteristic, that God's word is "an essential attribute, inseparable from God's being."[7] Therefore, the most important fundamental characteristic in the Bible lies in the premise that "God's word is God, and God is his word."[8]

The whole Bible is a book that records the word of the living God. The written words also have "the same authority" as God's voice.[9] This truth is the most important foundation for interpreting the whole Bible and our lives. The significant difference between the God of the Bible and the false gods of the world also comes from the God who "speaks" (1 Kgs 18:24–46; Pss 115:5–8; 135:15–18; Hab 2:18–20).[10]

In the Bible, God's speech also has the attributes of God: righteousness (Ps 119:7), faithfulness (Ps 119:86), wonderfulness (Ps 119:129), truth (Ps 119:142; John 17:17), eternity (Ps 119:89, 160; 1 Pet 1:25), omnipotence (Gen 18:14; Isa 55:11; Luke 1:37), perfection (Ps 19:7–11), goodness, and love.[11]

---

5. Frame, *Systematic Theology*, 522–23, 788.
6. Frame, *Doctrine of the Word*, 9.
7. Frame, *Systematic Theology*, 523.
8. Frame, *Doctrine of the Word*, 48.
9. Frame, *Doctrine of the Word*, 102.
10. Frame, *Systematic Theology*, 522; Frame, *Doctrine of the Word*, 66.
11. Frame, *Systematic Theology*, 522–23, 526.

Therefore, we as the image bearers of God can find the standard of truth in all areas of life only in the words of God. We can find the standards of God's love, wisdom, knowledge, righteousness, holiness, and goodness only in God's words (Eph 1:17; 3:18; 4:15–16, 24; 5:2, 8–9; Col 2:3; 3:10, 14; 1 Cor 1:30–31).[12] We must remember the standard of God's righteousness here. That is, as we saw earlier, we can find the standards of God's righteousness for all areas of life *only* in God's words.

B. The Covenant Lordship Attributes of God's Word

The covenant lordship (sovereign) attributes of God are also the important divine attributes revealed in the word of God.[13] God's words in the Bible essentially show these divine attributes, God's own nature. That is, God's words reveal God's covenant lordship as the covenant Lord of the universe and of all areas of life; he is Lord over every aspect of life. The God of the Bible is the Lord of the covenant. In the Bible, the important covenant lordship attributes of God revealed in his word include control, authority, and presence.[14]

In the word of God, we see the divine lordship attributes: (1) "*his control* in the word's powerful actions," (2) "*his authority* in his words addressed to us," and (3) "*his presence* in the inseparability of his word and Spirit."[15] Specifically, the Holy Spirit reveals the divine lordship attributes in our lives through God's word. The divine lordship attributes are also manifested in the providence of God within the events of nature and history. These lordship attributes of God demonstrate that God is directly

---

12. Frame, *Doctrine of God*, 446–51.

13. Frame, *Doctrine of the Word*, 50–68. As John Frame puts it, I am discussing here the covenant lordship attributes of God's word. I believe that this discussion is particularly helpful for understanding the nature of God's word, especially in relation to the importance of God's word and its application to our lives. We will explore this further.

14. Frame, *Doctrine of the Knowledge*, 15–18; Frame, *Doctrine of the Word*, 50–68. Modern liberal theology denies the covenant lordship attributes revealed in the word of God of the Bible. However, in liberal theology, human autonomy and reason are the standard for determining truth. This is a false theory. Cf. Frame, *Doctrine of the Word*, 15–25.

15. Frame, *Systematic Theology*, 522 (emphasis added). See also Frame, *Systematic Theology*, 523, 573–74; Frame, *Doctrine of God*, 472–75; Frame, *Doctrine of the Knowledge*, 10–11.

involved in his work of creating and of controlling with his power and authority through his word.[16]

Through his word, God has planned and fulfilled the redemptive work of Jesus with the divine attributes. God himself has demonstrated that he works through his word with the divine lordship attributes.

Why are these divine lordship attributes really that important for us?

They are important because they help us to understand the nature of God's word and to apply the word of God into our daily lives. Let's briefly examine the three aspects of God's lordship attributes as they appear in his word.

a. The Word of God as His Controlling Power

First, the controlling power of his word.

What does it mean that God controls with his word?

This means that God governs the entire universe and everything in it—but not in a way we can imagine (Ps 104). We cannot fully understand what the controlling power of God is. However, the Bible clearly states that God's word, with its legal authority as his word, has sufficient controlling power to govern creation, the human world, and the work of providence in his order.[17]

The power of the word in which God's lordship attributes are manifested in the Bible is a very important theme (Isa 55:11; Rom 1:16; 1 Thess 1:5; Heb 4:12; John 1:1). God's word sometimes appears as the omnipotence and omniscience of God himself in Scripture.[18] John's Gospel also says that God created the heavens and the earth by his word, and that the word is Jesus Christ (John 1:1, 14). John connects and explains Gen 1:1 and John 1:1–3 in this way.[19] Moreover, John introduces the Trinity (John 1:1–3; John 14–17) and emphasizes that the word was used as the means for the creation of the heavens and the earth (John 1:1–3). For this reason, "the power of the word" that created all things is also "the power of God's Spirit."[20]

16. Cf. Frame, *Apologetics*, 43–44.
17. Frame, *Doctrine of the Word*, 50–51.
18. Frame, *Systematic Theology*, 522nn8, 11.
19. Frame, *Systematic Theology*, 522–23.
20. Frame, *Systematic Theology*, 522, 528–29. Note that the word of God also has the power to fulfill God's promised judgment to those who disobey his word.

God also uses his word as the law to govern his kingdom. God has the power to execute his promises according to his words. If God does not have sufficient power to execute according to his own law, then his word has no power to control the world (*control*, controlling power). In other words, God's word has "controlling power" to govern the entire universe. God has controlling power to perform his marvelous works for us who have faith in Jesus Christ according to his word (Ps 107:15, 31).

> Then they cried to the LORD in their trouble, and he delivered them from their distress. He sent out his word and healed them, and delivered them from their destruction. Let them thank the LORD for his steadfast love, for his wondrous works to the children of man! (Ps 107:19–21)

The main point here is that God has the sufficient power to always keep his promises, his words, and his laws that govern the kingdom of God. God is the omnipotent God who can mobilize everything in order to fulfill his covenant word. That is, he has the power to accomplish all the words of his promises he has made, utilizing his own abilities without any help. For example, for the people of Israel, God's controlling power sometimes manifested as astonishing miracles during events like the exodus, the crossing of the Red Sea, and the fall of Jericho. God mobilizes his controlling power (control) to keep the words of his promises (Pss 105, 108, 111). In Isa 55:11, Scripture speaks of the divine lordship attribute of *God's control* (controlling power) present in the word of God.

> So shall my word be that goes out from my mouth; it shall not return to me empty, but it shall accomplish that which I purpose, and shall succeed in the thing for which I sent it. (Isa 55:11)

Therefore, we must not forget that God's powerful word promises both blessings to those who obey within the covenant and judgment to those who disobey.[21] Through the words of his commandments, God conveys his will and plan to humans with the covenant of promises and keeps his promises without fail.[22] The word of God's covenant is the word of the power that lasts forever.

What we need to remember is that the word of God has the power of salvation and the power of sanctification by God's grace.[23] First, the word

---

21. Deuteronomy 27–28 (Frame, *Doctrine of the Word*, 52).

22. Frame, *Systematic Theology*, 528–29; Frame, *Doctrine of the Word*, 10–11. Adam, Noah, and Abraham received God's will through the word of the covenant.

23. Frame, *Doctrine of the Word*, 51.

of the gospel has the power to bring the blessings of salvation through the work of the Holy Spirit. The Holy Spirit gives you this power by which you receive the eternal blessings of forgiveness of sins and justification before God. The power of this gospel message is also the power of the Holy Spirit.

> For I am not ashamed of the gospel, for it is the power of God for salvation to everyone who believes, to the Jew first and also to the Greek. For in it the righteousness of God is revealed from faith for faith, as it is written, "The righteous shall live by faith." (Rom 1:16–17)

> Because our gospel came to you not only in word, but also in power and in the Holy Spirit and with full conviction. You know what kind of men we proved to be among you for your sake. (1 Thess 1:5)

In addition, the word of God has the power to transform Christians and give assurance of faith. The word of God also has the power to bring wonderful blessings into the lives of those who respond to his word by faith and obey his word by faith, for God has the power to act according to the promised word for our sanctification. The power of the word for our sanctification is also the power of the Holy Spirit (1 Thess 1:5).[24]

Therefore, the word of God comes to humans with "absolute power" (Isa 55:11) to accomplish what he promises throughout human history when he gives his word to them.[25] In other words, the Spirit works within us by the word of God.

b. The Word of God as His Highest Authority

The word of God has not only the divine covenant lordship attribute of controlling power, but also the attribute of the highest *authority* in all areas. It is also important for us to understand that the word of the Bible has the highest sovereign authority in all areas.[26] As we saw earlier, God's word that is the legal commandment of God is based on God's righteousness.[27] In other words, God's righteousness becomes the most

---

24. Frame, *Systematic Theology*, 528–29; Frame, *Doctrine of the Word*, 52.
25. Frame, *Doctrine of the Word*, 11.
26. Frame, *Doctrine of the Word*, 37.
27. For God's righteousness, please refer to ch. 3 of this volume.

important foundation that establishes the most significant themes of the Bible. God's word has the highest authority based on his righteousness.

As a result, the word of God becomes the highest legal authority as the standard for judging all the truth in all areas of human culture and human life.[28] Similarly, the covenant document of the Bible is the highest "constitution of God's covenant people."[29] For Israel, as we saw earlier, the Mosaic covenant is the highest authoritative law in Israel.[30] And God commands with the supreme authority of his word and demands obedience of faith to humans through his word.[31] There are important characteristics of Scripture that support the divine sovereignty of the supreme authority of the word of God.

In addition to this, important characteristics of Scripture support the divine lordship attribute of the highest authority of God's word: inspiration, inerrancy, infallibility,[32] clarity, necessity, comprehensiveness, and sufficiency.[33] In particular, the comprehensiveness of Scripture means that Scripture fundamentally addresses "all aspects of human life."[34] And the sufficiency of Scripture implies that "Scripture contains all the divine words needed" for all aspects of human life.[35]

Why are these characteristics of Scripture, along with the authoritative nature of God's word, important to us?

It is because Scripture contains the highest authority that guarantees our salvation, justification, and sanctification. The authoritative attributes of God's word hold the highest authority as the ultimate truth for our salvation, justification, and sanctification. To be sure, these characteristics of Scripture are very important because they primarily support and prove the authoritative evidence about Jesus Christ presented in the Bible. Scripture testifies that Jesus came to this earth and completed the redemptive work for us. Also, Scripture testifies that Jesus is the way, and the truth, and the life.

---

28. Bavinck, *Reformed Dogmatics*, 1:463–65; Frame, *Doctrine of the Word*, 48, 54–56, 164–65, 216–20, 566; Frame, *Systematic Theology*, 530, 537–82.
29. Frame, *Doctrine of the Word*, 37.
30. Frame, *Systematic Theology*, 567, 570–71.
31. Frame, *Systematic Theology*, 530.
32. Frame, *Doctrine of the Word*, 140–42, 167–76, 241–53.
33. Frame, *Doctrine of the Word*, 201–28.
34. Frame, *Doctrine of the Word*, 216–19.
35. Frame, *Doctrine of the Word*, 220; see further 221–28.

> Jesus said to him, "I am the way, and the truth, and the life. No one comes to the Father except through me." (John 14:6)

> You search the Scriptures because you think that in them you have eternal life; and it is they that bear witness about me. (John 5:39)

If the Bible does not have the highest authority for truth, then we cannot acknowledge the authority of the word concerning Jesus Christ as described in the Bible. And if we disregard the authority of the Bible, we ultimately dismiss both Jesus and his redemptive work. By acknowledging the authority of the Bible, we also recognize the authority of the word of the gospel message. In other words, if we cannot accept the authority of the Bible, we cannot acknowledge the authority of the gospel.

If we cannot accept the authority of the Bible, we also cannot trust the authority of all words about Jesus, who has both divinity and humanity. If we disregard the authority of the Bible, we cannot accept the gospel of salvation. Without acknowledging the absolute authority of the Bible, we lose the basis and promise to "confess" Jesus Christ as our Savior since Scripture is also telling us about the gospel.[36] Without the words of the Bible, there can be no work of redemption by Jesus, no Mosaic law, and no gospel. Also, in this sense, the words of the disciples, such as the epistles of Paul and Peter and John, have full and eternal authority as the word of God over us. Therefore, we need the word of God for the assurance of our own salvation.[37]

Next, the authority of the Bible is important not only for salvation but also for the promise of sanctification. God's word has sufficient divine authority in Jesus to make our joy complete in him and enable us to overcome the world by faith. That is, the words of God's promises for Christian life also have the same highest authority. This becomes our assurance in the word of God's promise given to us. The authority of the Bible enables us to have confidence that God will work according to his promises for our faith life.

> These things I have spoken to you, that my joy may be in you, and that your joy may be full. (John 15:11)

> I have said all these things to you to keep you from falling away. (John 16:1)

---

36. Frame, *Systematic Theology*, 789, 573–90, 594–629, 679.
37. Frame, *Systematic Theology*, 562, 564, 582–85.

> I have said these things to you, that in me you may have peace. In the world you will have tribulation. But take heart; I have overcome the world. (John 16:33)

> Who is it that overcomes the world except the one who believes that Jesus is the Son of God? (1 John 5:5)

The main point of these texts is that when God approaches us, he does so with the highest authoritative word. When God gives us "the word of obedience," he comes with the word of the "supreme authority" that "creates" an obligation of obedience (Rom 4:20; Heb 11:6).[38] Therefore, to accept the word of God as the highest authority for all aspects of life is crucial, as it becomes the ultimate for the direction of our lives and our faith life. In other words, God's word is the highest authority for our faith and the ultimate foundation of our faith. The authority of the Bible gives us the utmost assurance that God will work according to his word.

> No unbelief made him waver concerning the promise of God, but he grew strong in his faith as he gave glory to God. (Rom 4:20)

> And without faith it is impossible to please him, for whoever would draw near to God must believe that he exists and that he rewards those who seek him. (Heb 11:6)

Thus, all people, especially God's children, must acknowledge this first and then believe that the words of the whole Bible are the words of the living God—because when God speaks to us, the word of God always carries the highest authority.[39] For this reason, God gives us the sovereignly authoritative word of promise and demands from us a response of faith and obedience of faith. This is also the most blessed path for us.

> But the word is very near you. It is in your mouth and in your heart, so that you can do it. See, I have set before you today life and good, death and evil. If you obey the commandments of the Lord your God that I command you today, by loving the Lord your God, by walking in his ways, and by keeping his commandments and his statutes and his rules, then you shall live and multiply, and the Lord your God will bless you in the land that you are entering to take possession of it. (Deut 30:14–16)

---

38. Frame, *Doctrine of the Word*, 10–11, 39. For the word of obedience, please refer to "3. The Purpose of God Giving His Word" in this chapter.

39. Frame, *Systematic Theology*, 530.

All Scripture is breathed out by God and profitable for teaching, for reproof, for correction, and for training in righteousness, that the man of God may be complete, equipped for every good work. (2 Tim 3:16–17)

c. The Word of God as His Presence

The last important covenant lordship attribute of God's word for us is the attribute of *presence*. Since God is a Spirit, he is present with us through his word with his sovereign power and authority.[40] Understanding the lordship attribute of the presence of God's word is also very important in our faith life because he comes to us by his word.

What does it mean that God comes to us by his word?

When God gives us his word, the word comes to us as "God's personal dwelling place," the word of "presence" (John 1:1; Heb 4:12–13).[41] Since "God's word is God himself," when his word is present with us, God's own "personal presence" is there.[42] Wherever the word of God is, his own personal presence is. Although God is everywhere (omnipresent), he particularly is there with us wherever his word is.[43] "When we encounter the word of God," we encounter God.[44] We need to further look at the attribute of the presence of God's word.

What does the Bible talk about the attribute of the presence of God's word?

Scripture teaches us that the word of God dwells in our hearts. In the Old Testament, the presence of God's word in our hearts is described as the word "on your heart" (Deut 6:6), the word "in your heart" (Deut 30:14), or the word "taken to heart" (Deut 32:46; Prov 22:17).[45] The Old Testament texts indicate that the word of God can be present in our hearts as God gives the words of his commandments. The Old Testament clearly helps us realize the fact that God demands us to obey his word with all our heart and faith (Exod 9:21; Deut 30:14; Job 22:22).

---

40. Frame, *Apologetics*, 42n23.
41. Frame, *Doctrine of the Word*, 11; Frame, *Systematic Theology*, 522.
42. Frame, *Systematic Theology*, 573–74; Frame, *Doctrine of the Word*, 63.
43. Frame, *Doctrine of the Word*, 63.
44. Frame, *Doctrine of the Word*, 68.
45. For the Old Testament Hebrew word for "heart" (mind, *lēb*, לֵב) and the New Testament Greek word for "heart" (mind, *kardia*, καρδία), refer to the section below, "The Power of Life, Work, and Judgment of God's Word."

> And these words that I command you today shall be on your heart. (Deut 6:6)
>
> He said to them, "Take to heart all the words by which I am warning you today, that you may command them to your children, that they may be careful to do all the words of this law." (Deut 32:46)
>
> Incline your ear, and hear the words of the wise, and apply your heart to my knowledge. (Prov 22:17)

In the New Testament, we can see the presence of God's word in terms of salvation (justification) and sanctification. With regard to the presence of God's word and the fruit of the word, the New Testament speaks more specifically of the parable of the sower (Matt 13:18–23; Luke 8:4–15) and the parable of the vine and the branches (John 15:1–17). The parable of the sower requires the result of salvation (Luke 8:12) and the fruit of our faith (Matt 13:23; Luke 8:15) after the word of God has come into our hearts. This also means that when the gospel word enters the heart, it can bear the fruit of salvation, and when the word of faith enters the heart, it can bear the fruit of faith. Ultimately, in these parables, Jesus desires obedient faith in the word that comes to all believers.

> The ones along the path are those who have heard; then the devil comes and takes away the word from their hearts, so that they may not believe and be saved. (Luke 8:12)
>
> As for that in the good soil, they are those who, hearing the word, hold it fast in an honest and good heart, and bear fruit with patience. (Luke 8:15)[46]

For this reason, Scripture mainly teaches that there is a very close relationship between the presence of God's word and the work of the Holy Spirit. The power of God's word to bear the fruit of salvation and faith is the power of the Holy Spirit that works within us as the life of Jesus (Gal 3:5; 2 Cor 4:10–12).[47] Before speaking the parable of the vine

---

46. "As for what was sown on good soil, this is the one who hears the word and understands it. He indeed bears fruit and yields, in one case a hundredfold, in another sixty, and in another thirty" (Matt 13:23).

47. For salvation, the life of the word and the life of Jesus, please see below: "The Power of Life, Work, and Judgment of God's Word."

"Always carrying in the body the death of Jesus, so that the life of Jesus may also be manifested in our bodies. For we who live are always being given over to death for Jesus'

and the branches, Jesus also teaches that the work of faith is the work of the Spirit. That is, the Spirit comes upon everyone who believes in Jesus. The Spirit that believers in Jesus receive is also the gift of salvation.

> Does he who supplies the Spirit to you and works miracles among you do so by works of the law, or by hearing with faith? (Gal 3:5)

> Whoever believes in me, as the Scripture has said, "Out of his heart will flow rivers of living water." Now this he said about the Spirit, whom those who believed in him were to receive, for as yet the Spirit had not been given, because Jesus was not yet glorified. (John 7:38–39)

Is there a term representing the covenant lordship attribute of *presence* as it relates to salvation and sanctification in the New Testament?

In the New Testament, the Greek word for "abide" (remain, stay, *meno*, μένω), related to the concept of presence, is used most frequently by John the apostle (sixty-seven times).[48] This Greek word for "abide" plays an important role in showing the characteristic of the presence of God's word in salvation and sanctification. In fact, the most important aspect of the presence of God's word in the Bible is about salvation. In John 5:38, Jesus emphasizes that believing in him through the *dwelling* of his word leads to salvation.

> And you do not have his word abiding in you, for you do not believe the one whom he has sent. (John 5:38)

Paul says in Rom 10:8 that the word of the gospel coming to us is the coming of the word of Christ, and receiving that word is accepting Christ. In this way, by accepting Christ, the word of Christ dwells in you.[49] The presence of Christ's word in our hearts is the dwelling of Christ.

---

sake, so that the life of Jesus also may be manifested in our mortal flesh. So death is at work in us, but life in you" (2 Cor 4:10–12).

48. *EDNT* 2:407. This Greek word (abide, remain, stay, *meno*, μένω) is used in John (forty times), 1 John (twenty-four times) and 2 John (three times) to represent the following: God's word (John 5:38; 1 John 2:14), Jesus' words (John 8:31; 15:7), the relationship between Jesus and believers (John 6:56; 15:4–5; 1 John 2:6, 24), the relationship between God and believers (1 John 3:24; 4:12, 15). See also BDAG 630–31.

49. Frame, *Systematic Theology*, 531. Frame uses Deut 4:7–8 and 30:11–14 to explain God's closeness to Israel. The aforementioned Rom 10:8 is derived from Deut 30:14.

"For what great nation is there that has a god so near to it as the Lord our God is to us, whenever we call upon him? And what great nation is there, that has statutes and rules so righteous as all this law that I set before you today?" (Deut 4:7–8).

> Because, if you confess with your mouth that Jesus is Lord and believe in your heart that God raised him from the dead, you will be saved. For with the heart one believes and is justified, and with the mouth one confesses and is saved. (Rom 10:9–10)
>
> So faith comes from hearing, and hearing through the word of Christ. (Rom 10:17)

The next thing to consider in the presence of God's word after salvation can be found in the relationship to the faith of God's children. Jesus teaches the relationship between the presence of God's word and the faith of salvation in the Gospel of John. This word (abide, dwell, *meno*, μένω) referring to the presence of God's word is also used to explain the relationship between the fruit of faith in those who are saved (the parable of the vine and the branches [John 15:1–17]) and discipleship.[50]

> So Jesus said to the Jews who had believed him, "If you abide in my word, you are truly my disciples, and you will know the truth, and the truth will set you free." (John 8:31–32)

Throughout the Gospel of John, the use of this Greek word, "abide" (dwell, *meno*, μένω), in the parable of the vine and the branches (John 15:1–17) should catch our attention. John uses this Greek word well to represent the presence (dwelling) of God's word here too.[51] In this parable, Jesus simultaneously teaches the relationship both between the presence (dwelling) of God's word (John 15:7) and the word of salvation (the remission of sin [John 15:3, 7]), and between the dwelling of God's word and the fruit of faith (John 15:7).[52]

> If you abide [dwell, *meno*, μένω] in me, and my words abide [dwell, *meno*, μένω] in you, ask whatever you wish, and it will be done for you. (John 15:7)

In this passage, when Jesus commands, "You abide in my word," it basically means "Do not depart from the word of God."[53] This is also

---

50. In 1 John 2:14, John says to the young men, "The word of God abides [*meno*, μένω] in you, and you have overcome the evil one." He also uses the term (abide, dwell, *meno*, μένω) to describe the dwelling of God's word.

51. BDAG 630–31; *EDNT* 2:407–8. This word essentially represents the continuation (progress) of time.

52. "Already you are clean because of the word that I have spoken to you" (John 15:3).

53. This is also used in relation to the following: teaching (2 John 9), faith and love (1 Tim 2:15), what you have learned (2 Tim 3:14), Jesus' love (John 15:9), and God's

the word of command that means "Do not depart from the word of the gospel (the basis for assurance in the faith life)," "Do not depart from the word of transformation," and "Do not depart from the word of obedience." In addition, it is also the word of the Lord's promise, saying, "If you do so, you will bear the fruits of the word given by the help of the Spirit!"

This is a word of exhortation and command for Christians: always remember what Jesus has fulfilled through his redemptive work for Christians, and never "depart" from the words of these teachings. This is a very important word for a life that bears the fruits of faith.

The coming of the Holy Spirit mentioned in the Gospel of John (14:16, 20; 15:7) is to help us not to depart from the word of God. Of course, before the work of the indwelling of the Spirit, Jesus Christ (the Word) himself became flesh for the work of redemption (John 1:14). Through Jesus' incarnation, the Word, which had been with the triune God alone, came into the world. In this way, Jesus prepared for the dwelling (presence) of God's word in our hearts through his redemptive work.

Thus, as seen earlier, the "abide in the word" in John 15:7 has a deep relationship with Jesus' work of salvation. The word that we should receive, believe, and trust is the word of salvation. This is because the word of salvation and the word of the gospel are the foundation of assurance (confidence) of faith.

> And the Word became flesh and dwelt among us, and we have seen his glory, glory as of the only Son from the Father, full of grace and truth. (John 1:14)

> In the beginning was the Word, and the Word was with God, and the Word was God. (John 1:1)

Therefore, unlike the words of the world, the Bible teaches that God's word is God. Where God's word is, "God is (God is present)."[54] Where God is, God's word is.[55] For this reason, there is nothing more

---

love (1 John 4:16) (BDAG 630–31).

54. John 14 and 15 speak of the presence of the word, the presence of salvation, and the dwelling of the Spirit. We will discuss the presence of the word and the fruit of the dwelling of the word more in "3. The Purpose of Giving the Word of God." To draw near to God's word is to draw near to God. James emphasizes the works of faith for the fruit of the presence of the word: "Draw near to God, and he will draw near to you. Cleanse your hands, you sinners, and purify your hearts, you double-minded" (Jas 4:8).

55. Frame, *Systematic Theology*, 531.

important in a believer's relationship with God than God's word. When we encounter the word of God through faith, we encounter God.[56]

In conclusion, we should note the work of God's word and the work of the Holy Spirit cannot be separated. The work of the Holy Spirit brings the word of faith to dwell in our hearts. The word of the Bible contains God's covenant lordship attributes of *control* (controlling power), *authority*, and *presence*. These three sovereign lordship attributes, revealed throughout the whole Bible, fundamentally go hand in hand with the work of the triune God.

God's word comes (*presence*) to us with the power of God (*control*) and the *authority* of God. Our attitude of faith toward the word of God, as we saw, is very important in our faith life, because the coming of God's word to us is the coming of God himself. Therefore, rejecting God's word is also rejecting God. Furthermore, when we encounter the word of God by faith, we encounter God.

I have summarized the covenant lordship attributes of God's word in terms of salvation (justification) and sanctification (to imitate Jesus, to live by faith) in relation to *The Kingdom of Justification* and *The Kingdom of Faith* in figure 1-B below. This figure shows the inseparability of the work of God's word and the work of the Spirit for our salvation and sanctification.

Figure 1-B Covenant Lordship Attributes of God's Word

The Covenant Lordship Attributes of God's Word	The Word of God and the Work of the Spirit	Connectivity with the Kingdom of God
God's Controlling Power God's Authority God's Presence	Salvation (justification)	*The Kingdom of Justification* John 1:12; 3:16; Rom 1:17; 3:21–22
	Sanctification (to imitate Jesus, to live by faith)	*The Kingdom of Faith* Rom 1:17; 8:1–2; Heb 11:6; Eph 4:23–24; Col 3:10

---

56. Frame, *Doctrine of the Word*, 68.

C. The Power of Life, Work, and Judgment of God's Word (Heb 4:12–13; 1 Pet 1:23)

For the characteristics of God's word, we have looked at the speaking God and the covenant lordship attributes of God's word. Now, we will explore the power of life, work, and judgment of God's word, which are the last important characteristics of it in this volume. We need to ask an essential question before we explore this topic: Is there another important difference between God's word in the Bible and the language of the world that we haven't looked at yet?

The fundamental difference lies in the covenant lordship attributes of God's word as we saw earlier, and the power of life, work, and judgment of God's word, which we are going to explore now. The latter difference also is a very unique characteristic of the biblical word that cannot be compared to any other language.

If the living God has given his unique word to humans, wouldn't there be a reason for it?

The most important reason I believe is that God's word contains the living God's will, plan, and thoughts. The sovereign attributes of God's word, we saw earlier, along with the living God's word, indicate the present reality of God's word in all areas of life today. That is, the word holds the highest authority in all areas of our present life. And this present reality of God's word also demands a total commitment to God from all of us, a response of faith and an obedience of faith to his word every person today.

The living God has given the Bible as the living word of life for all areas of our life and as God's presence. God has given us the Bible as a book of the recorded word of the living God's. God has given us the Bible to listen to as a story spoken by the living God. For this reason, words that appear in the Bible, such as faith, hope, love, gospel, and grace, are completely different than abstract nouns spoken in the languages of the world. The words of the Bible convey the word of the living God.

> For the word of God is living and active, sharper than any two-edged sword, piercing to the division of soul and of spirit, of joints and of marrow, and discerning the thoughts and intentions of the heart. And no creature is hidden from his sight, but all are naked and exposed to the eyes of him to whom we must give account. (Heb 4:12–13)

Hebrews 4:12–13 is a representative and important passage that shows the characteristics of the word of the living God. This text speaks of the characteristics of God's word showing a somewhat different perspective than the covenant lordship attributes of God's word.

In what ways, then, does this passage reveal the important characteristics of the word of the living God?

Here, we will try to show why the characteristics of the word of the living God in Heb 4:12–13 are important, and how they relate to all areas of our life. Now, we will look at the characteristics revealed in this text from three aspects: the power of God's word to live, work, and judge.

a. The Word of the Living God Has the Power of Life

The first characteristic of God's word in Heb 4:12 is the power of *life*. The living God is the source of life. So, the word that comes from God has the power of life. The word "living" in the phrase "the word of God is living and alive" from Heb 4:12 means that the word of God is living. That is, God's word has the power of life (life-giving power).[57]

In the New Testament, the word "live" (zaō, ζάω) is often used to describe the living God (Matt 16:16; Acts 14:15; Rom 9:6; 2 Cor 3:3; Heb 10:31), the living Father (John 6:57), living water (John 4:10–11; 7:38), living sacrifice (Rom 12:1), and a living being (Adam [1 Cor 15:45]).[58] The same holds true for the word "living" in Heb 4:12. In other words, the word of God is always "living and abiding" (1 Pet 1:23) and is "involved in everything" that God does.[59] The word of the living God is always the living word.

> Since you have been born again, not of perishable seed but of imperishable, through the living and abiding word of God. (1 Pet 1:23)

What does this mean to us?

In what sense is God's word said to be living?

The main point of this text lies particularly in the fact that the perfect sacrifice of Jesus has opened the way to the word of life for all believers. Jesus, who is the way, the truth, and the life (John 14:6), has made it

---

57. In Heb 4:12, the Greek term for "living" (zōn, ζῶν) comes from the verb "to live" (zaō, ζάω) (BDAG 424–26; Frame, *Doctrine of God*, 472).

58. Benjamin S. Davis, "Life," in Mangum et al., *Lexham Theological Wordbook*.

59. Frame, *Doctrine of God*, 472.

possible for us to live a new life that had been once closed to us (1 Cor 15:45; Heb 4:12; Rom 6:4). There is no word or language in this world that can give life to the dead souls of sinners. However, the word of God has a special power that can give life to the dead soul.

In the New Testament, the noun form, "life" (*zōe*, ζωή), of the verb "live" (*zaō*, ζάω) is also closely related to salvation. The word "living" (*zōn*, ζῶν) in Heb 4:12 is used many times in connection with salvation. For this reason, in the New Testament, "life" also describes an anticipation of eternal life after the resurrection of the dead. Paul also uses this word from a soteriological perspective, contrasting life and death.[60]

> There is therefore now no condemnation for those who are in Christ Jesus. For the law of the Spirit of life has set you free in Christ Jesus from the law of sin and death. (Rom 8:1-2).

John also uses this word, "live" (*zaō*, ζάω) to describe how those who believe in Jesus live beyond physical death. Jesus, who gives life and is the light of the world (John 8:12), not only provides the light of life of salvation to sinners (John 8:12), but also gives light and life (John 1:4). As the living bread (John 6:35, 48), Jesus is also the One who gives the bread of life (John 6:51) and living water (John 4:10-11; 7:38). Metaphorically, John often uses these words, "eating and drinking" (John 4:10-14; 6:35-40) and "believing" (John 3:16; 6:36, 40), as synonyms in the context of salvation. Therefore, only Jesus becomes life for us and gives us life.[61]

> Jesus said to her, "I am the resurrection and the life. Whoever believes in me, though he dies, yet shall he live." (John 11:25)

> Jesus said to him, "I am the way, and the truth, and the life. No one comes to the Father except through me." (John 14:6)

In other words, every believer in Jesus has the light of life through the word of God and the work of the Spirit. The word of God can become the word of life to sinners only through faith in Jesus (1 John 1:1; Phil 2:16; Acts 5:20).[62] God's word, which is the light of life, has the power of life to brighten dark hearts. Jesus' disciples also had this "life" when they

---

60. *EDNT* 2:106-7.
61. *EDNT* 2:108-9.
62. "Go and stand in the temple and speak to the people all the words of this Life" (Acts 5:20).

believed in Jesus (John 3:16, 36; 5:24, 40; 6:40, 47, 51, 53; 10:10; 20:31; 1 John 3:15; 5:12–13).[63]

> That which was from the beginning, which we have heard, which we have seen with our eyes, which we looked upon and have touched with our hands, concerning the word of life. (1 John 1:1)

> Holding fast to the word of life, so that in the day of Christ I may be proud that I did not run in vain or labor in vain. (Phil 2:16)

With Jesus' coming into the world, this life was introduced. Therefore, Jesus, through whom the word became flesh (John 1:14), also calls himself "the life" (John 1:4; 6:48; 11:25; 14:6), "the light of the world," and "the light of life" (John 8:12). Consequently, those who believe in Jesus are those who have the life of Jesus and the light of God's life (1 John 1:5, 7; 2:8–9).

Does Heb 4:12 talk about the life-giving power of the word only in relation to salvation?

The word "live" (*zaō*, ζάω) in this text refers not only to salvation, but to the power of life (the life-giving power) of the word working within God's children. In other words, the Holy Spirit works within those who believe in the word of God so that the word of God may dwell in us and work within us. In 1 Thess 2:13, Scripture says that God's word worked within the church members when they believed in God's word.

> And we also thank God constantly for this, that when you received the word of God, which you heard from us, you accepted it not as the word of men but as what it really is, the word of God, which is at work in you believers. (1 Thess 2:13)

This passage is about the work of the Holy Spirit, which gives the life-giving power of God's word in believers. This work of the Holy Spirit can take place only in God's children. In other words, the Spirit works within God's children to bear the fruit of God's word. The work of the life-giving power to God's word for their sanctification is entirely the work of the Spirit. Of course, before this happens to them, the Holy Spirit first brings the dead soul back to life when they believe in Jesus (Rom 8:1–2). However, the text (1 Thess 2:13) also means that the Spirit pours out the life-giving power of God's word into Christians so that they may

---

63. BDAG 430–31. The word of the living Jesus is also the word of life. "It is the Spirit who gives life; the flesh is no help at all. The words that I have spoken to you are spirit and life" (John 6:63).

bear good fruit by the Spirit. The word of the living God can give life to believers because the Spirit can provide life (Heb 4:12; Rom 7:10).[64]

In conclusion, every believer who is saved and justified in Jesus by God's grace alone will gain the life of Jesus (John 20:31; 1 John 5:12; Rom 5:18).[65] Those who believe in Jesus already have life in Jesus, and this results in having eternal life that continues even after the resurrection (John 6:40; 12:25; 1 John 3:14).[66]

However, for those who do not believe in Jesus, the words of the Bible are like a dead language. The word of the living God is dead in terms of the soul for those without faith. But for the believers, the word of God is *living* because of their faith in Jesus. The word of God does not automatically bring *life* to all believers or become the life-giving power to them. The work of God's word can bear fruit for believers when they respond to the word with faith in Jesus (1 Thess 2:13; Heb 4:11).[67]

> For good news came to us just as to them, but the message they heard did not benefit them, because they were not united by faith with those who listened. (Heb 4:2)

> Since therefore it remains for some to enter it, and those who formerly received the good news failed to enter because of disobedience. (Heb 4:6)

Therefore, whenever looking at Heb 4:12, which says, "the word of God is living and alive," God's children must always remember to have faith in the word of the living God.[68] This is important because the life-

---

64. BDAG 430–31.

65. Acts 11:18 refers to believing in Jesus and receiving salvation as "repentance that leads to life": "When they heard these things they fell silent. And they glorified God, saying, 'Then to the Gentiles also God has granted repentance that leads to life.'"

66. The word of God's commandment is eternal life (John 12:50). The saving faith is entirely the work the Spirit that brings life to the soul from death (John 5:24; 7:38–39; Rom 8:1–2; 2 Pet 1:3).

67. We can say that the words of the Psalms are involved in the word of God since Heb 4:2, which is essentially based on Ps 95:7–8, indicates that the words of the Psalms can also be considered God's word.

"For he is our God, and we are the people of his pasture, and the sheep of his hand. Today, if you hear his voice, do not harden your hearts, as at Meribah, as on the day at Meribah in the wilderness" (Ps 95:7–8).

68. Hebrews 4 introduces the words of the Old Testament as the word of the living God and the voice of the living God. It also introduces the Mosaic law as the word of God and discusses the voice of God's word through Joshua and David. Therefore, the Mosaic law is called "the god news" in Heb 4:2 and 6—indicating that Israelites received

giving power of the word in Heb 4:12, "living," is at work in God's children when they respond to and obey God's word by faith. Without faith, if you receive God's word, it has no life-giving power. And without faith, when reading the Bible, God's word becomes indistinguishable from the words of the world—there is no life-giving power.[69] God's word becomes beneficial and life-giving to us only when we read and accept it with faith in Jesus (Heb 4:2).

b. The Word of the Living God Has the Power to Work

The second characteristic of God's word in Heb 4:12 is the power to *work*. Hebrews 4:12 states, "the word of God is living and active," where the adjective "active" (effective, *energes*, ἐνεργής) demonstrates another difference from the language of the world.

What is the difference between this word ("active") from the term of the world?

The language of the world has no living and active power to work that is found in the word of God. However, Scripture, as the word of the living God, has active power to work.[70] Now, let's briefly look at the meaning of this word.

This word "active" in Heb 4:12 is primarily used to describe power in relation to Christ. This Greek word for "active" (effective, *energes*, ἐνεργής) clearly shows the characteristics of the word of the living God with the word "living" (*zōn*, ζῶν) that comes before it.[71]

> For the word of God is living and active, sharper than any two-edged sword, piercing to the division of soul and of spirit, of

---

the good news from God (Heb 4:6). Both the law and the gospel are the word of God.

69. *Justification and the Kingdom of God* as a whole is based on the premise that salvation and faith are gifts from God (Eph 2:8–9). However, we also have a responsibility for faith and obedience in the life of a Christian.

70. In Heb 4:12, the word "active" comes from a Greek adjective for "active" (effective, powerful, *energes*, ἐνεργής) (BDAG 335). Cf. L&N 162.

71. The English word "energy" comes from the Greek noun form *enérgeia* (ἐνέργεια) of this adjective "active" (*energes*, ἐνεργής [Heb 4:12]). This noun form is primarily used in the New Testament to mean power (*dunamis*, δύναμις). This word (*enérgeia*, ἐνέργεια) is primarily used to describe the power related to Christ: the power of Christ that transforms to glorious body (Phil 3:21), the power of the Father that gives to the believer (Eph 1:19), the power of God that gives the gospel (Eph 3:7), the power that works in the head and the body (Eph 4:16), the power at work within me (Col 1:29), the power of the resurrection (Col 2:12). For the power of the resurrection from the dead, please see Eph 1:19 and Col 2:12 (*EDNT* 1:453).

joints and of marrow, and discerning the thoughts and intentions of the heart. (Heb 4:12)

When we look at the verb form of the word "active" (*energes*, ενεργής) in Heb 4:12, "work" (be at work, *energeō*, ἐνεργέω), it will help us understand Heb 4:12. This Greek verb means "work (be at work)," that is, "put one's power into operation."[72] Thus, "the word of God is active" means that there is a working power in the word of God. That is, the word of the living God has the power to work. Therefore, the first part of Heb 4:12 means "the word of God has the working power to bring life into action by the Holy Spirit."

Earlier we mentioned that the word of God has a controlling power as the covenant lordship attribute.[73] This power is God's power that fulfills his promises through his word. As such, this Greek verb form "work" (be at work, *energeō*, ἐνεργέω), is also used to express the working power of God within us (Eph 1:11; 2 Cor 1:6; Gal 3:5).[74]

> Now to him who is able to do far more abundantly than all that we ask or think, according to the power at work within us. (Eph 3:20)

> For it is God who works in you, both to will and to work for his good pleasure. (Phil 2:13)

We should remember that the word of the living God has not only the life-giving power but also working power. This Greek word "work" (*energeō*, ἐνεργέω), as we saw, is mainly used to describe the power of God. Therefore, Heb 4:12 clearly says that the omnipresent and omniscient God always fulfills the words of his promises with his own power. God's word also has the working power to execute, achieve, and fulfill the promises of God. In other words, the word of the living God has sufficient power to work and accomplish according to God's promises. Notice that this is also the sovereign work of the Holy Spirit. The Spirit has the

---

72. The Greek verb for "work" (be at work, *energeō*, ἐνεργέω) of the adjective form "active" (*energes*, ενεργής [Heb 4:12]) basically means "put one's capabilities into operation." I translate it into "put one's power into operation" regarding Heb 4:12 (BDAG 335). Cf. In the New Testament, the Greek word for "work" (*ergon*, ἔργον) is often used to describe human works, mainly referring to the work of the law, rather than God's works (BDAG 390–91; *EDNT* 1:49–51). But as we saw before, salvation is entirely the work of God, a gift from God apart from human works. Cf. *TDNT* 2:639–43.

73. Please refer to our previous discussion in "1-B-a, The Word of God as His Controlling Power" in this chapter.

74. BDAG 335.

power to make the life of Jesus *active* in us through the word of the living God (2 Cor 4:10–12).[75]

> Does he who supplies the Spirit to you and works miracles among you do so by works of the law, or by hearing with faith? (Gal 3:5)

The main point here is that the words of the Bible are the words of the living and omnipotent God. The Holy Spirit is the One who has the power of God to give us salvation with the gospel message (Rom 1:17). Also, the Spirit has the sufficient power to give us love, hope, joy, and peace by his power when we believe the word and walk by faith according to the word of God (Rom 15:13; 1 Thess 1:6). Therefore, it is a great blessing that God has given us the ability to obey the living and powerful word. The word of God used by the Spirit has the working power to keep his promises.

> May the God of hope fill you with all joy and peace in believing, so that by the power of the Holy Spirit you may abound in hope. (Rom 15:13)

c. The Word of the Living God Has the Power of Judgment

> For the word of God is living and active, sharper than any two-edged sword, piercing to the division of soul and of spirit, of joints and of marrow, and discerning the thoughts and intentions of the heart. (Heb 4:12)

Last, the third characteristic of the word of God revealed in Heb 4:12 is the power of *judgment*. Since this power of judgment in the word of God comes from the attributes of God, it is necessary to briefly examine God's authority and power to judge. As we saw earlier, God is the only Lawgiver and Judge in the world. The righteousness of God serves as God's standards of governance, salvation, and a good life. We learned earlier that God works according to the law of his righteous nature.

Now we will look at the power of *judgment* of God's word as we did with the power of *life* and the power to *work*. Particularly, I want to see the power of judgment from the perspective of the standard of salvation and the standard of a good life, as spoken in Heb 4:12. The living God

---

75. "And you became imitators of us and of the Lord, for you received the word in much affliction, with the joy of the Holy Spirit" (1 Thess 1:6).

judges our hearts and works (Jer 12:3; 17:10; 20:12; Acts 1:24; 15:8; 1 John 3:20). As we saw earlier in the Mosaic covenant, the standard of God's word of judgment for the Israelites is the word of the Mosaic law.[76] Jeremiah 17:10 and 20:12 speak of God who judges our hearts and acts accordingly.

> I the LORD search the heart and test the mind, to give every man according to his ways, according to the fruit of his deeds. (Jer 17:10)

> O LORD of hosts, who tests the righteous, who sees the heart and the mind, let me see your vengeance upon them, for to you have I committed my cause. (Jer 20:12)

For this reason, Heb 4:12 focuses on the role of God's word as judge. That is, in Heb 4:12, "discerning" or "judging" (able to judge, *kritikos*, κριτικός) carries a judicial meaning.[77] Thus, the word of the living God has the power to directly judge all activities that occur within the human heart.[78] God judges human hearts and actions according to his word's law and renders a verdict.[79] As such, the word of the living God serves the role of a judge (Heb 4:12; John 12:48; Rom 3:19).

The main point of Heb 4:12 is that God has placed the power (ability) to judge and to render a verdict in the word of God on behalf of himself. This means that the word of God serves the role of a judge on behalf of God. In other words, the word of God is no different than God, who is the Judge of our thoughts and intentions in our hearts. The living God can see even the deepest parts of our hearts. The word of the living God also has sufficient power to judge all the activities of human hearts. Therefore, it is necessary for us to examine the word "heart" in Heb 4:12 more.

In the Bible, the word "heart" is primarily used in terms of the relationship between God and humans. However, "piercing" in Heb 4:12 means that God can "penetrate" into the deepest parts of human hearts through his word. Accordingly, the word of God has the power to judge all the inner activities of human hearts and actions that arise in

---

76. Please refer to the Mosaic covenant, which we discussed in ch. 2 of this volume.

77. BDAG 568–70; *EDNT* 2:322.

78. BDAG 570; *EDNT* 2:322. For reference, the Greek word for "judge" (verb form: *krinō*, κρίνω) is the verb of the Greek word for "discerning or judging" (adjective form: able to judge, *kritikos*, κριτικός [Heb 4:12]) (*EDNT* 2:319–20).

79. BDAG 568–69.

human relationships with God. First of all, the Greek word for "heart" (*kardia*, καρδία [Heb 4:12]) in the New Testament is not different than the meaning of the Old Testament "heart" (Heb. *lēb*, לֵב), for its meaning comes from the Old Testament.[80] Throughout the whole Bible, the word "heart" primarily refers to the human being's *self* or the source of the whole inner human with intellect, emotions, and will.

The word "heart" in the New Testament is used in various ways. In the New Testament, the activities of the heart include all the activities that arise through intellect, emotion, and volition: thoughts, decisions (general and moral), understanding, knowledge, expectation, hope, love, disappointments, anger, fear, courage, sorrow, joy, pain, and response of faith.[81] So, the "heart" (*kardia*, καρδία) in Heb 4:12 carries a comprehensive, holistic meaning, encompassing intellect, emotions, and will (all the inner activities of the whole person). In this passage, "the thoughts and intentions of the heart" include activities that arise from the heart, encompassing all activities that occur intellectually, emotionally, and volitionally.[82] Therefore, "discerning (judging) the thoughts and intentions of the heart" in Heb 4:12 means that the word of the living God "judges" (NIV) all the activities of the human heart.

As we discussed "power of *life*" and "power to *work*" with Heb 4:12 earlier, we will look at two aspects of what God's word primarily judges in the heart. Let us look at the judgment based on the center of our hearts from the perspective of salvation (justification) and sanctification (to imitate Jesus, to live by faith in Jesus).

First, the most important role of God's word as a judge in Heb 4:12 is the judgment concerning salvation (justification) to see whether a person is saved or not (John 3:18; 5:24).[83] God's word becomes the word that judges in regard to salvation. First and foremost, it looks at the human heart and makes a judgment concerning salvation.[84]

---

80. *TLOT* 638–42; BDB 524–25; BDAG 508–9; *EDNT* 2:249–51. This word "heart" (*kardia*, καρδία in the NT; *lēb*, לֵב in the OT) will be discussed further in "2. The Heart of Transformation," in vol. 3, ch. 2.

81. BDB 524–25; BDAG 508–9; *EDNT* 2:249–51.

82. Cf. *TLOT* 638–42. Wisdom books in the Bible, such as Proverbs, express that God knows all the inner activities of the heart very well and acts accordingly (Prov 16:1; 17:3; 19:21; 21:2) (*TLOT* 640–42).

83. *EDNT* 2:318–19.

84. Frame, *Doctrine of God*, 472.

> Whoever believes in him is not condemned, but whoever does not believe is condemned [be judged, passive of *krinō*, κρίνω] already, because he has not believed in the name of the only Son of God. (John 3:18)

As such, "judge (discern)" in Heb 4:12 clearly indicates the word of the living God judging even the hidden sins in our hearts (Rom 2:16; 3:19).[85] For this, the words of the law and the words of the gospel serve as judges. However, for those who receive God's grace and believe in Jesus, the word of judgment are transformed into the words of salvation in Jesus Christ (John 5:24). This is also the work of the Holy Spirit, given entirely by God's grace.

> On that day when, according to my gospel, God judges the secrets of men by Christ Jesus. (Rom 2:16)

> Truly, truly, I say to you, whoever hears my word and believes him who sent me has eternal life. He does not come into judgment, but has passed from death to life. (John 5:24)

Second, we need to consider the judge's role of God's word (Heb 4:12) in sanctification (to imitate Jesus, to live by faith in Jesus). God judges the hearts of his children through his word, no matter where we are or what we are doing, even "piercing to the division" of our hearts (Jer 11:20; 12:3; 17:10; 20:12; Heb 4:12–13; Ps 7:8–9).[86]

> For the word of God is living and active, sharper than any two-edged sword, piercing to the division of soul and of spirit, of joints and of marrow, and discerning the thoughts and intentions of the heart. (Heb 4:12)

> [Of David.] Vindicate me, O LORD, for I have walked in my integrity, and I have trusted in the LORD without wavering. Prove me, O LORD, and try me; test my heart and my mind. (Ps 26:1–2)

Remember here that Heb 4:12 also speaks of the role of God's word in judging the hearts of God's children who have received his love, discerning or judging their hearts in the process of sanctification. The Holy Spirit works to bring about a change in the hearts of those who have

---

85. "Now we know that whatever the law says it speaks to those who are under the law, so that every mouth may be stopped, and the whole world may be held accountable to God" (Rom 3:19).

86. Cf. BDB 524–25.

faith in Jesus, using the promises of God's word that have been given to them (Gal 4:6; Phil 4:6–7). Indeed, the Holy Spirit judges whether God's children respond in faith and obedience to God's word, and works accordingly.

To sum up, Heb 4:12–13 demonstrates the tremendous difference between the word of the living God and the words of the world. But we should not miss the essential point of Heb 4:12–13 that it teaches a good attitude toward the word of Scripture and how to respond to God's word by faith.

So how should we respond to Heb 4:12–13?

This passage clearly teaches us to believe that the word of God has the power of life, work, and judgment. First, in the Bible, the word of God and the work of God are closely related through Jesus Christ (Heb 4:14–16). It is crucial to see this relationship because it is through Jesus that the way of wisdom has been opened, and for us, the way of the work of the word, as spoken in Heb 4:12–13, has been opened. God reveals himself through the word, promises through the word, and works according to the word. Further, God shows the direction of God's providence through the word. God judges, bestows his grace, and enables our faith to grow through the living and powerful word (Heb 4:12–16). The word of God is a language of faith.[87] The word of God is the living word given by the living God.

What is the main point that the writer is trying to tell us in Heb 4:12?

The main point of Heb 4:12 is that those who have received the gospel (Heb 4:2, 6) should be united by faith with the word of the living God. In other words: Believe that God's word has the power of *life*, *work*, and *judgment*; be united with the word of the living God by faith; do not follow the path of the Israelites who wandered in the wilderness for forty years due to their unbelief, no matter what happens (Heb 3:7–19). Even when faced with trials (Heb 2:18; 3:8–9; 4:15; 11:17, 29, 36–37), believe in the promised word of Jesus Christ, who has become our High Priest (Heb 4:14–15; 5:1–10; 6:20; 7:1–28), and boldly draw near to the throne of God's grace again.

---

87. From Heb 4:14 to Heb 10, the writer discusses the Abrahamic covenant and the Mosaic covenant, explaining that Jesus Christ fulfilled the words of the Old Testament covenants. The importance of faith in Jesus is emphasized in Heb 11, which is known as the chapter of faith.

> Since then we have a great high priest who has passed through the heavens, Jesus, the Son of God, let us hold fast our confession. For we do not have a high priest who is unable to sympathize with our weaknesses, but one who in every respect has been tempted as we are, yet without sin. Let us then with confidence draw near to the throne of grace, that we may receive mercy and find grace to help in time of need. Let us then with confidence draw near to the throne of grace, that we may receive mercy and find grace to help in time of need. (Heb 4:14–16)

Therefore, the main point of Heb 4:12 encourages us to continually believe in God's promises, trust in Jesus, repent, and renew our faith (Heb 6:1–2; 10:36). As God's children who have been sanctified by God because of Jesus (Heb 10:10), it strongly encourages us to have the patience of faith and become those who inherit the promises of Jesus (Heb 6:11–18; 10:36; 11:1–2, 6), for this is the life of faith (Heb 10:38–39) that everyone who has received the gospel and become righteous in Jesus (Rom 1:17) must live out.

> And we desire each one of you to show the same earnestness to have the full assurance of hope until the end, so that you may not be sluggish, but imitators of those who through faith and patience inherit the promises. (Heb 6:11–12)

> And without faith it is impossible to please him, for whoever would draw near to God must believe that he exists and that he rewards those who seek him. (Heb 11:6)

For this reason, Heb 4:12 strongly emphasizes that the word of God has the power of *life*, *work*, and *judgment* by the work of the Holy Spirit. The Christian who has saving faith (Heb 10:39) and is justified by faith (Heb 10:38) should live by faith in Jesus (Heb 11:1–2; Rom 1:17). As for us who are saved by grace, we believe that the Spirit within us brings about the work of the life-giving power and the working power of God's word. Only God's word has the power to cause the work of the Spirit in those who believe.

As we have seen so far, I have summarized the characteristics of God's word revealed in Heb 4:12 in figure 1-C below—the power of *life*, the power to *work*, and the power of *judgment*. This table looks at the power of *life*, *work*, and *judgment* of God's word in terms of salvation (justification: being declared righteous) and sanctification (becoming like Jesus, living by faith). This means that the Holy Spirit works in our justification and sanctification through the power of *life*, *work*, and *judgment* of God's word. Note also here that God's word and the work of the Spirit cannot be separated.

Additionally, this passage has been summarized and organized along with *The Kingdom of Justification* and *The Kingdom of Faith*.

Figure 1-C The Power of Life, Work, and Judgment of God's Word
(Heb 4:12)

The Characteristics of God's Word	The Word of God and the Work of the Holy Spirit	Connectivity to the Kingdom of God
Power of *Life* Power to *Work* Power of *Judgment*	Salvation (justification)	*The Kingdom of Justification* John 1:12; 3:16, Rom 1:17; 3:21–22
	Sanctification (to imitate Jesus, to live by faith)	*The Kingdom of Faith* Rom 1:17; 8:1–2; Heb 11:6; Eph 4:23–24; Col 3:10

2. THE IMPORTANCE OF GOD'S WORD

The main theme of this volume, *The Kingdom of the Covenant*, is the importance of the word of God. Chapter 1 introduced the kingdom of God. Chapter 2 mentioned that the kingdom of God is established through God's covenant. Chapter 3 showed that the foundation of God's covenant is God's righteousness. And in chapter 4, we saw that the importance of God's word can be expressed in the special attributes of God's word. Through his word, God enters our lives, leads us with his love, and trains us. God is with us through his word.

Why is the word of God so important to us?

The importance of God's word lies in the fact that only the Bible contains the vital message that God gives to all humankind. Only the Bible reveals God's creation and the kingdom of God that God has established. Only the Bible shows that the relationship between God and humanity began in grace and love. Only the words of the Bible clearly answer the question "What has God done for humanity?" Therefore, the significance of God's word is that only the Bible introduces that the kingdom of God has been established through his sovereign grace.

But there is another reason the word of God in the Bible is so precious to us.

The Bible provides a clear answer to the question that all of humanity has been asking for ages, "How shall we live in this world?" The Bible has offered the word of God as the standards of truth in all areas of life, especially for those who have believed and become the citizens of God's kingdom. And it demands our responsibility of faith in God's grace given to his children. The Bible commands those who become righteous by believing in Jesus by God's grace alone (Rom 1:17; 3:21–22) to live by faith only in the word of God alone.

The highest importance of the word of God, therefore, lies in the fact that the Bible reveals the sovereign grace of God and demands our responsibility of faith. As I briefly mentioned earlier, *The Kingdom of the Covenant* (vol. 1) and *The Kingdom of Justification* (vol. 2) are about the sovereign grace of God, and *The Kingdom of Faith* (vol. 3) is about human responsibility. Now, we will look at the importance of God's word for God's grace and human responsibility.

A. The Importance of the Word of God for God's Grace

The main point of the kingdom of God in the Bible is that God has established this kingdom through his sovereign grace. In other words, the most important message in the whole Bible is the work of God's sovereign grace towards humanity. The Bible is full of stories about God's sovereign work to save sinful human beings, whom he created along with the world. In this sense, the story of Scripture is a story of how God saves sinners by his grace alone. The Old Testament is a story of preparing for the kingdom of God, and the New Testament is a story of accomplishing the salvation of sinners for the building of the kingdom of God.

As we saw earlier, this story of God's sovereign salvation by his grace alone is the redemptive-historical story of Jesus Christ. The Bible shows us God's powerful grace through redemptive history. In other words, God himself has directly come to us into human history through the redemptive work of Jesus Christ, as he promised. Thus, redemptive history reveals a very important point that God has established the kingdom of God in the events of human history. Redemptive history shows the process of God saving sinners through Jesus Christ and making them citizens of the kingdom of God in Jesus.[88]

Therefore, the work of God's grace introduced in the Bible is the most amazing and greatest drama in human history. The redemptive history that centers on Jesus Christ clearly introduces the Christian worldview of creation, fall, and redemption.

a. The Importance of Redemptive History

The importance of the redemptive history that the Bible speaks to us is incomparable to anything else. The amazing redemptive history that God has accomplished from the story of creation in heaven and earth to the birth of Jesus Christ cannot be found in any other human history.

For redemptive history so far, we saw God has mobilized many nations, many events, and many people over a long period of time. God not only used these things but also gave the word of God's covenant to many people who were not qualified, saved them, and protected them throughout redemptive history. God gave the word of God's covenant related to redemptive history through Adam, Noah, Abraham, Moses, David, and Jesus Christ. God revealed the law of the kingdom of God through the word of God's covenant. This is also the work of God's great grace.

As we saw before, the Old Testament covenants play an important role in connecting the redemptive history of the kingdom of God. God's covenants are like the backbone of the redemptive history of Jesus Christ. In the word of God's covenant, God's *power*, *authority*, and *presence* enabled redemptive history to be achieved through human history. These amazing lordship attributes of God's word still exist with us today.

Above all, the most important core of redemptive history that the Bible proclaims is the gospel, which gives us freedom from sin. In other words, there is no more important word of God for us sinners than the message of freedom from sin that the gospel gives us. The gospel is the grace of all grace, the greatest grace. Therefore, the most blessed day in our lives is the day we meet the freedom that the word of the gospel gives us. The day we believe in Jesus is the greatest day. It is another blessing that the word of the gospel becomes the basis for the assurance of faith for all believers throughout our lives (Rom 6:18, 22; Rev 1:5).

---

88. Frame, *Systematic Theology*, 540.

There is therefore now no condemnation for those who are in Christ Jesus. For the law of the Spirit of life has set you free in Christ Jesus from the law of sin and death. (Rom 8:1–2)

b. Redemptive History and Salvation

Salvation revealed by redemptive history is fulfilled through the work of God's total grace. We should remember that in the sovereign work of God's grace for human salvation, there is absolutely no merit of human autonomy to be found.[89]

The salvation of sinful humans is entirely the unilateral (one-sided) plan of God and the work of God's total grace. Salvation is entirely the work of God's grace beyond human imagination or planning. It is the powerful work of God the Creator, arising solely from God's total plan and authority. Only the Bible clearly tells us about this work of God's grace. That is why the word of God is incomparably superior to any knowledge in this world.

Through redemptive history, the Bible as a whole clearly shows that human salvation is entirely the work of God's grace. In fact, the Old Testament continuously prophesied the coming Messiah through the words of the covenant, preparing the way for the Messiah to come at the same time. The New Testament reveals the work of God in fulfilling all the covenant words of the Old Testament through the Messiah who has come.

God helps his children to firmly believe in the Lord who will fulfill the words of the promise in the *future*, ensuring their faith and trust in him for the days to come—trusting in the Lord who has kept the words of the covenant in the *past* by his sovereign redemptive work, and trusting in the words of the new covenant in the *present* by faith. The perfect fulfillment of the words of the covenant through Jesus' redemptive work serves as the foundation for trusting in God's other promises. The giving of the words of the new covenant is also a manifestation of God's grace.

The salvation given by Jesus Christ, the new covenant Representative, is indeed good news for sinners. Jesus was the greatest preacher in human history, possessing the highest authority of the word; he was also the One who listened and obeyed God's word most faithfully.[90] Therefore, the words spoken by the greatest prophet Jesus himself become a sure

---

89. Frame, *Systematic Theology*, 541; Carson, *Divine Sovereignty*, 201–3.
90. Frame, *Systematic Theology*, 557.

asset of faith for us. The word of God given by Jesus is a firm foundation for the faith life of God's children, including the disciples. Note that the words of Jesus, passed on by the disciples in the New Testament and the epistles that reinterpret them, all share the highest authority, which is a sovereign attribute of God.[91]

The Holy Spirit continues to persuade us sinners and leads us to the Lord through the words spoken by Jesus and the words of Jesus' witnesses, the disciples.

Indeed, redemptive work is a very important concept, but we must not forget about God's grace. We must consider God's purpose for us. We can become so focused on only the grace of salvation given by God that we can prevent the grace of God from being gracious. We often forget the reason God saved us by grace and the purpose for which God gave us the Bible. If we forget the purpose of the grace of salvation that God has given us and the purpose of his word, our growth in faith can stall. While knowledge of God's saving grace through the history of redemption is important, we must trust in the word more and advance in faith.

In the Bible, redemptive history is one of the "media of God's word" that conveys the message of God's grace to us. As we saw earlier, we should be able to see the power, authority, and presence of God's word conveyed through the redemptive history in the Bible.[92] When we encounter the word of God that testifies to redemptive work, we can meet God within it. When we meet God through the word that testifies of Jesus, we can be transformed into God's image by his grace. Therefore, we need to deeply recognize the importance of God's grace and its purpose through the redemptive history and salvation story testified in the Bible.

c. The Helper, the Holy Spirit

Last, in relation to the importance of God's word concerning God's grace, we will briefly examine the final topic, the Holy Spirit. The Holy Spirit is the One who makes us know the grace of God. Through the Spirit, God enables us to know the grace of the redemptive work fulfilled by Jesus and makes us bear fruit. This is also entirely the work of God's grace. For this purpose, the Holy Spirit, who came to apply Jesus' redemptive work,

---

91. Frame, *Systematic Theology*, 550–51.
92. Frame, *Doctrine of the Word*, 80.

cleanses us, justifies us, and sanctifies us.[93] The Spirit works within us using the word of God.[94]

The Holy Spirit has come to inspire, illuminate, and demonstrate the word of God.[95] The Spirit dwells in us for the completion of our salvation, and provides motivation for us to obey God's word.[96] This is also the work of the Spirit's sovereign grace. And the Spirit transforms us according to God's word. Therefore, the Bible is very important for believers because it teaches this work of God's grace through the Spirit. As we learn and keep the word of the Bible, we come to know the work of God's grace that is carried out through the Spirit.

B. The Importance of God's Word Concerning Human Responsibility

Now let's take a brief look at what the Bible says about human responsibility.[97] Living in a world that disregards human responsibility, it is necessary to emphasize that the Bible highlights the importance of individual responsibility. The Bible speaks of human responsibility being created in the image of God. Essentially, the human responsibility emphasized in the Bible focuses on obedience to God's word. Of course, in this regard, the ultimate model for human responsibility is the life of Jesus, who is the Fulfiller of the new covenant. The life of Jesus is a life of perfect obedience to the word.

Remember that Jesus astonishingly lived a life taking full responsibility for the sins of sinners while simultaneously living a life of perfect obedience to all the words given by God the Father. It is astonishing and marvelous that Jesus fulfilled both human responsibility in terms of redemptive work and obedience to the word simultaneously on our behalf. Therefore, in the Bible, Jesus is the ultimate *prototype* who demonstrates the most harmonious relationship between God's sovereign grace and human responsibility in faith.[98]

---

93. Frame, *Systematic Theology*, 673.

94. This is the reason I often mention the work of the Spirit in vol. 3. The more we know the Spirit, the more it will help us to understand our own sanctification.

95. Frame, *Systematic Theology*, 673–80.

96. Frame, *Systematic Theology*, 676.

97. For the application and practice of God's word, refer to vol. 3.

98. Cf. the New Testament scholar D. A. Carson, who calls Jesus "the best paradigm of the proper relationship" (*Divine Sovereignty*, 203). Here I call Jesus "the ultimate

Now, keeping in mind the life of Jesus, let's look at the importance of God's word as the standards of wisdom, knowledge, judgment, and deed.[99]

a. The Importance of God's Word as Wisdom and Knowledge

The living God is the source of wisdom and knowledge (Dan 2:20; Ps 110:10; Prov 1:7; 9:10; Isa 11:2). In fact, God's wisdom and God's knowledge are divine attributes.[100] Just like God's righteousness and God's goodness, true wisdom and true knowledge are divine attributes.[101] However, there is no way for us to find God's wisdom and knowledge anywhere in this world.

Where then can we find God's wisdom and knowledge?

Only the Bible teaches God's wisdom and knowledge. However, the true wisdom and knowledge spoken of in the Bible fundamentally differ from the wisdom and knowledge of the world.

So, what is that significant difference?

The biggest difference between the wisdom and knowledge in the Bible and what the world speaks of lies not in learning, but in "knowing." The true wisdom and true knowledge spoken of in the Bible begin with "knowing" God (the Old Testament) or "knowing" Jesus Christ (the New Testament).

God's wisdom stands out as a prominent theme throughout the book of Proverbs. Proverbs mainly refers to those with worldly wisdom as "the fool" and those with God's wisdom as "the wise." As a wisdom book in the Old Testament, Proverbs says that true wisdom and true knowledge come only from God. According to Proverbs, anyone who desires true wisdom and knowledge must first become someone who knows God. For God gives his wisdom and knowledge to those who know him.

> The fear of the LORD is the beginning of wisdom, and the knowledge of the Holy One is insight. (Prov 9:10)

---

prototype."

99. Here, we will examine the importance of God's word as the standard of wisdom, knowledge, judgment, and deeds. For the relationship between knowledge and change, refer to vol. 3, ch. 2, "Change Happens."

100. Frame, *Doctrine of God*, 479–84, 505–9; Frame, *Systematic Theology*, 569.

101. Frame, *Doctrine of God*, 480–81. Cf. Proverbs and Ecclesiastes.

> The fear of the LORD is the beginning of knowledge; fools despise wisdom and instruction. (Prov 1:7)

> For the LORD gives wisdom; from his mouth come knowledge and understanding. (Prov 2:6)

1. Wisdom and Salvation

Unlike the Old Testament, the New Testament does not directly say that knowing God is the beginning of wisdom. Instead, Paul says in 1 Cor 1:24 that Jesus is the wisdom of God. This is likely an answer to a question, "What is the wisdom of God?"

> But to those who are called, both Jews and Greeks, Christ the power of God and the wisdom of God. (1 Cor 1:24)

Some may have doubts about Paul's claim that Jesus is the wisdom of God. Even Paul, who was an expert in the Old Testament, did not begin to make such a claim immediately upon accepting Jesus. One curious fact is that in the four gospels, Jesus never explicitly referred to himself as wisdom.[102]

So, is Paul in 1 Corinthians claiming something that Jesus did not teach?

Is Paul's claim correct?

In order to answer these questions, we first need to examine whether there are expressions of wisdom in the New Testament related to "knowing" God, as described in the Old Testament (Prov 9:10), or related to "knowing" Jesus. For example, in John 17:3, Jesus' disciple John calls knowing God and Jesus "eternal life." First John 5:20 says that Jesus came and gave us understanding so that we may "know him" who is "the true God and eternal life." These passages use different expressions regarding eternal life.

> And this is eternal life, that they know you, the only true God, and Jesus Christ whom you have sent. (John 17:3)

> And we know that the Son of God has come and has given us understanding, so that we may know him who is true; and we

---

[102]. Luke 2:40 says that Jesus "grew and became strong, filled with wisdom." However, there is no statement saying, "Jesus is wisdom."

are in him who is true, in his Son Jesus Christ. He is the true God and eternal life. (1 John 5:20)

These texts clearly say that "knowing" Jesus is eternal life. However, John does not say that knowing Jesus is the beginning of wisdom or knowledge (like Prov 1:7 and 9:10).

So, how can we say that "knowing Jesus is the beginning of wisdom" like in Proverbs?

First, let's connect "Jesus is God" (1 John 5:20) and "knowing God is the beginning of wisdom" (Prov 1:7; 2:6; 9:10). According to these verses, "knowing Jesus is the beginning of wisdom" since Jesus is God. The same is true if we connect these to "Jesus is the wisdom of God" (1 Cor 1:24). That is, *knowing Jesus*, who is "the wisdom of God," becomes the beginning of wisdom. Also, since "Jesus is the wisdom of God," it can be said that *"knowing Jesus* is the beginning of *wisdom* and *knowledge."*

Second, let's connect *"knowing Jesus* is *eternal life"* and *"knowing Jesus* is the beginning of *wisdom* and *knowledge."* Combining these two ideas leads to an important premise that *"believing in Jesus* is the beginning of *wisdom."* In other words, "God's *true wisdom* begins for those who are saved." If we express the analysis up to this point, it can be summarized as follows in figure 1-D.

Figure 1-D Believing in Jesus is the beginning of wisdom.

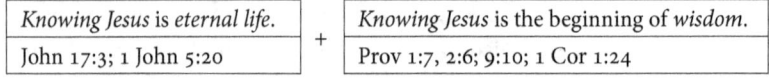

Knowing Jesus is eternal life.		*Knowing Jesus* is the beginning of *wisdom*.
John 17:3; 1 John 5:20	+	Prov 1:7, 2:6; 9:10; 1 Cor 1:24

It is interesting to see that the Bible uses different words (diversity) to express a single meaning (unity). Through a simple analysis of these texts, we can conclude that *"eternal life* is the beginning of *wisdom."* That is, *"believing in Jesus* is the beginning of *wisdom."* Scripture clearly teaches us that wisdom is deeply connected to salvation in Jesus.

One more important point: Can we find Paul's expression in 1 Corinthians that is very similar to that of John in this regard?

To answer this question, we need to examine Paul's interpretation and "the restored wisdom and justification." Let's first look at what Paul says in 1 Cor 1:18.

For the word of the cross is folly to those who are perishing, but to us who are being saved it is the power of God. (1 Cor 1:18)

This text says that those who have received the message of the cross, that is, the gospel, have obtained salvation and the power of God. That is, whoever believes in Jesus has obtained salvation and the power of God. Paul also says the same thing in Rom 1:16, that the gospel is "the power of God for salvation to everyone who believes." The gospel is the power of God. For the discussion of wisdom, note again Paul's words in 1 Cor 1:24, "but to those who are called, both Jews and Greeks, Christ the power of God and the wisdom of God."

To sum up, if we carefully observe these passages, Paul connects the gospel and Jesus (Rom 1:16), and then connects Jesus with God's power and God's wisdom (1 Cor 1:24). Therefore, according to Paul, everyone who is saved has God's power and God's wisdom. I think that we need to look at this more deeply to make clear the relationship between salvation (justification) and wisdom. We can apply this conclusion to 1 Cor 1:30. So, 1 Cor 1:30 declares that Jesus has become wisdom for those who are in Jesus.

> And because of him you are in Christ Jesus, who became to us wisdom from God, righteousness and sanctification and redemption. (1 Cor 1:30)

This passage is a significant declaration that reveals the relationship between wisdom, salvation, and justification (being justified). Therefore, combining this declaration with the conclusions above, we can say that "those who believe in Jesus obtain salvation and have the wisdom of Jesus." And these texts (Prov 1:7; 9:10; John 17:3; 1 John 5:20; 1 Cor 1:18, 24, 30) prove that the wisdom, righteousness, and holiness of Jesus become yours in Jesus Christ as a believer by God's grace alone, if you believe in Jesus.

We will examine the doctrine of justification and the relationship between the gospel and salvation and eternal life further in *The Kingdom of Justification*—justification means declaring us, who are sinners, as "righteous, considered righteous." From the perspective of this relationship, justification can also be called "the gospel," and in other words, also it can be called "salvation" or "eternal life." Now, we need to explore the relationship between the restored wisdom and justification.

II. The Restored Wisdom and Justification

One question regarding the relationship between wisdom, salvation, and justification is related to the statement that "Jesus becomes our wisdom" (1 Cor 1:30).

What is the connection between our lives and Jesus becoming our wisdom?

In 1 Cor 1–2, Paul contrasts biblical wisdom with worldly wisdom. Paul says in 1 Cor 2:7 that the mystery of Jesus' wisdom mentioned earlier has been hidden before the ages.

> But we impart a secret and hidden wisdom of God, which God decreed before the ages for our glory. (1 Cor 2:7)

Why is this secret of wisdom important to us today?

First, we cannot know this wisdom through worldly wisdom. Even if we mobilize the highest scientific knowledge, philosophical knowledge, and medical knowledge of this world, we cannot unlock the secret of this wisdom (Rom 16:26; 1 Cor 2:7; Eph 3:4; 5:32; 6:19; Col 1:26; 2:2; 4:3). The essence of Paul's explanation of the secret of wisdom is that only Jesus holds the key to unlocking this wisdom. As we saw earlier, for Paul, the statement that Jesus becomes our wisdom is related to the gospel.

We now need to consider how Paul compares and contrasts the wisdom of the world with the wisdom of God in 1 Cor 1–2 (1 Cor 1:17, 19–22, 24–27, 30; 2:1, 4–8). Above all, we must see ourselves as covenant breakers in the fall of Adam. We previously said that the image of God was marred because of Adam's sin. Due to Adam's fall, intellectual and moral excellence (God's image in a broader sense) has been marred. Further, the excellent abilities of wisdom and knowledge (God's image in a narrower sense), which are intellectual excellence, have been marred in him. No one in Adam can have God's wisdom or the wisdom of Jesus.

However, Jesus has restored the marred image of God through his perfect obedience for those of us in Adam. In Adam, we are the ones with the marred image of God. But in Jesus Christ we become the new self (Eph 2:15; 4:24; Col 3:10) with the restored image of God. In Jesus, our marred intellectual excellence is also restored. We are the ones with the restored excellence of wisdom and knowledge (the narrow sense). In other words, the path for God's wisdom and God's knowledge to enter has been opened for us in Jesus.

As we saw earlier, 1 Cor 1:30 speaks of the restoration of the marred wisdom and the restoration of the marred moral excellence (righteousness and holiness) in this way.

> And because of him you are in Christ Jesus, who became to us wisdom from God, righteousness and sanctification and redemption. (1 Cor 1:30)

In fact, it is interesting that Paul clearly explains the enormous difference between God's wisdom and worldly wisdom in terms of justification in 1 Cor 1–2. Paul makes a very firm assertion here. Paul's point is that only those who have been justified (declared righteous) in Jesus can have the wisdom of God. In other words, only those who believe in Jesus and come into him can have the wisdom of Jesus. This means that our marred intellectual ability has been restored, and we have come to know God's word.

There is no other way. Fallen humans cannot know or possess the wisdom of Jesus. In other words, in Adam, we do not have the wisdom of Jesus. Only in Jesus can we have his wisdom.

> But, as it is written, "What no eye has seen, nor ear heard, nor the heart of man imagined, what God has prepared for those who love him." (1 Cor 2:9)

Does this mean if one does not believe in Jesus, they cannot have true wisdom and true knowledge (Col 2:3; 3:10)?

Yes. Does that also mean that those who do not believe in Jesus and are not justified do not have the wisdom of Jesus?

Yes. Only through the grace of God can we know Jesus (Mark 10:27) to know God's wisdom.

> And this is eternal life, that they know you, the only true God, and Jesus Christ whom you have sent. (John 17:3)

> When the disciples heard this, they were greatly astonished, saying, "Who then can be saved?" But Jesus looked at them and said, "With man this is impossible, but with God all things are possible." (Matt 19:25–26)

For this reason, no matter how much outstanding scientific, medical, or philosophical knowledge a person may have, they cannot comprehend and know God's wisdom. Because sinners are in Adam, their intellectual ability (the excellence of wisdom and knowledge) to know the wisdom of God has been marred. Only through the work of the Holy Spirit can you believe in Jesus, and the door of wisdom excellence is opened to you. Only the Spirit can make you believe in Jesus and open the blocked door of wisdom. It is the door of the word of God that opens.

> These things [the wisdom of God] God has revealed to us through the Spirit. For the Spirit searches everything, even the depths of God. (1 Cor 2:10)

> And we impart this in words not taught by human wisdom but taught by the Spirit, interpreting spiritual truths to those who are spiritual (1 Cor 2:13).

The word of the gospel becomes the word of wisdom only when you believe in Jesus. When you believe in Jesus, you are saved and begin to realize the wisdom contained in Scripture. As such, the beginning of eternal life is the beginning of true wisdom and knowledge, for Christ is our wisdom in Jesus Christ (1 Cor 1:30). In this way, salvation opens the blocked door of wisdom and knowledge, and it restores the ability to know God's wisdom and God's knowledge, as revealed in the Bible. When you believe in Jesus, you are saved and justified and become a new creation, a new self. A new self must grow anew through the word of God, which is God's wisdom and knowledge.

Moreover, salvation opens the blocked door of truth. That is, those who believe in Jesus and have wisdom also become those who have the truth (John 14:6, 17; 15:26; 16:13; 17:17, 19). This also means that they are renewed in the truth in Jesus and abide in the truth (2 Cor 11:10; Eph 1:13; 4:21, 24; 1 Tim 2:4; 2 Tim 2:15; 1 John 2:4; 5:7; 3 John 1:3). However, not only do they have the truth, but also gain freedom from sin and become free from worldly philosophies and false truths.

> Jesus said to him, "I am the way, and the truth, and the life. No one comes to the Father except through me." (John 14:6)

> So Jesus said to the Jews who had believed him, "If you abide in my word, you are truly my disciples. And you will know the truth, and the truth will set you free." (John 8:31–32)

> See to it that no one takes you captive by philosophy and empty deceit, according to human tradition, according to the elemental spirits of the world, and not according to Christ. (Col 2:8)

Anyone who believes in Jesus no longer needs to be deceived by worldly philosophy or empty deceit (tricks). Therefore, when one believes in Jesus, they confess that all God's words are truth (John 17:17; see also 2 Sam 7:28; 1 Kgs 17:24; Ps 119:43, 89–90, 142, 151). Those who receive salvation come to realize that both the word of God and Jesus Christ are truth.

I have summarized and organized the old self in Adam and the new self in Jesus from the perspective of wisdom, knowledge, and truth in figure 1-E below.

Figure 1-E

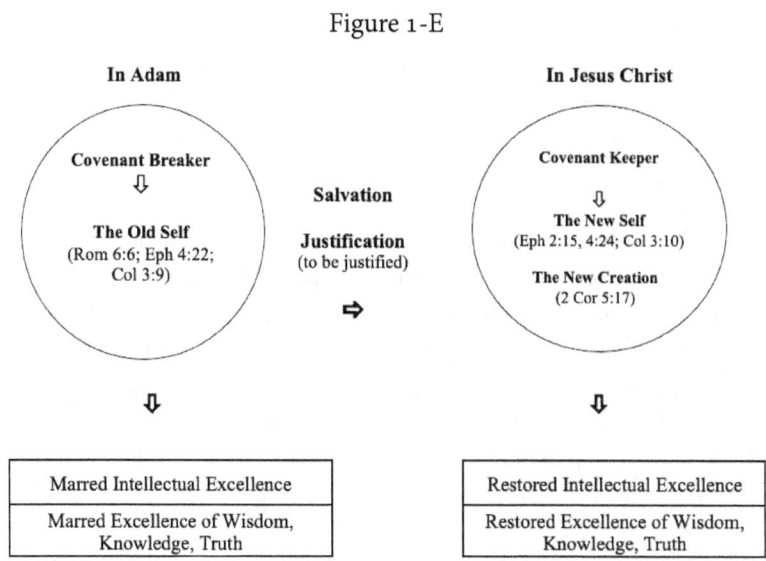

To sum up, everyone who believes in Jesus has obtained eternal life (salvation), is saved and justified, and has wisdom, knowledge, and truth—and has responsibility for them. This is because those whose image of God was marred in Adam have had their marred image of God restored in Jesus. In this way, those who believe in Jesus are born again as the new creation, the new self in Jesus. They are reborn as those who must live and grow in the word of God, containing God's wisdom and knowledge.

Justification (being justified) in Jesus reveals to us that we have become the new self in Jesus, as covenant keepers (1 Cor 1:30; Eph 4:23–24). After realizing the fact that we become the new self, there is something else that is important: to recognize the importance of God's word. Through his tremendous sacrifice, Jesus has opened the way of wisdom, knowledge, and truth that was blocked by sin. In other words, Jesus becomes the waymaker for us so that we can possess the word of God that is the precious wisdom, knowledge, and truth of the living God. However, we must not forget that we are still beginners concerning the word of God and need to grow by faith.

Whenever we encounter the word of God, we should remember that the gospel is the power of God, and the wisdom of knowing and believing in Jesus is also the power of God. That is, we must always remember that our faith is not in our wisdom or power, but in the power of the gospel (1 Cor 2:5; Rom 1:16–17). In other words, both faith in salvation and fruit in sanctification are gifts from the Holy Spirit (John 15:26; 16:13; Gal 5:22–23; Eph 2:8–10).

> For by grace you have been saved through faith. And this is not your own doing; it is the gift of God. (Eph 2:8)

In conclusion, a truly wise person is someone who has realized the importance of God's word. A wise person understands that true wisdom and true knowledge are found only in Scripture. The wise should be thankful to God for providing the living word as the source of wisdom and knowledge. And we must not forget that those with true wisdom, as mentioned in the Bible, are those who live according to the word of God. A truly wise person cannot live without the word of God. Note that Jesus himself set the best example by living according to the word of wisdom. Therefore, the true wise person is someone who reaps the fruits of God's word—someone who reaps the blessed fruit of the promised "covenant" by God.[103]

For this reason, a wise person is someone who accepts the word of God as the highest wisdom and knowledge in all areas of life (Jas 1:5; Eccl 2:26; Dan 2:23). In other words, the most important thing in our lives is the fact that the word of God has relevance in present reality.[104] Therefore, we should remember that all biblical wisdom, knowledge, and truth have also a present reality. This means that the word of God is absolutely necessary for us who are living on this earth.

---

103. Frame, *Doctrine of God*, 507.

104. Previously, we discussed the covenant lordship attributes of God's word and the power of life, work, and judgment of God's word—they are all related to present reality.

> Do you want to have true wisdom and true knowledge?
> Believe in Jesus and take the word of God!

b. The Importance of God's Word as the Standard for Judgment

We constantly make judgments, either consciously or unconsciously. Every person uses reasoning to make judgments in all areas of life.[105] We often judge the word of God with worldly knowledge. However, as we saw earlier, since the fall of Adam, the intellectual ability to know God's laws and truth has been marred. As a result, our ability to make accurate judgments of the truth has been marred. Also, all humankind in Adam has lost the ability to keep the word of God, which is the standard for judging the truth. The analysis we saw earlier regarding wisdom and knowledge can also be applied to the standard for judgment.

It is evident that relying on marred reason to make judgments, draw conclusions, and make decisions became human nature after the fall.[106] However, the gospel achieved through the redemptive work of Jesus the excellence of this marred intellectual ability.[107] This is the sovereign work of God's grace by the Holy Spirit. However, as we saw earlier, we must also remember the fact that even after we are saved, we must continue to grow with the proper judgment standard, which is the word of God.

1. Judgment Standard

As we have seen so far, the only place we can learn the righteous standard of the living is the Bible.[108] We saw earlier that God's righteousness in the Bible is revealed as God's command with legal authority. God's commandments given to human beings are God's words. God the Creator also appears as the Lord of the covenant, who has given the word of the covenant to humans.[109] In particular, the covenant word in the

---

105. Frame, *Doctrine of the Word*, 362.

106. Frame, *Doctrine of the Word*, 361. Frame points out that you cannot find the word "reason" in the Bible, but he correctly insists that Scripture evidently addresses the subject of reason.

107. Please refer to "4. Justification and the Restored Image of God," in vol. 2, ch. 3.

108. Frame, *Systematic Theology*, 522. "I will praise you with an upright heart, when I learn your righteous rules" (Ps 119:7).

109. We saw earlier that there are three important covenant lordship attributes of

Bible serves as the law of God's kingdom for all covenant people.[110] The word of the Bible provides the legal foundation for the kingdom of God. Therefore, God's word is the standard of rewards and punishments, as well as the standard for discerning the truth in all areas of life.

For this reason, you should ask yourself frequently, "What is my current judgment standard? Am I making judgments based on the word of God?" This is important because our judgment standard determines every direction of our thoughts and actions.

The most important thing is that the living God governs the kingdom of God through his word. We previously learned that the word of God in the Bible serves as the law of God's kingdom, based on God's righteousness. The standards of holiness and goodness in God's kingdom also fundamentally come from God's righteousness.[111] Therefore, the standards of holiness and goodness for God's kingdom and for humans come only from the righteous laws of God's word (Rom 7:12). For all who enter the kingdom of God by faith, the word of the living God becomes the highest standard of judgment.

In relation to God's kingdom, what is important is determining the most fundamental judgment standard for all areas of our lives. However, people do not change easily. To change, we must first clearly understand our identity of the new self in Jesus, while always remembering that there are still sinful remnants of the old self in us (Rom 6:6; Eph 4:22; Col 3:9). In other words, to believe in Jesus does not mean to change the judgment standard overnight. The judgment standard of the old self (old wineskin) and the judgment standard of the new self, which is God's word (new wine), cannot harmonize (Matt 9:17; Mark 2:22; Luke 5:37–38).

However, a society or a country that does not have the right standard of judgment is bound to fail. Only places where many of God's children who live with the proper judgment standard can truly have hope. Therefore, God's children have a much greater responsibility to choose the right standard, the word of God, more than anyone else. In this regard, we must choose and live by God's word every day. The whole Bible teaches the importance of the word as the standard of judgment for all areas of life. The Bible teaches all people that the word of God is the highest standard of judgment. But the Bible does not focus merely on knowing the highest standard of judgment. It also teaches the importance of

---

God's word: control, authority, and presence.

110. Horton, *Covenant Theology*, 127.

111. Frame, *Systematic Theology*, 233–35, 257–68, 276–79.

aligning one's hearts and actions with God's word in every aspect of life for a wholehearted human being (1 Tim 4:5–8, 15–16).

> But he answered, "It is written, 'Man shall not live by bread alone, but by every word that comes from the mouth of God.'" (Matt 4:4)[112]

> For it is made holy by the word of God and prayer. If you put these things before the brothers, you will be a good servant of Christ Jesus, being trained in the words of the faith and of the good doctrine that you have followed. (1 Tim 4:5–6)

Furthermore, the next important thing for us is the awareness of the practical blessings (benefits) that the living and accessible word can give us.

What practical blessings (benefits) can God's word provide us as the judgment standard?

God's word, first of all, grants us freedom from false truth and false knowledge in this age, where enormous amounts of information are overflowing.[113] It continuously liberates us from the challenges of incorrect philosophies and vain truths. That is, God's word continuously liberates us from the challenges of false philosophies, false truth, and empty deceits. This is particularly important because it can provide real and profound freedom and peace to those who have been pursuing truth. Colossians is filled with warnings about false philosophies and false truths. Especially, Col 2:8 is famous for its representative warning against philosophy and empty deceit.

> See to it that no one takes you captive by philosophy and empty deceit, according to human tradition, according to the elemental spirits of the world, and not according to Christ. (Col 2:8)

In Colossians, Paul presents a list of things that lead people away from the wisdom and truth of the words, causing confusion: deceptive philosophy and empty deceit, human traditions (Col 2:8); the elementary principles of the world (Col 2:8, 20); self-imposed worship, false wisdom (Col 2:23); human commands and false teachings (Col 2:20); false

---

112. "And he humbled you and let you hunger and fed you with manna, which you did not know, nor did your fathers know, that he might make you know that man does not live by bread alone, but man lives by every word that comes from the mouth of the LORD" (Deut 8:3).

113. Please refer to the discussion on the change in practical knowledge in vol. 3, ch. 2, "Change Happens."

humility and worship of angels (Col 2:18); self-imposed worship focused on religious ceremonies and formalism (Col 2:16–18).

Paul, however, strongly encourages those who possess wisdom and knowledge in Jesus (Col 2:1–3; 3:3) to receive the renewal of knowledge (Col 3:10) and to let the peace of the Lord rule in their hearts (Col 3:15). He then emphasizes the importance of God's word and commands them to give thanks to the heavenly Father who has granted great grace. It is important that they have become free from deceptive philosophy and empty deceit through the wisdom and knowledge of Jesus.

> And let the peace of Christ rule in your hearts, to which indeed you were called in one body. And be thankful. Let the word of Christ dwell in you richly, teaching and admonishing one another in all wisdom, singing psalms and hymns and spiritual songs, with thankfulness in your hearts to God. (Col 3:16–17)

So, the believers who have eternal wisdom and truth in Jesus (Col 2:1–3, 9–15) are eternally free from idolatry, deceptive philosophy, empty deceit, and false teachings (John 8:31–32). This freedom is not imaginary, theoretical, conceptual, or abstract. This freedom is accompanied by the practical rest and peace that the Holy Spirit gives to our hearts. This freedom occurs when the Holy Spirit uses the word of God within our hearts. The Holy Spirit works within us by using the word of God, which has the covenant lordship attributes and the power of life, work, and judgment. The Spirit gives this freedom, one of the practical benefits (blessings) given to God's children who live by faith with the word of God as their judgment standard. The Spirit always helps us to apply it to ourselves.

11. Love Yourself

One of the issues that churches often face today is the issue of equality. This leads to endless debates depending on each person's perspective. In fact, the Bible provides a clear answer regarding equality. The most important biblical response to this issue begins with the fact that humans are made in the image of God. For example, Jesus, who knows all human beings best, once gave a very clear message. Jesus' teaching, "Love your neighbor," has become famous even in the world (Matt 5:43; 19:19; 22:39; Mark 12:31; Luke 10:27; Rom 13:9; Gal 5:14; Jas 2:8).

> You shall love your neighbor as yourself.

The most fundamental reason we should love our neighbors is that all humans are made in the image of God. However, we must remember the fact that all humans started to have a problem with the image of God by Adam's fall. Along with the concept of being made in the image of God, the most important issue is whether we and our neighbors are in Jesus or not. Moreover, we should also pay attention to the fact that the main point of Jesus' teaching on loving our neighbors starts with "love yourself."

The theme of "love" stands out as a characteristic throughout the whole Bible. Jesus' teachings on love (Matt 5:43; 19:19; 22:39; Mark 12:31; Luke 10:27; Rom 13:9; Gal 5:14; Jas 2:8) mainly speak about "loving" with God's love. Jesus' teachings fundamentally mean "love yourself" even when you cannot find a reason to love yourself. Jesus is saying, "I have made it possible." However, in this world, there are surprisingly many people who cannot love themselves for various reasons. These reasons take hold as the basis for judging oneself. The negative factors mainly stem from the environment in which one was raised, feelings of inferiority, talents, appearance, and family issues.

> And to put on the new self, created after the likeness of God in true righteousness and holiness. (Eph 4:24)

> And have put on the new self, which is being renewed in knowledge after the image of its creator. (Col 3:10)

Where do we start then?

Therefore, first, the most important thing in the change of judgment standard for the new self (Eph 2:15; 4:24; Col 3:10; 2 Cor 5:17) is the judgment standard for oneself. In other words, it is the question of whether one has a new, clear identity in Jesus after believing in him. Obviously, the importance of a healthy identity is already well established among experts. The greater you have a healthy identity, the more you can live a healthy life in various ways. Having a new identity (a new self) in Jesus after believing in him is especially of utmost importance. This new identity in Jesus helps one to shake off difficulties and rise again. This means that the believers with this new identity become capable of loving their neighbors according to the words of Jesus.

Second, you need to acknowledge that the Bible clearly teaches what a healthy identity is. In order to have this healthy identity, it is essential for us to know what the Bible teaches "about the world and about ourselves."[114] A person who has a biblical healthy identity in Jesus has the wisdom to see themselves and the world through the image of God in Jesus. This identity in Jesus can also establish a healthy relationship between oneself and the world. And the believers with this healthy identity in Jesus have eyes to see themselves through the words of the Bible. This is the identity of faith given by the Spirit.

> For God so loved the world, that he gave his only Son, that whoever believes in him should not perish but have eternal life. (John 3:16)

Ultimately, the best healthy identity comes from believing in Jesus. Those who are with a healthy identity start to see themselves in Jesus as the word of God. The new self (Col 3:10) is someone who never looks at themselves by the world's evaluation or judgment standard again (Col 2:8–23). A person with a healthy identity takes the word of God as the standard for judging themselves. In other words, the word of God has become their thoughts. To them, all the words of grace, love, gospel, salvation, forgiveness of sins, justification, sanctification, and glorification in Jesus also become the eternal standards for judging themselves. However, if you lose sight of this truth, you may also lose the blessings of the gospel. By continually focusing on this understanding, you will begin to love yourself. This is a very important issue.

In this way, those with a healthy identity as a new self in Jesus Christ begin to "love themselves." Such a person discards the judgment criteria of the old self (Rom 6:6; Eph 4:22; Col 3:9) like trash (Phil 3:8) and loves themselves with the love that God has for them (John 3:16).

> But God shows his love for us in that while we were still sinners, Christ died for us. (Rom 5:8)

> I have been crucified with Christ. It is no longer I who live, but Christ who lives in me. And the life I now live in the flesh I live by faith in the Son of God, who loved me and gave himself for me. (Gal 2:20)

---

114. Frame, *Doctrine of the Word*, 350.

In summary, a person with a biblical healthy identity is someone who sees themselves in Jesus Christ through the eyes of God. This person views themselves as clothed in the righteousness of Jesus Christ.[115] Never forget this truth. After the conversion on the road to Damascus, Paul also started to see himself in Jesus. This is the reason Paul says, "I do not even judge myself" in Jesus (1 Cor 4:3–4). Therefore, we should remember that God looks at us with the eyes of love in Jesus.

> But with me it is a very small thing that I should be judged by you or by any human court. In fact, I do not even judge myself. For I am not aware of anything against myself, but I am not thereby acquitted. It is the Lord who judges me. (1 Cor 4:3–4)

> So we have come to know and to believe the love that God has for us. God is love, and whoever abides in love abides in God, and God abides in him. (1 John 4:16)

Furthermore, we should not only be not viewing ourselves by the standards of the world or our own standards, but also seeing ourselves through worldly thoughts or our own thoughts is an act of unbelief. We must first cultivate the ability to see ourselves through the gospel message in Jesus Christ as we believe in him, apart from our old thoughts. Only then can we see ourselves as justified in Jesus Christ by God's grace. If you apply this truth to yourself, you will receive its blessings. Through Jesus Christ alone, and by faith alone, Jesus becomes our wisdom, knowledge, righteousness, holiness, and redemption.

> That their hearts may be encouraged, being knit together in love, to reach all the riches of full assurance of understanding and the knowledge of God's mystery, which is Christ, in whom are hidden all the treasures of wisdom and knowledge. (Col 2:2–3)

> And because of him you are in Christ Jesus, who became to us wisdom from God, righteousness and sanctification and redemption. (1 Cor 1:30)

When the eyes of faith are opened by the work of the Holy Spirit, one begins to live a life that boasts only in Jesus (1 Cor 1:31; 2 Cor 10:17).[116] When you see yourselves through faith in Jesus, you will taste the

---

115. For justification and the robe of Christ's righteousness, see "2. The Imputation of the Perfect Righteousness of Christ," in vol. 2, ch. 3.
116. "Let the one who boasts, boast in the Lord" (1 Cor 10:17).

blessings of freedom that the gospel brings. Those who love themselves through faith in Jesus can overcome the world. These are the blessings given to those who see themselves through the word of God.

> For everyone who has been born of God overcomes the world. And this is the victory that has overcome the world—our faith. (1 John 5:4).

c. The Importance of God's Word as the Standard of Deeds

The phrase "by Scripture alone" (*sola Scriptura*) implies that the word of God is not only the ultimate standard for judgment but also the highest authority for action. Acknowledging the word as the highest authority for action also means agreeing to apply it to our lives.[117] So, the importance of the word as a standard for action cannot be overemphasized.

As we saw, the analysis of the restored image of God can also be directly applied to the importance of the word of God as a standard of deeds. Citizens of God's kingdom have a standard of behavior that matches their dignity. In other words, there is a proper standard of behavior for those who have become a new self in Jesus Christ (John 3:16; Eph 2:15; 4:24; Col 3:10; 2 Cor 5:17): the words of God in the Bible.

"To become a new self (person) in Jesus," as we saw earlier, can be expressed as "to be justified in Jesus," and in another way as "to have the restored image of God in Jesus." It is heartbreaking that God-given moral excellence in humans was marred by the fall of Adam. This moral excellence is deeply related to our moral standard of behavior. This marred moral excellence caused by Adam's fall has made all humanity lose the ability to obey the word as the standard of deeds. However, amazingly, the punishment proclaimed to Adam, who disobeyed the word "In the day you eat of it you shall surely die" (Gen 2:17), was fulfilled on the cross of Jesus Christ. Jesus, as the Representative of God's children, restored the marred image of God through his perfect obedience.[118]

Therefore, it can be said that the ability or qualification to obey the holy, righteous, and good word of God (Rom 7:12) has been restored by his perfect obedience.

---

117. For the application of the word, refer to "3. The Purpose of God Giving His Word" in this chapter; and vol. 3. The word of truth is also an "ethical truth" (Frame, *Doctrine of God*, 478–80).

118. For the restored image of God, refer to "4. Justification and the Restored Image of God," in vol. 2, ch. 3.

What an amazing grace of God this is!

The next important thing to realizing God's grace is the answer to a question, "Have I spoken and acted according to God's word today?" Notice that it is not granted to live in disobedience to God's word at will just because one has become a child of God.

> What shall we say then? Are we to continue in sin that grace may abound? By no means! How can we who died to sin still live in it? (Rom 6:1-2)

Now, living according to the word of God, the standard for action, has become our sole responsibility. Indeed, it is a burden, but it means that obeying the word of God given to us is up to us. Therefore, setting up a model for our life has also become the most important thing for Christians as new people in Jesus Christ.

THE LIFE OF JESUS CHRIST AND YOURSELF

"Has Jesus become the greatest teacher for you who have become a new self?"

If the answer yes does not come easily, it is necessary to consider the life of the perfect obedience of Jesus. The life of the perfect obedience of Jesus Christ is *the greatest prototype* that shows the most balanced relationship between the sovereign grace of God and the human responsibility in faith.

First, the life of Jesus' perfect obedience is a life that fulfills all the conditions for the justification of sinners.[119] This will be discussed in detail when we address the life of perfect obedience in the broad sense in the upcoming chapter 2 of volume 2.

Second, the life of Jesus' perfect obedience is the model for our lives, the model of living out the standard of deeds, which is the focus here.

The life of Jesus' perfect obedience accomplishes these two things.

In other words, in order to fulfill the purpose of establishing the kingdom of God, Jesus restored the marred image of God and showed clearly and marvelously how God's children, bearing the image of God, should live.

Throughout his entire life, Jesus fully acknowledged the authority of God's word as the standard of deeds and perfectly obeyed it in our

---

119. Refer to vol. 2, ch. 2, "The Condition of Justification: The Perfect Obedience of Jesus Christ."

place. That is, on the one hand, Jesus perfectly obeyed all the words of God given by God the Father, fulfilling all of God's will for himself. On the other hand, this was a life of perfect obedience for us. Through his life of perfect obedience, Jesus personally showed that in all areas of life, the highest authority is the word.[120]

Therefore, throughout his life on earth, Jesus demonstrated the importance of the word as the standard of deeds. Jesus' life is the ultimate example for all of our lives. In other words, Jesus is the first true human who, throughout his entire life, believed, acknowledged, and accepted God's covenant lordship attributes of control (controlling power), authority, and presence as revealed in the word and obeyed them. Moreover, even when Jesus faced tremendous suffering, he took it as an opportunity for obedience to the word.

> Although he was a son, he learned obedience through what he suffered. (Heb 5:8)

Jesus Christ, in his divine nature, has granted eternity to the effects of salvation he has already fulfilled, and in his human nature demonstrated the true human life that God desires. Jesus' fulfillment of all the requirements of obedience to the words of the Old Testament shows the importance of the word as the standard of our deeds.

> Do not think that I have come to abolish the Law or the Prophets; I have not come to abolish them but to fulfill them. For truly, I say to you, until heaven and earth pass away, not an iota, not a dot, will pass from the Law until all is accomplished. Therefore whoever relaxes one of the least of these commandments and teaches others to do the same will be called least in the kingdom of heaven, but whoever does them and teaches them will be called great in the kingdom of heaven. For I tell you, unless your righteousness exceeds that of the scribes and Pharisees, you will never enter the kingdom of heaven. (Matt 5:17–20)

Now let us ask some questions about the importance of God's word as the standard of deeds.

"What does the whole life of Jesus' perfect obedience have to do with me?"

"Do I want to accept and live by God's word as the standard of deeds in my life, just like Jesus did?"

---

120. Cf. Carson, *Divine Sovereignty*, 159–60; Frame, *Systematic Theology*, 542–59.

In summary, Jesus' entire life is the best model of a life that obeys all the words of God, the laws of God's kingdom. The purpose of Jesus, who is both fully God and fully human (God-man), is to accomplish salvation and demonstrate the true human life. Therefore, the relationship between the sovereign grace of God and the responsibility of human faith is in perfect harmony in Jesus' life.

> Have this mind among yourselves, which is yours in Christ Jesus, who, though he was in the form of God, did not count equality with God a thing to be grasped, but emptied himself, by taking the form of a servant, being born in the likeness of men. And being found in human form, he humbled himself by becoming obedient to the point of death, even death on a cross. (Phil 2:5–8)

As we have seen so far, living according to God's word, the standard for action, like Jesus did, is entirely my responsibility. However, we should not forget that a life lived according to God's word is a life with God's promises. This is also the reason God has given us his word.

3. THE PURPOSE OF GOD GIVING HIS WORD

When discussing the topic of "the purpose of God giving his word," the most important thing is the beginning of creation.

Why is that?

From creation, the whole Bible finds both the necessity of Jesus' redemptive work and the need for the restoration of identity through the gospel. As mentioned earlier, we referred to the restoration of identity as the restoration of the marred image of God. Therefore, when considering the restoration of identity through the gospel, the most appropriate starting point for discussing the purpose of God giving his word would indeed be creation.

God created humans in his image in order to establish the kingdom of God according to his good pleasure. And he has given his word as the law of the kingdom of God. He wanted humans bearing his image to live according to the holy, righteous, and good word (Rom 7:12).

By looking at the beginning of creation in this way, the purpose of God giving his word to humans becomes clear. The ultimate purpose of God giving his word is to serve as a guide for living a life that increasingly resembles God's image. If God made humans in his image, then this is only natural.

Let's look at three points to remember when discussing the purpose of God giving his word.

First, the word of the Bible is the greatest gift to God's children. The word of the Bible is like a daily essential that we need to use every day. The word of the Bible is a gift given to us to use daily. Especially the New Testament guides us with "how to live" according to the words based on historical facts about Jesus.

Second, the word of the Bible, given by the living God, always has a present reality (1 Pet 1:23; Heb 4:12–13). The covenant lordship attributes of God's word, its power of life, work, and judgment—as we saw earlier—also apply to this present reality. In other words, this means that the word of God can be fulfilled as promised.

Third, the word of the Bible is the word given by the living God to living believers. Although this is related to the previous two points, the Bible is not for the dead but for the living people of faith. All these discussions, including the fact that the word is the standard in all areas, have discussed the importance of God's word for the living people. We can talk about the need for the word of living God in various ways. However, the key point in all these discussions is that in order to fulfill the purpose of giving the living word, there must be faith in the living God.

> And without faith it is impossible to please him, for whoever would draw near to God must believe that he exists and that he rewards those who seek him. (Heb 11:6)

We will now divide the purpose of God giving his word into two major categories: the purpose of assurance and the purpose of obedience. Of course, there are also words that show both the purpose of assurance and obedience, as well as words for the purpose of exhortation. Although we can discuss various other purposes, in this book, we will examine the purpose of God giving his word in these two categories. As we will see later, I think that it is appropriate to divide the purpose into assurance and obedience in a way that harmonizes with the entire *Justification and the Kingdom of God* set.

A. The Purpose of Assurance (Trust)

The first purpose of God giving his word is the assurance of faith to his children. The word of assurance serves as an important starting point that helps us better understand God and ourselves. In other words, the more we know the word of assurance, the more we can establish the assurance of faith in God and our identity as a child of God within him. A correct understanding of our identity according to the word of assurance can provide great confidence in our faith.

Therefore, the word of assurance plays the most important role as the foundation stone in our faith life. We can always stand firm on the eternal promise of God's word. This is the reason God has given us the word of assurance. God has given his word to his children so that they can believe in his promises and have the confidence of faith in his word.

a. The Words of Assurance (Trust)

What are some examples of the words of assurance?

Before answering this question, remember that the fundamental purpose for which God has given his word is essentially about trust. God has given us his word so that we can trust in him. Trusting in him means trusting in his word. When God sets boundaries, you set boundaries according to his word. Therefore, the first and most important thing is the word of assurance (trust). Without the word of assurance, it is difficult to build a house of faith.

Representative words of assurance include words about God (who God is; what God does for us), words about Jesus (who Jesus is; what Jesus did for us), and words of the gospel. In the Old Testament, representative words of assurance include words about God, covenant words, and messianic prophecy words. In the Old Testament, the representative words of assurance can be found in David. In particular, there are important words of assurance that we can learn through the songs of David. David praises God, who saved him from all his enemies and Saul, in 2 Sam 22. David, using the language of a soldier who has participated in many battles, praises God with assurance (trust) of faith for saving him in the midst of war.

> He said, "The LORD is my rock and my fortress and my deliverer, my God, my rock, in whom I take refuge, my shield, and the

> horn of my salvation, my stronghold and my refuge, my savior; you save me from violence." (2 Sam 22:2–3)

To David, God is his rock, his fortress, his deliverer (2 Sam 22:2–3, 32–33), his shield, the horn of his salvation (2 Sam 22:3, 31), his stronghold, his refuge, his savior (2 Sam 22:1–3, 33). In this way, David is a representative person who shows us the assurance of faith in God. David clearly demonstrates his faith in God as a shield that protects him from all the attacks in his life. Through David, God gives us words of assurance (2 Sam 22:31; Ps 18:30).[121]

Like David, when we encounter God's word, we too can have the assurance of faith in the power of God who protects us.

> This God—his way is perfect; the word of the LORD proves true; he is a shield for all those who take refuge in him. (2 Sam 22:31)

Throughout his life, David believed in and relied on the living God, who became the savior of his life and a lamp (2 Sam 22:29; Ps 18:28). David also had the assurance of faith that God would grant him victory whenever he fought against enemies in numerous battlefields or jumped over the walls (2 Sam 22:30; Ps 18:29).

In fact, the living God still speaks to us today and gives us words of assurance through the language of David. Through his word, God invites us all to believe and rely on him who becomes our Rock and our Shield (2 Sam 22:31; Pss 18:2; 27:1; 118:14).[122]

God uses the people of faith like David throughout the Bible to give us words of assurance. God invites us to believe in, rely on, and trust in the words of assurance (Ps 23).[123] The core message of the Old Testament words of assurance is that when we believe David's word of assurance, we too can encounter the God whom David encountered.

> The LORD is my rock and my fortress and my deliverer, my God, my rock, in whom I take refuge, my shield, and the horn of my salvation, my stronghold. (Ps 18:2)

---

121. Psalm 18 is where David's song in 2 Sam 22 reappears.

122. "The LORD is my strength and my song; he has become my salvation" (Ps 118:14).

123. The famous Ps 23 by David is also a word of assurance. In this psalm, David introduces God as the Good Shepherd. Through Ps 23, God introduces himself as a good shepherdlike figure and invites us to believe, trust, and follow him.

> [Of David.] The LORD is my light and my salvation; whom shall I fear? The LORD is the stronghold of my life; of whom shall I be afraid? (Ps 27:1)

In the New Testament, there are also some representative words of assurance that are connected to the words of the Old Testament. For example, in the Old Testament, the good shepherd God of David and Jesus in the New Testament are seen as the same. The good shepherd God whom David encountered (Ps 23) is introduced in the New Testament as Jesus, who laid down his life to atone for our sins (John 10:7–18). Such interpretations also help strengthen our assurance of faith. The God who keeps his promises in the Old Testament appears in the New Testament as the God who fulfills his promises through the Messiah. In other words, the invisible good shepherd God came to this earth as the visible good shepherd Jesus Christ. The Gospel of John proclaims the fact that the God of David remains an unchanging good shepherd for God's children.

> I am the good shepherd. I know my own and my own know me, just as the Father knows me and I know the Father; and I lay down my life for the sheep. (John 10:14–15)

The coming of Jesus, the Fulfiller of the covenant, strengthens our faith through the words of the Old Testament covenant. Jesus came to this earth and became the Fulfiller of all the covenants, connecting the God of the Mosaic law and the God of the gospel. With this tremendous event of grace, the church offers a solution to humans who bear the marred image of God.

The church proclaims that the problem of the marred image of God can be solved by encountering Jesus Christ. The main point of this proclamation is that Jesus has become the Mediator of the covenant of grace, connecting God and sinners. This message of assurance that Jesus has become the life-giving Spirit gives life to souls that would inevitably die due to sins (2 Cor 3:6).

> Thus it is written, "The first man Adam became a living being"; the last Adam became a life-giving spirit. (1 Cor 15:45)

> It is the Spirit who gives life; the flesh is no help at all. The words that I have spoken to you are spirit and life. (John 6:63)

b. The Word of the Gospel

To reiterate, if you do not trust the gospel and the words of the gospel, then you do not trust God. Consider this: if you do not trust the words of the gospel, you have no relationship with God. In this sense, the words of the gospel are the most typical word of assurance in the New Testament.

The gospel is the word of assurance that reveals "who Jesus is" and "what he has done for us." The word of the gospel gives us the assurance (trust) that our salvation is accomplished by God's grace alone (*sola gratia*), apart from our works. Whoever believes in Jesus receives forgiveness of sins and attains salvation (Luke 1:77; Acts 16:31; Rom 10:9). This is very important. The word of the gospel gives us the assurance of the forgiveness of sins that Jesus has eternally atoned for the sins of sinners through his death on the cross.

> In him we have redemption through his blood, the forgiveness of our trespasses, according to the riches of his grace. (Eph 1:7)

> But if we walk in the light, as he is in the light, we have fellowship with one another, and the blood of Jesus his Son cleanses us from all sin. (1 John 1:7)

These texts provide assurance of faith in the blood of Jesus.

On the one hand, these texts contain God's promise that the blood of Jesus saves sinners from their sins.

On the other hand, these words of assurance also have the power of cleansing the filthiness of believers' sins and bringing light to their dark souls. Of course, the saving and life-giving work is also the work of the Holy Spirit. In other words, the living words of the gospel are also essential for living believers. The Holy Spirit revives dead souls through these life-giving words.

The New Testament, in particular, has many words that give assurance about Jesus' redemptive work. These words of assurance become the source of courage, boldness, comfort, love, and joy in our lives. For example, words about grace (Eph 2:8–9), love (Rom 5:5; 8:35–39), atonement (2 Cor 5:21), reconciliation (Rom 5:1, 9–11), sacrifice (Heb 9:26; Eph 5:2; 1 Cor 5:7), redemption (Rom 6:18; Titus 2:14; Col 1:13–14), ransom (Matt 20:28; 1 Tim 2:6; Rom 3:24) and victory (Col 1:11; 2:13–15; 1 Cor 15:57) also belong to the words of assurance (trust). The gospel is the word that deeply implants assurance (trust) in God's grace and love.

Paul's epistles especially use various expressions to convey the accomplishments achieved through Jesus' death and resurrection, which are words of assurance. The words of redemption, salvation, forgiveness, and justification clearly show how great a work God has greatly accomplished for us through and in Jesus Christ.[124] Paul, in this way, proves that the core of the gospel is justification, connected with the Old Testament covenants.[125]

> For in it the righteousness of God is revealed from faith for faith, as it is written, "The righteous shall live by faith." (Rom 1:17)

> But now the righteousness of God has been manifested apart from the law, although the Law and the Prophets bear witness to it—the righteousness of God through faith in Jesus Christ for all who believe. For there is no distinction. (Rom 3:21-22)

Paul's epistles suggest that justification in Jesus can be referred to as the gospel, and in another sense, it can also be called salvation. I have summarized the content of the word of assurance in figure 1-F below, as we have discussed.

Figure 1-F The Word of Assurance and the Work of the Spirit

The Purpose of the Word	The Word of Assurance and the Work of the Spirit	Connectivity to the Kingdom of God
Word of assurance (trust)	Assurance of faith Assurance of Christian identity Assurance of justification (the gospel, salvation)	The Kingdom of Justification John 1:12; 3:16; Rom 1:17; 3:21–22

It is the Holy Spirit who comes to our hearts with the words of assurance (the gospel and justification) and works within us. That is, the Holy Spirit helps us to have faith and assurance in God and Jesus Christ through these words. Moreover, the Holy Spirit is the One who makes us boast in Jesus with great confidence in our faith (1 Cor 1:30–31). When the words of assurance are present in our hearts, we encounter Jesus. When the word of love is present, we encounter Jesus. When we encounter these words of assurance, we meet the living God.

---

124. Kang, *Living Out the Gospel*, 113–38.
125. Kang, *Living Out the Gospel*, 149–269.

c. The Presence of the Word of Assurance

> For this is the covenant that I will make with the house of Israel after those days, declares the Lord: I will put my laws into their minds, and write them on their hearts, and I will be their God, and they shall be my people. (Heb 8:10)

After believing in Jesus and acknowledging that the word of assurance (trust) dwells in our heart (Jer 31:33; Heb 8:10; 10:16), we must accept the word by faith (John 15:7; Jas 1:21). In other words, we should start to live by the word of assurance (Matt 4:4). We then must pray for the word to rule over our hearts and hold onto the word with faith in Jesus.[126]

> And you show that you are a letter from Christ delivered by us, written not with ink but with the Spirit of the living God, not on tablets of stone but on tablets of human hearts. (2 Cor 3:3)

For example, when the word of justification (Rom 1:17; 3:21–22) comes into "your heart," you should start seeing yourself according to the word in Jesus—you are justified by faith in Jesus Christ. This means that you should learn how to change your old judgment standard for yourself based on the word of assurance present in your heart. If you don't see yourself through the word and accept yourself according to that word, you should hold onto the word and pray until you grasp that word and change your old judgment standard. The reason the word of assurance was given is because God wants you to change your old way of thinking, your old judgment standard to see yourselves according to the word.

Therefore God wants his children to know first and foremost what he has done for them through the word of assurance.

How can we live by faith in this world without knowing God's love (Rom 8:28–39)?

Here, we must first remember that we cannot understand the word of assurance without first using and applying God's word (God's love) to ourselves. You cannot understand yourself apart from God's word. And remember that God wants us to change our thoughts according to the word of assurance in Jesus, such as Rom 6:11.[127]

---

126. For this dwelling and ruling of the word, please refer to figs. 1-I and 1-J in the discussion about the ruling of the word below.

127. In Rom 6:11, the term "consider" (*logizomai*, λογίζομαι) is a commandment (an imperative mood) that we must change our thoughts according to God's thoughts (God's grace here). This Greek word "consider" (*logizomai*, λογίζομαι) is used eleven

So you also must consider yourselves dead to sin and alive to God in Christ Jesus. (Rom 6:11)

This passage teaches us how we should respond to the word of assurance (Rom 6:3–10). In other words, it calls us to "accept the word of assurance" and to "consider" (Rom 6:11).

Why should we change "our thoughts according to God's thoughts (words)," as Paul says?

The reason we need to change "our thoughts according to God's thoughts (words)" is because the Holy Spirit gives us life through the word and transforms us anew. The Holy Spirit first gives new hearts and spirits to dead souls through the gospel word, forgives their sins, leads them to salvation, and guides the process of sanctification.[128]

> Then he said to me, "Prophesy over these bones, and say to them, O dry bones, hear the word of the LORD. Thus says the Lord GOD to these bones: Behold, I will cause breath to enter you, and you shall live." (Ezek 37:4–5)

In conclusion, the word of the gospel (justification) used by the Holy Spirit is like a seed planted in our hearts. This seed of the gospel must be planted deep within our hearts to be beneficial (blessings). The deep roots from the gospel are like a house built on a solid foundation. Jesus himself becomes the solid foundation for this house of faith (Acts 4:11–12).[129]

> "Everyone then who hears these words of mine and does them will be like a wise man who built his house on the rock. And the rain fell, and the floods came, and the winds blew and beat on that house, but it did not fall, because it had been founded on the rock. And everyone who hears these words of mine and does not do them will be like a foolish man who built his house on the sand. And the rain fell, and the floods came, and the winds blew and beat against that house, and it fell, and great was the fall of it." And when Jesus finished these sayings, the crowds were

---

times in Rom 4 to explain how God made Abraham's faith righteous by God's grace alone—to explain the concept of the imputation of Jesus Christ's righteousness (Kang, *Living Out the Gospel*, 189, 217–20). For the concept of imputation, refer to "2. The Imputation of the Perfect Righteousness of Jesus," in vol. 2, ch. 3.

128. Ezekiel 37:14 says, "I will put my Spirit within you." This not only speaks of Ezek 37:1–14, coming alive from the dead with the breath of life, but also indicates that the Holy Spirit pours out a new heart upon a soul that is dead in sin (Bavinck, *Reformed Dogmatics*, 4:514, 650; Frame, *Systematic Theology*, 401).

129. Bavinck, *Our Reasonable Faith*, 481–86.

astonished at his teaching, for he was teaching them as one who had authority, and not as their scribes. (Matt 7:24–29)

Therefore, the word of assurance regarding the grace and love given by the Holy Spirit bears fruits like a wellspring of joy, hope, love, thankfulness, and peace in our daily lives (Col 3:16). The word of assurance is also very useful when praying with total dependence on the Holy Spirit because it supplies us with the energy to pray with patience of faith. Ultimately, the Holy Spirit enables us, who possess the word of God, to overcome the world through faith in Jesus.

> For everyone who has been born of God overcomes the world.
> And this is the victory that has overcome the world—our faith.
> (1 John 5:4)

As we have seen so far, the word of assurance comes into us through the work of the Holy Spirit. In other words, the dwelling of the word of assurance in our hearts is the work of the Holy Spirit. The Holy Spirit enables us to encounter the living Jesus when we encounter the word of assurance. Therefore, encountering the word of assurance is of utmost importance to God's children. The Holy Spirit strengthens the bones of our faith through this word and prepares us for a healthy life of faith. Figure 1-G below summarizes the responses of faith to the word of assurance that comes to us through the work of the Holy Spirit.[130]

Figure 1-G

The Work of the Holy Spirit		
The Presence of the Word of Assurance	⇨	Response of Faith

B. The Purpose of Obedience

After the word of assurance, the next important word is the word of obedience. As we have seen so far, God has promised his children the words of assurance and obedience. In particular, the word of obedience is given for the transformation of God's children and for Christian leaders. In the Old Testament (Hebrew) and the New Testament (Greek), the words for "obedience" are primarily composed of imperative commands.

---

130. For the response of faith to God's word, refer to vol. 3, ch. 1, "God Demands Faith."

a. The Words of Obedience

In the Old Testament, the most representative word of obedience is undoubtedly the Mosaic covenant given to the Israelites. The purpose of God giving the Mosaic law to the Israelites was to teach them how to live. Among all the words of obedience in the whole Bible, from the Hebrew word for "hear" (shema, שְׁמַע) in Deut 6:4, we can especially see the reason for giving the Mosaic law.[131] In other words, the analysis of Deut 6:4 helps us understand why the word of the Bible demands obedience.

> Hear therefore, O Israel, and be careful to do them. (Deut 6:3)

Why should we obey the word?
Deuteronomy 6:4–5 answers that question:

> Hear, O Israel: The LORD our God, the LORD is one. You shall love the LORD your God with all your heart and with all your soul and with all your might. (Deut 6:4–5)

As this text says, the greatest reason God gave the word of obedience is to love God. Thus, the act of keeping God's word becomes an act of loving God. God's basic evaluation standard for human "good works" and "evil works" is no different. Obeying God's word is a good deed, and disobeying God's word is an evil deed (Deut 6:17–18).

On the one hand, God gave the word of obedience to Israel to "love God."

On the other hand, for Israel, obedience to the word is not only a matter of life and death (Deut 6:10–15), but a matter of blessings (Deut 6:17–19; 28:1–14) and curses (Deut 27:26; 28:15–68).

> You shall diligently keep the commandments of the LORD your God, and his testimonies and his statutes, which he has commanded you. And you shall do what is right and good in the sight of the LORD, that it may go well with you, and that you may go in and take possession of the good land that the LORD swore to give to your fathers by thrusting out all your enemies from before you, as the LORD has promised. (Deut 6:17–19)

---

131. The Hebrew word for "hear" (shema, שְׁמַע) in Deut 6:4 is the imperative form of the Hebrew verb "listen" (shama, שָׁמַע). Deuteronomy 6:4 is widely known as the Shema (shema, שְׁמַע) because it comes from the pronunciation of the imperative form of this verb.

In this way, in the Mosaic law, there was fundamentally a promise of life and blessings (Deut 6:24) for those who obeyed the word of the living God.

Which way did Israel, led by Moses, go?

Despite God's earnest persuasion, Israel did not keep the blessed word of God for a long time. Israel had to first realize their sins (Rom 3:19–20) through the holy, righteous, and good words of the law (Rom 7:12). They had to recognize their sins and come before the God of grace. However, they failed to see their own sins through the Mosaic law and did not seek God's grace by coming before him. The people of Israel should have believed that God's word is always alive and that God is the One who always keeps his promises.

In the New Testament, the most important word of obedience also coincides with the Old Testament. By far the most important word of obedience is undoubtedly Jesus' word, "Love one another" (John 13:34). Jesus summarizes the Mosaic law as "love God and love your neighbor" (Luke 10:25–37) and directly shows God's love in his life by a supreme example. Through his redemptive work, Jesus proved that the foundation of God's love in both the Old and New Testaments is the same.[132] The entire New Testament commands us to love one another with the love of Jesus (John 3:16; 14:21; 15:9, 17).

> A new commandment I give to you, that you love one another: just as I have loved you, you also are to love one another. By this all people will know that you are my disciples, if you have love for one another. (John 13:34–35)

Therefore, this love of Jesus is the source of the love of all God's children. All the strength and power to practice the word "love one another" comes from the love of Jesus who performed it. The Holy Spirit does this in us. The Spirit comes into our hearts (John 14:16–17, 20–21, 26; 2 Cor 1:22) and supplies us with the power of Jesus' love (John 15:4, 7, 10; Rom 5:5; 8:1–2, 38–39; Gal 5:22).

The Holy Spirit, who is with us, enables us to keep the word "make disciples" (Matt 28:18–20). Jesus the King sits on the throne in heaven, ruling over all things, while the Spirit works in us.

> And Jesus came and said to them, "All authority in heaven and on earth has been given to me. Go therefore and make disciples

---

132. For this, refer to "1-B-b-iv. Obedience to the Word and the Fruit of Love," in vol. 3, ch. 3, "Obedience of Faith and Fruit of Faith."

of all nations, baptizing them in the name of the Father and of the Son and of the Holy Spirit, teaching them to observe all that I have commanded you. And behold, I am with you always, to the end of the age." (Matt 28:18–20)

A common characteristic of the New Testament epistles is that they reinterpret and teach on the word of Jesus' command "love one another." These epistles teach the word of obedience, "love one another" (unity), in various ways (diversity), based on the redemptive work of Jesus' love. In other words, these epistles command the word of obedience on the basis of the words of assurance such as the gospel and justification. Figure 1-H below summarizes the word of obedience in connection with sanctification and *The Kingdom of Faith*.

Figure 1-H The Word of Obedience and the Work of the Spirit

The Purpose of the Word	The Word of Obedience and the Work of the Spirit	Connectivity to the Kingdom of God
Word of obedience	Sanctification (to imitate Jesus, to live by faith)	*The Kingdom of Faith* Rom 1:17; Heb 11:6; Eph 4:23–24; Col 3:10

What we should note here is that the New Testament epistles give us the word of obedience in relationship with union with Jesus (in Jesus).[133]

In particular, Paul uses the phrase "in the Lord (Jesus)," meaning union with Jesus, many times for this purpose. This phrase presupposes justification and sanctification by God's grace alone. As we will see in volume 2, this means that God sees us "in Jesus." That is, only those who have been justified in Jesus by grace alone are qualified to obey the word. Therefore, we must always remember this tremendous blessing in Jesus whenever we obey God's word.

> Rejoice in the Lord always; again I will say, rejoice. Let your reasonableness be known to everyone. The Lord is at hand; do not be anxious about anything, but in everything by prayer and supplication with thanksgiving let your requests be made known to God. (Phil 4:4–6)

Then, what happens when we keep the words of God's commandment in the New Testament?

---

133. For union with Christ, see vol. 2, ch. 3, "1. Union with Christ."

We must first remember, as we saw in the Old Testament, that there are promises in the New Testament about obedience to the word. Of course, there are cases in the New Testament where God's promises do not appear to be directly stated. However, there are cases where we can find God's promises within the chapter of the verse or in the context that precedes or follows it. For example, Phil 4:8–9, which follows right after Phil 4:4–7, also unfolds nearly the same promise of the word.

> And the peace of God, which surpasses all understanding, will guard your hearts and your minds in Christ Jesus. (Phil 4:7)

> Think about these things. What you have learned and received and heard and seen in me—practice these things, and the God of peace will be with you. (Phil 4:8b–9)

Therefore, these texts promise "the peace of God" when we obey God's word. When we obey the word of God's commandment in this way, we encounter the peace of Jesus. As we saw earlier, this is not much different than the case of the Old Testament. Second Timothy 2:7 is also a good example of God's promise appearing in the same verse right after the word of obedience:

> Think over what I say, for the Lord will give you understanding in everything. (2 Tim 2:7)

b. The Presence of the Word of Obedience

In order for God's promises to be fulfilled, the word of obedience must first be present in the heart. That is, the word of God's commandment must be given first. The presence of the word of obedience is also the work of the Holy Spirit. The order should be that the word of assurance should first occupy the heart, and after being ruled by that word, the word of obedience comes. In other words, this means that the word of obedience comes after trust in God has been established. For example, the famous story of Abraham is a good inspiration for the presence of the word of obedience.

Could Abraham have accepted God's word in Gen 12:1–3 if he had not had faith in God?

> Now the LORD said to Abram, "Go from your country and your kindred and your father's house to the land that I will show you. And I will make of you a great nation, and I will bless you and

make your name great, so that you will be a blessing. I will bless those who bless you, and him who dishonors you I will curse, and in you all the families of the earth shall be blessed." (Gen 12:1–3)

Uncertainty is said to be one of the factors that cause fear in people. In this passage, God commands Abraham to "go to the land that I will show you." However, God gives Abraham his word that demands obedience without explanation of the final destination. Of course, it is somewhat shocking to Abraham, who is not young, but seventy-five years old. As we saw earlier in Philippians, there is clearly a promise of God in this passage as well. But if Abraham could not have firmly trusted in God, he would not have been able to obey as the word said.[134]

The story of Abraham asks us an important question: "What will we do when the word of God's commandment comes to us?"

This word, of course, included God's providence (Messiah), but it also coexisted with a promise given to an individual. However, when the word of God's commandment came upon him, Abraham might have had an internal conflict, but he eventually chose obedience, and God finally made him the father of faith as promised (Gen 17:4–7; 22:17–18; Rom 4:16).

Therefore, the lesson of Abraham's story is clear. God gives us his word and wants us to think and act according to that word.[135] This transformation that God desires is a real transformation that takes place throughout the entire life of God's children.

> Do not be conformed to this world, but be transformed by the renewal of your mind, that by testing you may discern what is the will of God, what is good and acceptable and perfect. (Rom 12:2)

As the story of Abraham shows, the word of the living God has a promise of eternal blessing. The promised work of God's grace takes place when we have unyielding determination and will to keep the word of obedience. This is also the work of the Holy Spirit, who continuously help us after coming into our hearts. In the Bible, there is God's promise that those who live "by the Spirit" in obedience to the word will bear fruit (Rom 8:11).

> But I say, walk by the Spirit, and you will not gratify the desires of the flesh. (Gal 5:16)

---

134. For the presence and the total control of the word of obedience, see figs. 1-I and 1-J in the discussion on the total control of the word below.

135. For transformation, refer to vol. 3, ch. 2, "Change Happens."

> But the fruit of the Spirit is love, joy, peace, patience, kindness, goodness, faithfulness, gentleness, self-control; against such things there is no law. (Gal 5:22–23)

The reason God gives us his word is to bless us with the transformation that comes from following his word. The greatest blessing lies in receiving the promise given by the word of assurance (trust) after believing in Jesus. Following this blessing, another great blessing is receiving the promise given by the word of obedience and undergoing transformation to imitate Jesus.

c. Are You Totally Controlled by the Word of God?

So far, we have looked at the meaning of the word of God's commandment and the presence of his word in our hearts. Now, we will briefly look at how the word that dwells in our hearts rules our lives.

"Am I being controlled by the word of God?"

To answer the question, we can say that another way of saying "to be controlled" is "to obey" or "to keep." The discussion about this will help us understand a life that fulfills the purpose for which God has given his word.

As we saw, the word of assurance dwells first in our hearts through the work of the Holy Spirit. That word of assurance rules and moves our hearts, and then the word of obedience can dwell in our hearts.

At this point, we may start to ask a question, "Am I being controlled by the word of obedience?"

In other words, "Am I obeying the word of commandment?"

The process up to this point is summarized in figure 1-I below.

Figure 1-I

The Holy Spirit Working According to God's Word

Heart — Presence of the Word of Assurance	⇨	Heart Controlled by the Word of Assurance — Presence of the Word of Obedience	⇨	Heart Controlled by the Word of Assurance — Controlled by the Word of Obedience

THE WORD OF GOD

With figures 1-I and 1-J (below), I am not presenting the stages from the presence of God's word to the total control of God's word over us. I am also not trying to generalize or formulate how the Holy Spirit works in various ways according to God's pleasing will. I have simply focused on two aspects of the work of the Spirit (fig. 1-I) to emphasize the reality of the work of God's word in our hearts:

1. The reality of the presence of the word in our hearts
2. The reality of the works of the word and of the Holy Spirit

Figure 1-J below reorganizes figure 1-I above to include our responsibility in our faith regarding the word's working within us.

The figure below signifies that only when we continue to obey the word by being under its rule and control through the working of the Holy Spirit, the Spirit enables the word to bear fruit.

Figure 1-J

The Holy Spirit Working According to God's Word

Heart ⇨ Heart (Presence of the Word of Assurance, Presence of the Word of Obedience) ⇨ Heart (Fruit Bearing: Controlled by the Word of Assurance, Controlled by the Word of Obedience)

⇧
Response of Faith
Response of Obedience

In Luke 8:15, Jesus also says that the fruit of the word requires patience to obey the word by faith (see also John 15).

> As for that in the good soil, they are those who, hearing the word, hold it fast in an honest and good heart, and bear fruit with patience. (Luke 8:15)

For example, when Jesus says, "Love one another," it cannot be considered as the word controlling us solely by its presence in our hearts. The presence of the word itself does not guarantee its application. It takes time for this "love one another" to continue to control our hearts, and it takes time for it to actually manifest itself in our lives as controlling our thoughts and actions. We may have to go through a process of overcoming difficulties before we can actually put this command into practice in our lives. In John 15:10, Jesus speaks of going through this process as follows.

> If you keep my commandments, you will abide in my love, just as I have kept my Father's commandments and abide in his love. (John 15:10)

As such, Scripture says that when we love one another, all people will recognize us as Jesus' disciples (John 13:35), we will gain boldness (1 John 3:21), and our prayers will be answered (1 John 3:22). In other words, if we obey the command to "love one another" (John 13:34; 1 John 3:11) and continue to be controlled by that word (1 John 3:21–24), we abide in God's love. Additionally, the Holy Spirit shows us that God loves us and enables us to bear fruit.

> In that day you will know that I am in my Father, and you in me, and I in you. Whoever has my commandments and keeps them, he it is who loves me. And he who loves me will be loved by my Father, and I will love him and manifest myself to him. (John 14:20–21)

Therefore, a life controlled by the word of God comes from a life where we see, hear, speak, think, and act according to the word. When the word of obedience is made present through the working of the Holy Spirit, it is up to you to begin to be controlled by the word. The Spirit helps you when you seek to continue believing God's word and practicing God's word with the assurance of faith in the love of Jesus. God wants to see faith in you even after you are saved.

> And without faith it is impossible to please him, for whoever would draw near to God must believe that he exists and that he rewards those who seek him. (Heb 11:6).

This text emphasizes the importance of going forth in faith and believing in God's word for the word of obedience to enter our hearts. In this regard, the faith of Heb 11 is faith in the word. Furthermore, faith in the word is faith in God, that is, faith in the living God who gives the word. If we live each day under the control of the word of God, we can see the Holy Spirit fulfill the promise of God's word through our lives.

For this reason, as we continue to encounter God's word in faith and are controlled by it, we can encounter God anew.

In conclusion, the purpose of the word is for us to see, hear, and keep the word of God. Therefore, everyone who prays and endures to keep the word and overcomes with patience will receive its promise and bear fruit in the end (2 Tim 3:16–17; 4:4; 6:12; Phil 4:4–6; Gal 5:22–23). Our faith grows and bears fruit as we see, hear, and keep the word (2 Tim 2:5–6). As such, when the word of the living God is present and rules our lives, the Spirit changes our words, actions, and lives. As we are transformed by the word of God, we finally bear the fruit of the word.

> An athlete is not crowned unless he competes according to the rules. It is the hard-working farmer who ought to have the first share of the crops. (2 Tim 2:5–6)

When hardships, loneliness, pain, troubles, difficulties, sufferings, despair, and feelings of frustration occur, those who hold onto the promised word and endure with faith will change and bear fruit (Luke 8:15). Those who obey in faith to keep the word of obedience until the end overcome the world (1 John 5:5; Rev 1:3; 21:7; 22:7, 12).[136] The following figure 1-K summarizes the obedience of faith to the word of obedience that comes to us through the work of the Spirit.

Figure 1-K

The Work of the Holy Spirit	
The Presence of the Word of Obedience ⇨	Obedience of Faith

4. THE WORK THAT FULFILLS THE PURPOSE OF GOD'S WORD

As previously explained, the Christian life not only begins with faith in Jesus (the word of assurance), but also continues by faith in Jesus (the word of obedience). The most important thing in this life of faith is the word of God. Similarly, it is important to recognize that the living God gives us the word. That is, this recognition that God, who loves *me* to the

---

136. Kang, *Living Out the Gospel*, 270–98. For the obedience of faith, refer to "1. Obedience of Faith," in vol. 3, ch. 3.

point of death (John 15:13; 1 Thess 2:8), has given *me* the best word for *me*. This awareness is a very important faith recognition. In 1 John 3:16, Scripture testifies to the love of Jesus like this.

> By this we know love, that he laid down his life for us, and we ought to lay down our lives for the brothers. (1 John 3:16)

However, even if we have an awareness of this love, a crisis of faith can arise when God's given word does not agree with our thoughts. In some cases, the assurance of faith in God's love for us can be shaken. Remember that such moments of faith crisis can come to anyone.

Therefore, the most important thing that fulfills the purpose of the word is to thoroughly believe in God's love. In other words, when a faith crisis arises, it can be used as an opportunity to check on God's love. Depending on the situation, it may be necessary to pray and repeatedly confess God's love with our mouths. When we can restore confidence in God's love through God's word, we fulfill the purpose for which God gave the word.

So, what do we do if we want to actually fulfill the purpose for which God gave his word?

We should first remember that God's sovereign work and the work of fulfilling our responsibility of faith must go hand in hand (concur). Thus, we will now briefly discuss what we should keep in mind for the work of fulfilling the purpose of the word. For this discussion, we will first look at the Holy Spirit and the vine, and then conclude with Paul.

A. The Holy Spirit and His Work of Fulfilling the Word

The Holy Spirit always works according to the word of God from the beginning to the end of the Christian life. God has given the Spirit into our hearts to bring us a new life (2 Cor 1:22; Rom 5:5; Acts 15:8; Gal 3:10). Therefore, the Spirit leads us in the direction of a new life through God's word. As we saw, the Spirit does this work through the word of assurance and the word of obedience.

To explain this, the Bible introduces a very unique relationship between the Holy Spirit, Jesus, and the word. This is not an ordinary relationship. At first, this relationship may not make sense to you. When that happens, we can only pray. Let us first briefly look at the relationship between Jesus and the Holy Spirit.

The New Testament is very specific about the presence of the invisible Holy Spirit. Because the Holy Spirit is invisible, Jesus' promise of the Holy Spirit's presence is of utmost importance. For this reason, the event of the Holy Spirit's presence (Acts 2), which fulfilled Jesus' promise, is the second greatest event after the first coming of Jesus. We may look at this incident without much thought, but for the Jews, it was a shocking event. Before that, Jesus had already clearly promised the presence of the Holy Spirit, the Helper and Spirit of truth who can help us (John 16:7, 13).

> And I will ask the Father, and he will give you another Helper, to be with you forever, even the Spirit of truth, whom the world cannot receive, because it neither sees him nor knows him. You know him, for he dwells with you and will be in you. (John 14:16–17)

As this text says, the Holy Spirit, the Spirit of truth, dwells in our hearts and guides us into all truth (John 16:13). When you believe in Jesus and receive salvation, the Holy Spirit comes, makes your heart a temple, dwells in you, and pours out God's love into your heart (Rom 5:5; 1 Cor 3:16; John 14:16–17).[137] The Spirit's great power to save us and sanctify us generally comes through the power of God's word (1 Pet 1:23, 25; Jas 1:18). In other words, the presence of the Spirit fulfills in us the sovereign lordship attributes of God's word, which we saw earlier. To accomplish this, the Spirit comes and dwells in our hearts (John 14:16–17, 20) to save us and sanctify us.

For example, the Greek word for "dwell" in John 14:17 and 15:4–8 (remain, stay, *meno*, μένω) is a representative word expressing the attribute of God's presence through the word.[138] This word has the concept of "duration of stay." What is important for us here is the fact that the Holy Spirit begins to actually dwell in us. Now we must ask ourselves whether we believe in the presence of the Holy Spirit, who is the fulfillment of this promise of Jesus. For the Holy Spirit becomes the subject leading our new life.

---

137. "And hope does not put us to shame, because God's love has been poured into our hearts through the Holy Spirit who has been given to us" (Rom 5:5).
"Do you not know that you are God's temple and that God's Spirit dwells in you?" (1 Cor 3:16).

138. This Greek verb is most used often by the apostle John (sixty-seven times) (*EDNT* 2:407). Please see "1-B, The Covenant Lordship Attributes of God's Word," which we discussed earlier in this chapter.

The next important thing to this promise of Jesus is the explanation of the relationship between the presence of the Holy Spirit and the presence of Jesus. That is, Jesus says that the presence of the Holy Spirit is the presence of Jesus (John 14:18, 23) and the presence of the triune God.

> In that day you will know that I am in my Father, and you in me, and I in you. (John 14:20)

Jesus especially introduces the triune God in John 14-17. This teaching about the existence of the triune God is not a parable. Jesus teaches clearly about it, "speaking clearly" (John 16:25, 29). Therefore, in the whole Bible, this teaching of Jesus can be said to be the most important teaching not only about the existence of the triune God, but also about the providential work of God.

Jesus is the God of Immanuel, who is with us through the Holy Spirit (Matt 1:23; 28:20). Jesus, who has both divinity and humanity, revealed the invisible God through himself when he was on this earth, and continues to reveal God through his word (John 1). Jesus also says, "Whoever has seen me has seen the Father" (John 14:9). Now the Holy Spirit is the God who dwells in us and is with us. Remember that the importance of the presence of the Holy Spirit lies in his presence within us to fulfill the purpose for which the word is given, the word for us. The Holy Spirit leads us to obey the word of God's truth (John 14:20-21; Matt 28:20).[139]

> Whoever has my commandments and keeps them, he it is who loves me. And he who loves me will be loved by my Father, and I will love him and manifest myself to him. (John 14:21)

> When the Spirit of truth comes, he will guide you into all the truth, for he will not speak on his own authority, but whatever he hears he will speak, and he will declare to you the things that are to come. (John 16:13)

We also should remember that the Holy Spirit has the power to bear fruit in our lives through the word of God (John 15:2-3). The Holy Spirit, as we saw, is the One who directly carries out and fulfills the work of the covenant lordship attributes of God's word and the power of life, work, and judgment of God's word. In other words, the Spirit has the power to surgically remove and eliminate things that prevent us from bearing

---

139. Frame, *Systematic Theology*, 676.

fruit through the word (John 15:2–3; Heb 4:12–13; 2 Tim 3:16–17).[140] The importance of the Bible lies in the promise of the Holy Spirit's work being with us.

> All Scripture is breathed out by God and profitable for teaching, for reproof, for correction, and for training in righteousness, that the man of God may be complete, equipped for every good work. (2 Tim 3:16–17)

Therefore, if you want God's word to work in your life, you must pray for the help of the Holy Spirit. Not praying for help from the Holy Spirit can be seen as an act of denying the presence of the Spirit. Now we need to take a closer look at the parable of the vine to understand the work of the Spirit more. Jesus' parable of the vine helps us better understand the work of the Spirit in fulfilling the purpose of the given word.

B. The Vine and the Work of the Holy Spirit Through the Word

I believe that Jesus' parable of the vine (John 15) is the most important teaching about the work of the Holy Spirit who dwells in us. Through the parable of the vine, Jesus teaches the beginning of the Christian life (salvation) and its fruit (sanctification, growth of faith). This parable also helps us understand the work that the Spirit accomplishes within us with the words of assurance and obedience.

Through the story of the vine, we can see how the Holy Spirit bears the fruit of the word. When first encountering the story of the vine, it might seem like the story speaks only of the sovereign work of God's grace. But Jesus is also talking about the obedience of our faith. To properly understand the story of the vine, we must first remember that John 1:1–14 equates Jesus with the word of God and God himself. In other words, when discussing the work of God's word, Jesus, the Word, and God can never be separated.

> In the beginning was the Word, and the Word was with God, and the Word was God. (John 1:1)

> And the Word became flesh and dwelt among us, and we have seen his glory, glory as of the only Son from the Father, full of grace and truth. (John 1:14)

---

140. Bavinck, *Reformed Dogmatics*, 4:652; Frame, *Systematic Theology*, 401.

As we saw, it is quite intriguing that the Gospel of John uses "God" and "Jesus" and "the word" interchangeably. That is, from the very beginning, the Gospel of John emphasizes the importance of the word of God, that the word is God. John is telling us that there is nothing more important than the word of God. In other words, it means, "Treat the word of God as you would God, and as you would Jesus. The most important change for Christians lies in treating the word of God as God himself."

This analysis can be applied to John 14 and 15. It is amazing that Jesus uses the parable of the vine to specifically teach the work of the word under the guidance of the Holy Spirit, along with this analysis. In fact, Jesus presents a new interpretation of the work of Trinity—God the Father, God the Son, and God the Holy Spirit in the Gospel of John.

According to Jesus, the Holy Spirit works within us through the word of God for salvation and sanctification. We will first look at how the Spirit forgives the sins of sinners and leads them to salvation through the word (John 15:3). Then, we will briefly look at the work of the word for our sanctification.

First, the Spirit cleanses the sins of sinners (guilt) with the word of the gospel (salvation [John 15:3]).[141] Here is the sovereign work of grace by the Holy Spirit for salvation. Jesus compares this to a farmer pruning (cutting) the branches of a vine. Here the farmer is God the Father ("my Father" [John 15:1]). Therefore, the pruning (the word "clean") in John 15:3 refers to the work for salvation.

> Already you are clean [pure, *katharos*, καθαρός] because of the word [*logos*, λόγος] that I have spoken to you. (John 15:3)

This passage figuratively compares receiving freedom from guilt and salvation to God's pruning of vine branches. So, the Greek word for "clean" (*katharos*, καθαρός) in John 15:3 used for this parable means "to clean (to prune, to cut) from sins."[142] In other words, it means that the problem of sin (guilt), which hinders the salvation of sinners, has been

---

141. The Trinity—God the Father, God the Son, and God the Spirit—always work together in all ministries. They always cooperate with each other for all the works. However, before Jesus ascended into heaven and the Holy Spirit came upon the disciples, the forgiveness of sins by the word was led by the Father (John 15:1–4; 17:6–8, 17).

142. Here the Greek word for "clean" in John 15:3 (pure, clean; adjective: *katharos*, καθαρός) means "(to make) clean" in connection to "to (cut) clean" (to cut, prune, clean; verb: *kathairō*, καθαίρω) in John 15:2. These two words belong to the same word group with the sense of purity or cleanliness (BDAG 488–89; *EDNT* 2:217–20). From the perspective of repentance, we will explore John 15 in vol. 3, ch. 3.

"cut off and cleansed" by the words that Jesus has spoken (word, *logos*, λόγος).

Jesus compares the forgiveness of sins for salvation to the pruning branches by the Spirit with the word. This parable brings to mind Paul's word that the word of God is "the sword of the Spirit" (Eph 6:17).[143] Of course, there is a difference in expression between Paul and John. For Paul, the word is the sword of the Spirit used when we stand against the devil's schemes (Eph 6:17), whereas for John, the word is the sword of the Spirit used to cut off (remove) sinners' guilt of sin for their salvation (John 15: 3). It is worth noting, however, that these texts all refer to the word as the sword of the Spirit. The same interpretation also appears in the ministry of the Spirit's word in the lives of Christians as spoken in John 15:2.

Second, the Spirit cuts the branches of the sinful nature with the word so that Christians can bear fruit (the fruit of Christians [John 15:2]). The main point of John 15 is the life of a Christian bearing fruit. Thus, John 15:2 first talks about fruit, and 15:3 briefly mentions salvation in relation to it. Then it continues to speak about bearing fruit in John 15:4–17. The importance of the process of fruit bearing spoken directly by Jesus cannot be emphasized enough. We will now briefly examine the principle of fruit bearing starting from John 15:2.

> Every branch in me that does not bear fruit he takes away, and every branch that does bear fruit he prunes, that it may bear more fruit. (John 15:2)

Jesus first emphasizes that it is God who makes us bear fruit. However, while John 15:2 speaks from the perspective of God's sovereign work of grace, it is important to remember that John 15:4–17 focuses on our responsibility of our faith. In other words, God doesn't prune just any branch. There is a condition for God's pruning branches. That is, those who are saved (John 3:16; 15:3) must hold fast to (abide in) Jesus, the vine.

> Abide in me, and I in you. As the branch cannot bear fruit by itself, unless it abides in the vine, neither can you, unless you abide in me. I am the vine; you are the branches. Whoever

---

143. Ephesians 6:17 refers to the word as the sword of the Spirit, used in wrestling against the schemes of the devil. In Eph 5:26, "that he might sanctify her, having cleansed her by washing of water with the word," Paul uses the Greek verb for "to cleanse" (purify, cleanse, *katharizō*, καθαρίζω) (BDAG 488–89; *EDNT* 2:217).

> abides in me and I in him, he it is that bears much fruit, for apart from me you can do nothing. (John 15:4–5)

What must we do to stay attached to (abide in) the vine that is Jesus?

The problem here is that the vine used in the parable is visible to the eye, but Jesus is not. There is only one way to stay attached to (abide in) Jesus. We must stay attached to the word of God that is visible to our eyes. Jesus refers to staying attached to the word as "if my words abide in you" (John 15:7). In fact, John 15:7 also presents the most fundamental reason Christians should pray.

> If you abide in me, and my words [*logos*, λόγος] abide in you, ask whatever you wish, and it will be done for you. (John 15:7)

Therefore, in this text, Jesus equates being attached to the vine with *abiding in the word*. As we saw earlier, we can consider that after the word is implanted in the heart, one continues to stay attached to the word and comes under the rule of the word. Just as time is needed for a flower to bloom and bear fruit, time of patience in faith is needed to come under the rule of the word and bear fruit.

This means that the unique power of God's word (God's covenant lordship attributes, and the power of life, work, and judgment) will come into play only after the time of patience in faith. However, in order for Christians not to be discouraged during this period of patience and to go through this process well, they must pray (John 15:7). For only those who pray can bear the fruit of this word.

Now we can summarize the two characteristics of God's word and John 15:2–3, as we see in figure 1-L below. This figure is a recapitulation of how the Holy Spirit works in both our salvation and sanctification through the two characteristics of God's word, as seen in John 15:2–3. As we saw earlier, I have also organized this in connection with *The Kingdom of Justification* and *The Kingdom of Faith*.

Figure 1-L The Characteristics of God's Word and John 15:2-3

The Characteristics of God's Word	The Work of the Holy Spirit		Connectivity to John 15:2-3 and the Kingdom of God
The Covenant Lordship Attributes of God's Word	Heb 4:12	The Work of the Sovereign Grace of the Spirit	"Already you are clean because of the word [logos, λόγος] that I have spoken to you." (John 15:3)
		(justification, salvation)	**The Kingdom of Justification** John 1:12; 3:16; Rom 1:17, 3:21-22
Controlling power of God Authority of God Presence of God	Power of life Power to work Power of judgment	The Work of the Sovereign Grace of the Spirit and Christian Responsibility	"Every branch in me that does not bear fruit he takes away, and every branch that does bear fruit he prunes, that it may bear more fruit." (John 15:2)
		(sanctification: to imitate Jesus Christ, obedience, to live by faith)	**The Kingdom of Faith** Rom 1:17; Heb 11:6; Eph 4:23-24; Col 3:10

In summary, the Gospel of John teaches two important points that Christians should always remember for their lives.

1. The importance of God's word
2. The importance of the presence of the Holy Spirit

As we saw, it is the living God who has given Christians the word of life. For Christians, the word of God is God himself and Jesus (John 1:1-2, 14). After Jesus completed the work of redemption, rose, and ascended into heaven, the Holy Spirit dwells in us as Jesus (John 14:16, 20, 23; 15:4-7). Therefore, for Christians, in this sense, the Holy Spirit is Jesus. When Christians encounter the word of God, they must encounter the invisible God through faith in Jesus.

The relationship between the word of God and the work of the Holy Spirit is that the Gospel of John reveals to us is something we must understand. This relationship explains the biggest reason we need to pray (John 15:7).

> If you abide in me, and my words [logos, λόγος] abide in you, ask whatever you wish, and it will be done for you. (John 15:7)

As we have seen so far, it takes time to bear the fruit of God's word. In other words, we need patience in faith to bear the fruit of the word. If we endure with faith, the Spirit does everything that God has promised through his word.[144]

During this period of patience in faith, the Holy Spirit is the One who is pleased to help us to *abide* in the word of God. The Spirit (John 14:18, 20, 23; 15:7; 16:13) is the One who continues to supply us with life through the word of God (John 1:4; 3:8; 5:24, 26, 29; 6:33, 35, 48, 51, 63; 7:39; 8:12; 10:10; 11:25; 14:6, 26; 20:31; cf. Ps 1, 23). The Spirit is the great One who enables us to encounter the invisible God when we encounter the word of God.[145]

Therefore, the life that fulfills the purpose of God's word given to us is a life that bears the fruit of the word in Jesus (the Spirit). And the most important thing in bearing fruit is our attitude and action toward God's word and Jesus (the Spirit). In other words, when we encounter God's word, we must obey it as encountering God and Jesus (the Holy Spirit) Himself. This is because the fruit of God's word is produced when we see, hear, speak, think, and live according to the word in Jesus (the Spirit).

> See, hear, speak, think, and live according to the word in Jesus (the Spirit)!

C. Paul and the Work of God's Word

The work of the Holy Spirit in Christians through God's word is extensively recorded in the book of Acts. The book testifies to us that the Holy Spirit is the One who is still at work within us for justification and sanctification. Of course, the writer also tells us that our lifelong process after becoming a new self in Jesus can be different.

Acts contains many incidents that illustrate this. There are many examples in the book, but as we conclude the first volume, *The Kingdom of the Covenant*, we will take a brief look at Paul's life.

a. Paul's Story

The road to Damascus–event where the apostle Paul met Jesus was a moment when his theology of the law transformed into a theology of grace.

---

144. Frame, *Doctrine of God*, 470–75.

145. We will discuss the reasons why we obey God's word in "iii. Why Obey the Word of God?" under "1-B-b. God's Word and Obedience," in vol. 3, ch. 3.

This incident well illustrates the presence and control of the gospel word that came to Paul. The story of Paul the apostle tells us that Paul, like us, lived with the same human nature, body, and problems. The work of the word that happened to Paul didn't happen only to him. Although the aspects of the work of the word may vary among individuals, the same work can be manifested in us to achieve the purpose for which God has given us his word.

b. Paul's False Assurance of the Word

Paul had knowledge of the Old Testament Messiah. However, for Paul, an expert on the Old Testament, the knowledge of the Old Testament Messiah did not become a word of assurance for a time. Paul's misperception of the Messiah put him in conflict with the shocking words about the Messiah on the road to Damascus (Acts 9:3–5). It must have been the most shocking event of his life. Until then, he had been persecuting Jesus and the Christians with deep conviction in the Old Testament. Paul firmly believed that he was doing God's work. However, his persecution of the Christians stemmed from a mistaken conviction about the Messiah.

Then one day, the word of the gospel came to Paul. In fact, Scripture indicates that when the word of the gospel reached him, his reaction was one of tremendous shock. On the one hand, it was a day of great upheaval for Paul, but on the other hand, it was the day of the greatest blessing because it marked the beginning of the tremendous blessing of Jesus in his life. It was the moment he became a new person (self) by the grace of God (Eph 2:15; 4:24; Col 3:10). On that day, Paul's understanding of the Messiah began to change.

> Now as he went on his way, he approached Damascus, and suddenly a light from heaven shone around him. And falling to the ground, he heard a voice saying to him, "Saul, Saul, why are you persecuting me?" And he said, "Who are you, Lord?" And he said, "I am Jesus, whom you are persecuting." (Acts 9:3–5)

c. Paul and Ananias

A big shock from the word of God can come as a blessing of thought change for anyone. For Paul, this shock was the word of the gospel. Like Paul, the word of God can come as a great shock to us. God commanded

Ananias to go find Saul (Paul), who was praying and unable to see due to the great shock (Acts 9:10–12). The word of obedience, "Go to Paul," came to Ananias, who was already being ruled by the word of the gospel (the word of assurance).

> And the Lord said to him, "Rise and go to the street called Straight, and at the house of Judas look for a man of Tarsus named Saul, for behold, he is praying, and he has seen in a vision a man named Ananias come in and lay his hands on him so that he might regain his sight." But Ananias answered, "Lord, I have heard from many about this man, how much evil he has done to your saints at Jerusalem. And here he has authority from the chief priests to bind all who call on your name." (Acts 9:11–14)

If the gospel word came as a shock to Paul, the word of obedience came as a shock to Ananias. Ananias already knew about Paul's wrongdoings. Ananias conflicted with God's word by referring to the rumors about Saul (Paul), "how much evil he has done to your saints" (Acts 9:13). Obviously, Ananias already knew about Paul's evil deeds.

However, Ananias accepted the authority of the word through the work of the Holy Spirit and, in obedience to the word, went to Paul. By Ananias's obedience, Paul could receive the presence of the word of God and be filled with the Spirit. He recovered his sight again and was baptized. Through this analysis, we should remember that it was the result of Ananias's decision to obey. Ananias's obedience was a great blessing to Paul.

> So Ananias departed and entered the house. And laying his hands on him he said, "Brother Saul, the Lord Jesus who appeared to you on the road by which you came has sent me so that you may regain your sight and be filled with the Holy Spirit." And immediately something like scales fell from his eyes, and he regained his sight. Then he rose and was baptized. (Acts 9:17–18)

This also can happen to us when we act according to the word of obedience. Paul's story is a good example of what to do when our thoughts conflict with the word of assurance or the word of obedience. When we obey the word with the help of the Holy Spirit, our neighbors can receive God's blessings just like Paul did.

Paul, whose thoughts about the Old Testament Messiah changed, became a person who testified "Jesus is the Christ" (Acts 9:22) and boldly preached the gospel "in the name of the Lord Jesus" (Acts 9:28).

Amazingly, he became a person sharing the greatest blessing on earth. This, of course, is entirely a work of God's grace alone.

But we should remember that Paul continued to obey the word even after this conversion event. Paul then continued to do missionary work according to the word and came to know the Holy Spirit, who enabled him to bear the fruit of the word through missionary endeavors. He continued to fulfill God's call to evangelism and missions.[146]

d. Paul and the Work of the Word After the Road to Damascus-Event

For Paul, the encounter with the word (Jesus) of the gospel (assurance) changed his thoughts and life. This word of assurance made Paul know Jesus. That is, the work of the word of life saved Paul through the work of the Spirit. When the word came to Paul through the work of the Spirit, he accepted the authority of the word, believed it, and obeyed it.

After realizing this principle of faith, Paul did not stop there. He became a minister of the church, living a life fulfilling the word of God given to him for the church. This work of the word can also happen to all of us.

> Now I rejoice in my sufferings for your sake, and in my flesh I am filling up what is lacking in Christ's afflictions for the sake of his body, that is, the church, of which I became a minister according to the stewardship from God that was given to me for you, to make the word of God fully known. (Col 1:24-25)

The Holy Spirit used Paul as a minister of the church for the ministry of God's word. And Paul continued to teach the gospel and the life ruled by the word through his epistles of the New Testament. The Spirit still uses Paul's epistles, in which his understandings are revealed.

Paul's interpretation of the Old Testament and Jesus' words is a great help to us. For example, his epistles like Romans and Galatians connect and explain the Old Testament covenants and the new covenant Mediator, Jesus Christ. Paul is not arguing philosophical ideas or theories, but explaining the preparations God the Father made to save us through Jesus Christ, and how the words of the covenants have been fulfilled.

---

146. Acts 9-28 primarily tells the story that the Holy Spirit continued to establish churches through the ministry of Peter and Paul.

Not only that, but the word of the covenant was also fulfilled in Paul's own life. For this reason, as God's servant, Paul experienced the love of Christ (Phil 1:9, 16; 2:1; 4:8), the word of life (Phil 2:16), and that the Spirit is the One who gives power (Phil 4:13) according to the word of God (Phil 4:8–9).

Paul was a man who learned, received, heard, saw, and also acted according to the word in various situations (Phil 4:8). Thus, Paul was able to meet the God of peace (Phil 4:9) through the work of the word given by the Spirit and give thanks to God with joy (Phil 4:4). This shows that in Paul's life the purpose of God's word given to him was fulfilled through the work of the word (Col 1:24–25). We can live like Paul.

Paul clearly explains to us "why the word of God is important and why the coming of Jesus Christ is important." He clearly states why the presence of the Holy Spirit is important. Paul's main point in all his epistles is to hear the voice of our Heavenly Father's love through the word of the living God in the Bible. He urges us to listen and obey the word of God.

Paul's conclusion is no different than that of John's we saw earlier.

See, hear, speak, think, and live according to the word in Jesus (the Holy Spirit)!

5

Conclusion: God's Word Is the Most Important

GOD CREATED HUMANS IN his image and wanted to establish the kingdom of God. There is something we need to know about this kingdom that God has established. Scripture teaches that God has established this everlasting kingdom on the foundation of the eternal righteousness of God. This righteousness of God revealed in the Bible becomes the legal basis of God's kingdom. That is, God's righteousness becomes the legal standard that governs God's kingdom, the standard of salvation and judgment, and the standard of the good life for citizens of God's everlasting kingdom.

God's eternal righteousness gives us a glimpse of his holiness and goodness. Therefore, if you want to know God's righteousness, you must look to the word of God's covenant, which is revealed in the Bible as God's law. For God has given us humans his word, a word that never fails us.

The next important thing to know is the meaning of God's word as revealed in the Gospel of John. Scripture says that the word of God is God (John 1:1–2).

Why does John call the word of God, God?

The word of God is called God in the Gospel of John because the word of God is actually the most important thing in our lives. More importantly, the word of God is called God because God has given the covenant lordship (sovereign) attributes of God to the word of God. As we saw, God has endowed the word with the three major covenant lordship (sovereign) attributes of control (controlling power), authority, and presence. Of equal importance is also the fact that God has endowed God's word with the power of life, work, and judgment (Heb 4:12–13). Just as God's righteousness is eternal, so the word of God is eternal.

Why has God given the word the covenant lordship attributes and the power of life, work, and judgment?

God has given the characteristics of God (his own attributes) to his word because he has a special purpose for humankind. Note that we have no way to encounter the invisible God. The only way to meet God is through the word of God. God's word is the only authoritative representative with his full authority in his place on earth. Therefore, God wants us to encounter the living God every time we encounter the word of God.

The whole Bible story is not just a simple story of success and failure. But the Bible is full of stories of encountering the living God through the word of God. We should note that in the Bible, God works through his word in the lives of many people.

For this reason, God gave the Mosaic law in the Old Testament so that the Israelites could encounter him. The reason God has given the word of the gospel in the New Testament is also to meet with sinners. When sinners encounter the word of the gospel, they can meet Jesus. That is, the Holy Spirit gives life to those who are dead in sin and revives them through the word of the gospel (Rom 1:17; 2 Pet 1:3). The Spirit gives sinners faith through the word of the gospel to become children of God. The Spirit enables us to encounter the love of Jesus through the gospel. This is the most important reason God's word is called God himself (John 1:1–2, 14).

Therefore, we must treat the word of God as we would treat God himself, for whoever ignores God's word ignores God. Also, whoever encounters the word of the gospel by faith in Jesus encounters Jesus by the work of the Spirit. The Holy Spirit orchestrates these encounters through the word of God by faith alone.

The most important work of the Spirit is to fulfill the purpose of God's word given to us. The Spirit leads God's children to have conversation with God to let them know the love of God the Father. Especially, the Spirit helps us to have communication between God the Father and his children through God's word. This communication begins with an encounter with God's word in Jesus.

When we encounter God through his word, the presence of the word of God manifests as the personal presence of the living God. Through this encounter with God's word, God's children begin to change their thoughts and actions. The Holy Spirit is the subject of the presence of God's word and all the works that follow it.

Christians who accept the word of God as God gradually make the word of God the standard of truth in all areas of life. For them, the word of God becomes the standard for wisdom, knowledge, judgment, and action. God's children can grow through this process of encountering God's words in Jesus. The Holy Spirit rules us, educates us, trains us, and helps us grow (2 Tim 3:16–17) with the righteous, holy, and good word (Rom 7:12). The Spirit is the One who can fulfill the purpose for which God gave his word in the lives of God's children.

Therefore, we should remember that when we encounter the living word, we can encounter the living God. We must remember that the Spirit, through the living word, enables us to fight and overcome the temptations of the world and the habits of our sinful nature.

We also need to remember that we have work to do in order to fulfill the purpose for which God has given his word. Every time we encounter the word of God, we must continually meet him through prayer by faith in Jesus and with the help of the Spirit. We must live each day by grace alone, by Scripture alone (*sola Scriptura*), with the help of the Holy Spirit alone, and by faith alone.

In conclusion, we must always remember the importance of God's word and the presence of the Holy Spirit working within us. The Spirit works in us through the eternal word. The Spirit works in us when we believe in Jesus, hold onto the word, believe in the word, and pray. The Spirit also works in our lives as we believe in the promises of the word and fulfill the purposes for which God has given the word. Whatever we do according to the eternal word of God has eternal value, because the Bible contains many of God's covenant promises. For example, by believing in Jesus, the Spirit conforms us to the image of Jesus through God's word.

> For those whom he foreknew he also predestined to be conformed to the image of his Son, in order that he might be the firstborn among many brothers. (Rom 8:29)

Once the word of God starts to work within you, you will come to realize that no one loves you more than God. Learning to love God and encouraging yourself with the word, by the word, and through the word is a lifelong process. You will come to realize that there is no one who wants you to be conformed to the image of God more than God.

In other words, you deeply understand how precious God is to you. The Holy Spirit works within you through the word of God.

No one is more important to us than God!

No one is more important to us than Jesus!

No one is more important to us than the Holy Spirit!

Therefore, there is nothing more important to us than the word of God!

Bibliography

Bavinck, Herman. *Our Reasonable Faith: A Survey of Christian Doctrine*. Translated by Henry Zylstra. Grand Rapids: Eerdmans, 1975.
———. *Reformed Dogmatics*. Edited by John Bolt. Translated by John Vriend. 4 vols. Grand Rapids: Baker Academic, 2003–8.
Berkhof, Louis. *Systematic Theology*. Grand Rapids: Eerdmans, 1996.
Calvin, John. *Commentary on the Epistle of Paul to the Corinthians*. Grand Rapids: Baker, 1989.
———. *Commentary on the Epistle of Paul to the Romans*. Grand Rapids: Baker, 1989.
Carson, D. A. *Divine Sovereignty and Human Responsibility: Biblical Perspective in Tension*. Eugene, OR: Wipf & Stock, 1994.
Christian Reformed Church. *Ecumenical Creeds and Reformed Confessions*. Grand Rapids: CRC, 1988.
Crowe, Brandon. *The Last Adam: A Theology of Obedient Life of Jesus in the Gospels*. Grand Rapids: Baker Academic, 2017.
Fesko, J. V. *The Trinity and the Covenant of Redemption*. Fearn, Scot.: Mentor, 2016.
Frame, John M. *Apologetics*. Phillipsburg, NJ: P&R, 2015.
———. *The Doctrine of God*. Phillipsburg, NJ: P&R, 2002.
———. *The Doctrine of the Christian Life*. Phillipsburg, NJ: P&R, 2008.
———. *The Doctrine of the Knowledge of God*. Phillipsburg, NJ: P&R, 1987.
———. *The Doctrine of the Word of God*. Phillipsburg, NJ: P&R, 2010.
———. *Salvation Belongs to the Lord: An Introduction to Systematic Theology*. Phillipsburg, NJ: P&R, 2006.
———. *Systematic Theology: An Introduction to Christian Belief*. Phillipsburg, NJ: P&R, 2013.
Hendriksen, William. *More Than Conquerors: An Interpretation of the Book of Revelation*. Grand Rapids: Baker, 1990.
Hoekema, Anthony A. *The Bible and the Future*. Grand Rapids: Eerdmans, 1979.
———. *Created in God's Image*. Grand Rapids: Eerdmans, 1986.
———. *Saved by Grace*. Grand Rapids: Eerdmans, 1989.
Horton, Michael. *Covenant and Salvation: Union with Christ*. Louisville: Westminster John Knox, 2007.
———. *Introducing Covenant Theology*. Grand Rapids: Baker, 2006.
———. *Justification*. 2 vols. Grand Rapids: Zondervan, 2018.

Irons, Charles Lee. "Kline on the Works Principle in the Mosaic Economy: An Exposition." Upper Register, Apr. 25, 2015. http://www.upper-register.com/papers/works-principle-mosaic-economy-exposition.pdf.

Johnson, Gary L. W., and Guy P. Waters. *By Faith Alone*. Wheaton, IL; Crossway, 2007.

Kang, Paul ChulHong. *Justification: The Imputation of Christ's Righteousness from Reformation Theology to the American Great Awakening and the Korean Revivals*. New York: Lang, 2006.

———. *Living Out the Gospel*. Seoul: Christian Literature Center, 2015.

Kline, Meredith G. *Images of the Spirit*. N.p.: Kline, 1986.

———. *Kingdom Prologue*. Eugene, OR: Wipf & Stock, 2006.

———. *The Structure of Biblical Authority*. N.p.: Kline, 1989.

Luther, Martin. *The Bondage of the Will*. Translated by J. I. Packer and O. R. Robinson. Grand Rapids: Revell, 1997.

———. *Commentary on Galatians: Modern English Version*. Grand Rapids: Revell, 1999.

Mangum, Douglas, et al., eds. *Lexham Theological Wordbook*. Lexham Bible Reference Series. Bellingham, WA: Lexham, 2014. Digital Logos ed.

McGrath, Alister. *Iustitia Dei: A History of the Christian Doctrine of Justification*. 3rd ed. New York: Cambridge University Press, 2005.

———. *Justification by Faith*. Grand Rapids: Academie, 1990.

Muller, Richard A. *Dictionary of Latin and Greek Theological Terms*. Grand Rapids: Baker, 1985.

Murray, John. *Collected Writings of John Murray*. 4 vols. Carlisle, PA: Banner of Truth Trust, 1982.

———. *The Epistle to the Romans*. Grand Rapids: Eerdmans, 1968.

Ridderbos, Herman. *The Coming of the Kingdom*. Philadelphia: P&R, 1962.

———. *Paul: An Outline of His Theology*. Grand Rapids: Eerdmans, 1984.

Sandel, Michael J. *Justice: What's the Right Thing to Do?* New York: Farrar, Straus & Giroux, 2009.

Schreiner, Thomas. *Faith Alone: The Doctrine of Justification*. Grand Rapids: Zondervan, 2015.

Sproul, R. C. *Justified by Faith Alone*. Wheaton, IL: Crossway, 2010.

Swanson, James, ed. *A Dictionary of Biblical Languages with Semantic Domains: Greek (NT)*. Oak Harbor, WA: Logos, 1997. Digital Logos ed.

———. *A Dictionary of Biblical Languages with Semantic Domains: Hebrew (OT)*. Oak Harbor: Logos, 1997.

Thiselton, Anthony C. *The Hermeneutics of Doctrine*. Grand Rapids: Eerdmans, 2015.

Vos, Gerhardus. *Biblical Theology: Old and New Testaments*. Grand Rapids: Eerdmans, 1948.

———. *The Pauline Eschatology*. Phillipsburg, NJ: P&R, 1991.

———. *Redemptive History and Biblical Interpretation: The Shorter Writings of Gerhardus Vos*. Edited by Richard B. Gaffin Jr. Phillipsburg, NJ: P&R, 1980.

Westminster Assembly. *The Westminster Confession of Faith*. Edinburgh ed. Philadelphia: Young, 1851.

Subject Index

ability, 64, 151
  human, 46
  intellectual, 141, 145
  of judgment, 125 (word)
  of knowing God's wisdom, 142
  moral, 47
  of obedience, 152
  of presence, 14 (Jesus), 90 (word)
  rational, 47
Abraham, 55
  and covenant. See Abrahamic covenant
  descendants of, 53 (great nation), 55
  and eternal blessing, 169
  faith of, 50n79, 55
  as father of faith, 54–56
  gospel to, 93
  for great nation, 53, 56
  and justification, 38n41, 50n79, 54–55, 93
  justified by faith, 56
  justified by work, 55
  and lineage to Jesus, 54, 71n137
  obedience of, 168–169
  offspring of, 56 (Messiah), 67
  saved by God's grace, 53–55
Abrahamic covenant (53–57), 36n38, 54–55
  and covenant of grace. See covenant of grace
  by grace alone, 53
  and Messiah, 54
  requirement of obedience, 57

Adam
  as covenant breaker, 39, 62n114, 83
  creation of, 41, 43
  disobedience of, 40, 46, 62n114, 82
  fall of, 5, 33, 35, 37, 40–41, 45, 49, 61n112, 70, 82, 88n33, 95, 140, 145, 152
  and marred image. See image of God
  office, 40–41, 40n48
  representative (all human kind), 5, 38, 40, 44–45, 47n74, 49, 54, 62n114, 83
  sin of, xi, 45, 47n74, 83, 85, 39n43, 45, 45n62, 46, 62n114, 82n21, 140
  and tree of knowledge of good and evil, 35, 44, 88
Adamic covenant (38–49), 53, 55–57, 59n104, 65, 67, 70–71
  biblical reference of, 38n41 (Hos 6:7)
  continuity of, 68
  and covenant of grace. See covenant of grace
  and covenant of works. See covenant of works
  and cultural mandate. See cultural mandate
  and first gospel, 48–49
  and image of God. See image of God
  and judging righteousness. See judging righteousness
  and Messiah. See Jesus Christ

Adamic covenant (continued)
  offspring in, 67
  and origin of sin. *See* original sin
  as post-fall covenant, 44–45,
    61n112
  as pre-fall covenant, 40–44
  and tree of the knowledge of good
    and evil, 44, 88
age to come, 9, 12, 15
alien righteousness, 93
already and not yet, 9, 9n17, 10, 10n22
amillennialism, 10n22
Ananias, 183–84
apostles, 17, 102
application, 102, 104n13, 171
Aristotle, 43n55, 99n66
assurance, 156–64
  of faith, xx, 23, 107, 115, 132, 158,
    160, 172–74
  false, 183
  of God's promises, 109
  of grace, 95
  of justification, 95
  of love, 95
  of salvation, 4, 95, 109
  of word, 110
  words of, 157–59 (trust), 160–62,
    164, 167–68, 170, 174, 177,
    183–85
atonement, xii, 8, 160
authority, 111, 116, 124, 152, 176, 181,
  184–85, 187–88
  Adam as king, 40, 40n48, 41
  of Bible, xi, 109
  of God, 13n29
  of God's children, 41n51
  of God's righteousness, 95, 145; *see
    also* God's righteousness
  of God's work, 133
  of gospel, 109, 185
  of Jesus, 13–14, 133–34, 166
  of Scripture, 108
  of word of God. *See* word of God
authority (word: 107–11), 116, 187
  of Bible, 145
  as eternal authority, 109
  as highest (legal) authority, 108–10,
    117, 133–34, 152
  as highest sovereign authority, 107–8
  as supreme authority, 108, 110
autonomy, 104n14, 133

Babel, 53
baptism, 50–51
  of believers, 50
  and flood judgment, 50
  of Jesus, 50
  Peter (1 Pet 3:20–22), 51
  as sign and seal, 50
  and union with Christ, 51 (flood)
Bavinck, Herman, 42n54, 42n55,
  44n59, 46n70, 91n36, 163n128
  on covenant of grace, 39n43
  on covenant of works, 39n43
  on human creation (pre-fall), 44n59
beauty, ix
belief, xxii, 10, 20
Bible. *See* Scripture
biblical theology, 9
blessing(s), xi, xiii, 11, 24, 69, 107, 132,
  166, 183–85
  in Adam, 41
  of application, 151
  as benefits, 147, 163
  eternal blessing. *See* eternal blessing
  of faith, 95
  of forgiveness, 68
  of freedom, 152
  of gospel, 33, 150
  obedience to word of, 25–26, 41,
    124, 167
  of promise, 57, 106, 170
  of salvation, 107
  of the righteous, 11
  for world, 16
blessings and curses, 57, 59n104, 61,
  61n112, 73, 165
blood covenant, 29n11, 36, 36n37, 37,
  57n99, 65, 72
breath, 163n128
bride
  and eternal kingdom of God, 19
    (victorious church)
  image of, 19
  by Christ alone
    justification, 49, 51

SUBJECT INDEX

by grace alone (*sola gratia*), 69, 189
  Abraham, 54
  gospel, 73
  justification, 22, 33, 37, 43n58, 55, 71, 167
  salvation, 53, 71
by faith alone, 151, 189
  Abraham, 54
  and Holy Spirit, 188
  justification, 66, 69, 74, 93
  and kingdom of God, 7n11, 22
by Scripture alone (*sola Scriptura*), 152, 189

calling, 55 (Abraham)
Calvin, John, 61n110, 73n142, 93n42, 94n44, 98n64
  on covenant of grace, 35n36 (unity)
Carson, D.A., 135n98 (Jesus: prototype)
change, xxi, 146, 149, 173, 178, 183, 188
  of heart, 127
  judgment standard of, 149, 162
  in status, 74
  of thinking(thought), 162, 162n127, 163, 183 (Paul)
characteristics of God's words (103–30); *see also* power of life, power of work, and power of judgment
Christ. *See* perfect obedience
Christian life, 26, 73, 73n142, 173–75
  beginning of, 174, 177
  and eschatology, 9–12
  growth of, xi
  and image of God, xi
  obedience of, 173
  as the righteous, 51
  word for, 109
Christian worldview, 132
church, 16–20, 17n44, 159, 185
  as bride, 19
  and Christian life, 20
  as God's covenant people, 17
  as greatest blessings, 16
  as greatest hope, 16
  head (Jesus Christ) of, 16
  and Holy Spirit, 20
  as kingdom of God, 16–20, 16 (identical in Jesus)
  as one in Jesus Christ, 17
  as people of God in all ages, 17
  in Revelation, 18–19
  as solution to marred image, 159
  victorious, 18–20, 19 (eternal victory)
  worship in, 20
circumcision, 57n99
common goodness (ethical goodness), 47
common grace, 46, 73n142
control (word: controlling power, 105–7), 116, 154, 187
  of blessings, 107
  of keeping God's promises, 106
  of salvation, 106
  of transformation, 107
  of world, 106
conversion, 151, 185
corruption, 102n3
  result of, 46n69
  in whole person, 46n69
covenant (27–75)
  Abrahamic covenant. *See* Abrahamic covenant
  Adamic covenant. *See* Adamic covenant
  covenant of grace. *See* covenant of grace
  covenant of redemption. *See* covenant of redemption
  Davidic covenant. *See* Davidic covenant
  Mosaic covenant. *See* Mosaic covenant
  Noahic covenant. *See* Noahic covenant
  party of, 27, 35
  and Trinity, 31–33
  word of covenant, 53
covenant breaker, 39, 62n114, 83
covenant faithfulness, 44
covenant keepers, 40 (in Jesus), 143 (as new self)
covenant of grace (33–38), 31–32, 34, 40n46

covenant of grace (continued)
    and Abrahamic covenant, 36n38,
        54n92, 55–57, 68 , 70
    and Adamic covenant, 57, 68, 70
    in Bible's story, 38
    conditions of, 35
    continuity of, 35, 35n36, 36
    and Davidic covenant, 57, 66,
        68–69
    definition of, 33
    as external covenant, 33
    fulfilment of, 33, 71
    and God's eternal decree, 44
    in human history, 33
    in human salvation, 34
    and Jesus Christ, 33, 159
    and justification, 34, 37
    and Mosaic covenant, 65–66, 68, 70
    and Noahic covenant, 49–50, 53, 68
    and redemptive work, 24
    and salvation, 35, 39n43
    unity of, 35n36, 37–38
covenant of nature, 38n41 (Adamic
    covenant)
covenant of nature preservation, 52
    (Noahic covenant)
covenant of redemption, 30, 31, 31n18,
    33, 39n42, 67
    definition of, 31
    and God's eternal decree, 33
    in human history, 32, 33
    as internal covenant, 33
    and Jesus Christ, 32, 33, 39n43
    Mediator of, 66
    and new covenant, 70
    and redemptive history, 32
    Trinitarian, 32, 33
    and union with Christ, 46n68
covenant of works, 61n112
    and Adamic covenant, 39, 39n43,
        61n112
    and Adam's disobedience to,
        61n112
    Bavinck on, 39n43
    and Mosaic covenant, 61n112
    and original sin, 39n43
    and pre-fall, 40n46
    WCF on, 38n41

covenant promises, 57, 72, 189
creation, xvii, 29–31, 33, 52, 52n88,
    105, 130, 132, 155
    of Adam, 41, 43
    before creation, 31
    God's image in, 5
    God's purpose of. 41–42. 70
    heavens and earth, 105, 132
    human creation, 5, 35, 42
    and plan of salvation, 31
    redemption before, 32–33, 39n42
cross, xi, 37, 71, 81n20, 86, 89, 92, 139
    as eternal atonement, 160
    fulfillment of, 152
    and perfect obedience. *See* perfect
        obedience
    as punishment, xx
    and resurrection, 13
cultural mandate, 41 (Adam), 41n49,
    51 (Noah)
curse, 45
    on all humanity, 45
    as promise to Abraham, 169
    and sin, 24
curses
    for Adam's disobedience, 62n114
    for disobedience, 57, 59n104, 61,
        61n112, 73n142, 85
    of Israel, 165
    for sin, 66

Damascus
    Paul, 151, 182–183
David
    assurance of faith in, 158
    descendant of, 68n127, 69
    and forgiveness of sins, 68–69
    God as the Good Shepherd, 158
    God as rock, 158–59
    and justified, 69
    as king, 66–67
    promises to, 69
    and redemptive history, 132
    as soldier, 157
    words of assurance in, 157–58,
        158n123
Davidic covenant, 66–70
    and Abrahamic covenant, 67, 71

SUBJECT INDEX

and Adamic covenant, 67–69, 71
and covenant of grace. *See* covenant
 of grace
and covenant of redemption, 67
and everlasting covenant, 68
and fulfilment, 68
and King, 68, 68, 85
and Messiah, 66–68
and Mosaic covenant, 59, 67, 69,
 71, 85
and new covenant. *See* new
 covenant
and Noahic covenant, 68, 71
and obedience of faith, 69
dead soul, 119–20
death, xix, 19, 32
 and Adam's sin, 45
 and blood covenant, 36n37, 37
 and Jesus, 160–161, 174
 and life, 119, 121n66
 and perfect obedience, 63, 65
 and punishment, 83
 and resurrection, 13, 50–51
Decalogue (Ten Commandments), 10, 61
 and moral law, 61
 and Mosaic law, 61
 and sacrificial law, 61
 and social law, 61
 summary of, 64
disobedience, 39, 59n104, 82, 121, 153
 of Adam. *See* Adam
 and curses, 61, 61n112, 73, 85
 and penalty, 71
diversity
 unity in, xii, xiin1, 30, 42, 73, 138, 167

Enlightenment, xii
eternal blessing, 24, 35, 68, 107, 169
eschatology, 9, 10n22, 11, 11n22
 personal eschatology, 11
eternal life, 6–7, 87n31, 119
 and beginning of wisdom, 138, 142
 and fulfillment, 39n43
 and good deeds, 95n50
 and gospel, 21
 and kingdom of God, 7, 7n11, 19,
  21, 39n43
 and knowing Jesus, 137–38

and promise, 39
and resurrection, 121
and salvation, 7n11, 39n43, 143
eternal value
 of belief, xxii
 of eternal word, 189
 of faith, 3, 12
 fruit of, 11
 of Jesus' redemptive work, 3
 of obedience, 12, 24
 of present reality, xx
eternity
 God's eternity. *See* God's eternity
 of gospel, 23
 of kingdom of God, 9, 21
 of salvation, 154
ethical goodness (common goodness),
 47
Eve, 84
evil
 and Adam's fall, 35
 and all human beings, 48
 evil deeds, 165, 184
 evil hearts, 51
 evil sins, 64
 evil works, 165
 in Noah's time, 50
 standard of, 28, 77, 165
 of world, 47, 51
external actions, 61, 63

faith
 content of faith, xxi (God's word)
 fruit of, xxi-xxii, 112, 114
 obedience of, 3, 110, 117
 object of, xxi (Jesus Christ)
 response of, xxii, 3, 110, 117, 126,
  164
false knowledge, 147
family of God, 75
fear of God, 85
feelings, 149, 173
first gospel, 48–49 (Gen 3:15)
flesh, 69, 99, 113n47
 of Jesus Christ, 115
 as sinful nature, 48
 word of becoming, 120

fall, xviii, 5, 29, 33–37, 40–42, 44–49,
    51, 82, 101, 132, 145, 163
  of Adam, 5, 33–37, 40–41, 44–49,
    46n69, 70, 82, 88n33, 95, 140,
    145, 149, 152, 163
  and image of God, 42
  of Israelites, 38n41
  pre-fall, 40, 40n46, 44, 48, 61n112
false truths, 147
forgiveness of sins, 72, 150, 160,
    178n141, 179
  as blessing, 68
  as eternal blessings, 107
  for God's children, 87
  gospel as, xi
  by Jesus Christ alone, 65
  and salvation, 160
Frame, John, 30n13
  on covenant lordship attributes
    (103–16), 104n13
  on God's attributes, 80n13
  on God's righteousness, 80n13,
    84n27
freedom, 73, 99, 132, 147–48
  as benefit (blessing), 148, 152
  from false truth, 147
  from guilt, 178
  Sandel on, 84n28
  from (of) sin, 74, 132, 142
Fulfiller
  of all covenants, 66, 159
  of covenant, 159
  of new covenant, 75, 135
future, xvii, 10, 72, 133

genealogy
  of Jesus, 41n51, 68n127
  of Messiah, 52–53
gift of grace, 6
glory, 25–26
glory of God, 41, 41n51, 75
God
  as attributes of, xix, 3–4, 28 (word),
    73, 76 (righteousness), 80n13,
    96–97, 103–118, 124, 130, 132,
    136, 148, 154, 175–76, 180–81,
    187–88
  eternity of, xviii, 3–4, 12, 73

  ethical character of, 98
  as Father, 118 (living Father),
    122n71, 135, 148, 154, 176, 178,
    178n141, 185, 188 (love of)
  faithfulness of, 44, 73, 103
  goodness of, ix, 80, 80n13, 96n52,
    96, 104, 136, 187
  grace of. See God's grace
  holiness of, 80, 80n13
    (righteousness), 98 (ethical
    character)
  of Immanuel, 176
  immutability of, 73
  as Judge, 22, 49, 78–79, 78n3,
    124–25
  justice of (87–89), 28, 77, 87
  knowledge of. See God's knowledge
  as Legislator, 79
  Lordship attributes of (104–18); see
    also Lordship attributes
  love of. See God's love
  omnipotence of, 103, 105
  omniscience of, 105
  perfection of, 103
  promises of, 4–5 (word), 68n127,
    75 (fulfilment of), 101 (word),
    109 (word), 123, 129, 155, 168
  providence of, xi, xx, 33, 104 (in
    history), 105 (control of), 128
    (word), 169 (word)
  righteousness of. See God's
    righteousness
  sovereignty of, 69, 108
  Trinity. See Trinity
  wisdom of. See God's wisdom
  wrath of, 24, 47–48
God-man, 155
God's grace (87–89, 131–132), xix, xxii,
    33, 35, 74, 94–95, 128, 131, 153,
    162n127
  and Abrahamic covenant, 53–54
  and Adamic covenant, 48, 70
  and covenant of. See covenant of
    grace
  and covenants, 39n43
  and forgiveness, 69
  and God's kingdom, xviii, 5, 10
  and gospel, 160

SUBJECT INDEX

and Holy Spirit, 24–25, 127, 134–35, 145
and human creation, 5
and human history, 132
and Israelites, 65
and justification, 55, 66, 69, 74, 93–94, 96, 121, 151, 167
and Mosaic covenant, 57
and Mosaic law, 63, 70, 166
and new covenant, 73, 133
and Noahic covenant, 50, 53
and our faith, 9, 177
and our obedience, 29, 74, 169, 177
and our righteousness, 91 (in Jesus), 92, 96
and Paul, 185
and redemptive history, 134
and redemptive work, 134
and righteousness, 139
and sanctification, 74, 106
and salvation, 5, 7n11, 33, 66, 69, 93–94, 102, 106, 121, 127, 133, 160, 167
and wisdom, 139
God's knowledge, 102, 104
as divine attribute, 136
path for, 140
as restored, 140–41
God's love, ix, xiii, 4, 95
abide in, 172
in Bible, 149
confession of, 174
faith in, 174
as God's ethical character, 95, 98
and Holy Spirit, 175
in Mosaic law, 64
in word, 104, 106
God's righteousness (justice: 76–100), xi-x, xix, 14, 49, 76–77, 79, 81, 84, 88, 92, 94–95, 98, 100–101, 104, 130, 187–88
as assurance of salvation, 4
of being word, 12, 79, 102, 107–8, 146
and Bible, 81, 145
concept of, 77, 77n3, 79, 79n10, 81n20, 92
in covenants, 78

as eternal, 4
as God's attributes, 3–4, 73, 76, 136
and God's covenants, 76
as God's ethical character, 98
and God's goodness, 80
and God's grace, 87, 89
and God's holiness, 80
and gospel, 87
and human efforts, 63
for innocent people, 78 (protect)
and Jesus, 91
Judge of, 79
and judging righteousness. See judging righteousness
and justification, 12, 92–95
in kingdom of God, 79
King of, 79
law of, 45
law of God's kingdom, 76
as means of salvation, 82
and Mosaic law, 45, 78–79, 87, 98
most important thing for humans, 80
nature of, 86
and perfect obedience, 49
and saving righteousness. See saving righteousness
as standard of a good life (95–100), 98–99
as standard for governance (legal standard: 77–81)
as standards of holiness and goodness, 146
as standard of judgment, 77
as standard of right and wrong, 83
as standard of salvation (81–95), 82, 89
as structure for goodness, 80, 80n13, 97–98
training in, 98
God's speech, 103
God's wisdom, 102, 102n3m
as attribute of, 36
in Bible, 136
greatness of, 42
growth in, 143
of Jesus, 140 (in believers)
Jesus as, 137

God's wisdom (continued)
    of knowing Jesus, 141
    and new self, 142
    as restored, 142
    and salvation, 139
good life
    highest, 99, 100
    in politics, 99n66
    standard for (95–100), 77; see also
        God's righteousness
goodness
    common goodness, 47
    ethical goodness, 47
    growth in, xxi
    highest goodness. See highest
        goodness
    as human, 96–97
    as image of God, xiii, 5, 42–44,
        43n58, 46, 46n69; see also image
        of God
    of Jesus, 97
    life of, 99
    marred goodness, 96n51
    standard of, 99, 146
gospel, 4, 87, 102, 109, 132, 139–40,
    183, 188
    and assurance, 160–61, 167
    authority of, 109
    as blessings, 150
    and covenant of redemption. See
        covenant of redemption
    and first gospel, 48, 84
    and freedom, 152
    and God's righteousness, 87
    as good news, 15
    by grace alone, 73
    of John, 105, 114, 159, 178, 181, 187
    and justification, 87–88, 161
    necessity of, 64
    and New Testament, 86
    and perfect obedience. See perfect
        obedience
    power of, 107, 122n71, 139, 144
    and restoration of identity, 155
    and the righteous, 129
    and salvation, 139
    of salvation, 109
    seed of, 163
    as word of, 23, 112–13, 115, 127,
        132, 142, 160–61, 163, 183–85
    as word of wisdom, 142
grace. See God's grace
grace and law, 59 (Mosaic covenant)
great blessing
    of ability to be transformed, 170
    of ability to obey word, 124
guilt
    and freedom from, 72, 178
    and Hoy Spirit, 178–79
    and pollution of sin, xx, 10, 45,
        47n74, 72, 83
    and price for, 23n69
    and responsibility for sin, 10, 83

habits
    sinful habits, 23n69
    of sinful nature, 189
heart, xiii, 37, 63n116, 125
    actions of, 45n63
    activities of, 126, 126n82
    Bavinck on, 44n59
    dwelling (presence) of word in,
        162, 168
    God's love in, 175
    as good heart, 112
    gospel word on, 112
    Hebrew and Greek of, 111n45, 126
    implanted word in, 180
    and Mosaic law, 62
    as new heart, 163n128
    sin in, 63n116, 64
    as temple, 175
    thoughts of, 47 (post-fall)
    word on, 111
hearts, 47, 98, 119, 125, 147–48, 172
    activities of, 125
    actual change of, xxi
    blessings of, 163
    change of, 127
    coming of kingdom of God to, 7, 21
    dwelling of Hoy Spirit in, 175
    dwelling (presence) of word in, 111,
        113, 115–16, 161, 170–71
    evil, 151
    freedom in, 148
    God's judgment on, 125–27

SUBJECT INDEX

and Holy Spirit, 127, 148, 161, 164, 166, 169, 174–75
new heart, 163
planted word in, 163
ruled by word, 162, 170–71
thoughts of, 83
work of God's word in, 171
Helper. *See* Holy Spirit
highest goodness, 98–99
history, 11n22, 19, 35, 104
  Christian, xix
  human, 15–16, 19, 28, 30–33, 35, 49, 53, 69–70, 107, 131–33
  of Israel, 58, 59n104, 65
  of kingdom of God, xviii, 17
    (present reality), 53
  providence in human, 33
  redemptive history. *See* redemptive history
holiness, xiii, xxi, 46n69, 97, 146
  Bavinck on, 44n59
  developing, 44 (Adam)
  as fact and norm, 80n13
  and God's attributes, 80n13, 96
  and God's ethical character, 98
  and God's righteous words, 97
  and God's righteousness, 80, 80n13, 97, 187
  and God's word, 104, 146
  and goodness, 80
  growth in, xxi
  and justification, 97
  as marred holiness, 43n58, 46
  as moral excellence, 5, 42–43, 43n58
  narrow sense of, 43n58
  as restored holiness, 141
  standard of, 97
  yours in Jesus, 139, 151
Holy Spirit
  as Helper, 134–135, 175
  and justification, 24, 94, 107, 116, 130, 161, 163, 181
  and lordship attributes, 104, 116, 148, 175–76, 181–82
  presence of, 175–76, 181, 186, 189
  salvation by, 94, 116, 130, 161, 181

sanctification by, 74, 107, 116, 120, 127, 129–30, 144, 163, 167, 178, 181–82
sword of, 179, 179n143
of truth, 175
and word of God, *See* word of God
works of, 15, 171
hope, 126
  Bible of, 117
  in first gospel, 49
  for God's children, 146
  greatest hope, 16 (church)
  and Holy Spirit, 124
  Jesus Christ as, 47
  in Messiah, 85, 86
  in Mosaic law, 60
human beings, 31, 77n3, 78, 145, 148
  as evil, 48
  and God, 76, 79
  and God's righteousness, 80
  as image of God. *See* image of God
  and responsibility. *See* human responsibility
  as sinful, 93, 131
  as sinners, 64, 93
  human history of. *See* history
human merit, 63n114
human responsibility, 135–36
  and God's grace, 131, 153
  and God's sovereignty, 69, 75, 135
  and *Kingdom of Faith*, 131
  and ultimate model (prototype), 135
human traditions, 147
human wisdom, 43, 51, 142

identity, xviii-xx, 146, 149–50, 161
  as child of God, 157
  healthy identity, 149–51
  new identity, 149 (new self)
  restoration of, 155
image of bride
  in eternal kingdom of God, 19
    (victorious church)
image of God (40–44), x-xi, xiii, xxi-xxii, 40n47, 41, 41n48, 42n54, 45–47, 48, 135, 143, 148–50, 190
  in Adam, 40, 43–44, 43n58

image of God (continued)
  in Adam's office, 40
  in broad sense, 42–43, 43n58, 46n69
  in Christian life, xi
  and cultural development, 47
  growth in, xi, xiii, xxi
  as holy image, 26
  in humans, 5
  in human rational ability, 47
  in intellectual excellence, 46, 46n69
  in justification, 40
  as lost (Lutheran), 45n62, 46
  as marred image (45–48), xi-xiii, xx-xxi, 5, 43n58, 45n62 (Reformed), 46, 46n69, 47, 49, 83n25, 140, 143, 152–53, 155, 159
  as moral excellence (broad sense), 46, 46n69
  as narrow sense (biblical sense), 42–43, 43n58, 46
  as post-fall, 45–48
  as pre-fall (before), 40–44
  as restored image, ix-x, xii, xx-xxi, 5, 43n58, 46, 140, 152
  in sense of the whole person, 42–43, 46, 46n69
imitating Christ, 11n23, 98, 116, 126–27, 130, 167, 170, 181
imitating God, 97–98
Immanuel, 176
imputation (transferring, counting)
  of Christ's righteousness, 46, 51, 94–95, 163n127
  in Jesus, 94n45
  of perfect righteousness, 57
  of righteousness, xx
  of sin, 45, 47n74, 83, 140
inability
  obedience to word, 88
  of sinners, 63
incarnation, 58, 115
indwelling grace, 62n112
inerrancy. See Scripture
infallibility. See Scripture
inheritance, 6, 41n51, 67

intellectual excellence. See image of God
Israel
  and church, 17
  as covenant people, 5, 60, 65, 108
  and God's righteousness. See God's righteousness
  liberation of, 84 (type of salvation)
  and Mosaic covenant. See Mosaic covenant
  and Mosaic law. See Mosaic law
  as shadow of God's kingdom, 16, 60n108
Issac, 54n92, 55, 57 (sacrifice), 59, 65, 84 (offering)

Jacob, 54n91 (covenant), 55, 59, 65
Jesus Christ
  as author and perfecter of faith, 21
  in Christ alone, 66, 94
  and church, 16
  and covenant. See covenant
  cross of, 37
  divinity and humanity of, 12–13, 19, 90n35, 94, 109, 154, 176
  and eternal life, 21, 39, 87n31
  final judgment of, 11
  first coming of, 8, 52, 175
  as Fulfiller. See Fulfiller
  as fulfilling office, 6, 39n43, 69, 71, 74, 82, 91, 152, 154, 185
  genealogy of, 68n127
  and God's righteousness. See God's righteousness
  as Good Shepherd, 159
  and guilt, 10
  and Holy Spirit, 74, 161
  and image of God. See image of God
  incarnation of, 58, 115
  as Judge, 49, 99
  and judging righteousness. See judging righteousness
  and justification. See Justification
  as King (12–16), 21, 68
  and kingdom of God. See kingdom of God
  lineage of, 54

as Mediator. *See* Mediator
as Messiah, 16–17, 35, 37, 49, 52,
    54, 61, 63, 65, 67–68, 70, 79,
    83n25, 89, 93
and new self, 140, 150
obedience of, xx, 40, 92 (cross)
office of, 12n25 (three), 31 (servant)
as our inheritance, 6
as our model, 153
perfect obedience of. *See* perfect
    obedience
perfect righteousness of. *See* perfect
    righteousness
as Redeemer, 49
and redemption, 30, 32, 34, 66, 69,
    72, 115
as Representative. *See*
    Representative
and restoration. *See* restoration
and righteousness. *See*
    righteousness
and salvation, 7–8, 39, 56–57, 69,
    72, 87n31, 94, 127, 131, 133
as saving righteousness. *See* saving
    righteousness
second coming of, 7–8, 10–11, 52
as single coming, 8
as truth, 143
union with. *See* union
wisdom of. *See* God's wisdom
and word. *See* word of God
judging righteousness, 53, 83, 81n20,
    83n25
in Abrahamic covenant, 84
in Adamic covenant, 84, 88
in Adam's fall, 82, 83n25
in animal sacrifices, 85
definition of, 82
in gospel, 87
of Jesus, 91, 93
and lawlessness (unrighteousness),
    63, 82
and marred image, 83n25
as Messiah, 60
in Mosaic covenant, 84
in Mosaic law, 60, 63–64, 82, 84–85,
    88
in New Testament, 86

in Noahic covenant, 84
and perfect obedience, 92
and perfect righteousness, 91
and sin, 63
as solution, 64
as standard of, 81
John the Baptist, 90
judgment
    day of, 11, 52
    as final judgment, 11, 50, 52
    as flood judgment, 50–51
    God's judgment on sinners, 83
    of God's word, 103, 112n47, 117,
        124–30, 136n99
    power of, xix, 124, 129–30, 181
    and punishment, 45
    standard of, 28, 58, 60, 77, 145–48;
        see also God's righteousness
    of world, 50
judgment standard (word), 145–50,
    152, 156, 162, 176, 180–81,
    188–89
justice, 77–78n3, 78–80, 84n28, 99n66
    concept of, 78n3
    of Israel, 80
    Sandel on, 84n28, 99n66
justification, 26, 40, 42, 49, 55, 71,
    81n20, 94n45, 108, 112, 116,
    126, 130, 150, 167, 181–82
    as act of God, 96
    as covenantal, 35
    definition of, 95, 91–95
    doctrine of, 11, 12, 37, 38, 38n41,
        39n43, 41n38, 42, 43n58,
        50n79, 61, 61–62n112, 62–
        63n114
    as eternal blessings, 107
    by faith, xxii, 22, 54, 88–89, 129,
        162
    and God's righteousness, 89; *see
        also* God's righteousness
    and God's word, 116, 130, 161–62,
        181
    and gospel, 88, 16–63, 167
    by grace alone, 33, 37, 43n58, 55,
        71, 94n45, 167
    grace of, 71

justification (continued)
    and holiness and goodness, 97,
        97n54
    and Holy Spirit, 182
    and image of God, 43
    and Jesus Christ, 11, 24, 54–56, 87,
        87n31, 90–92 (Jesus), 93–97,
        151, 161–62, 181
    by Jesus Christ alone, 55
    and Mosaic law, 88–89
    and Old Testament covenants, 161
    by perfect obedience. See perfect
        obedience
    and redemptive work. See
        redemptive work
    of sinners, 51, 89, 91–93, 153
    and sufficient conditions of, 91–93
    union with. See union
    and wisdom, 138–45

Kant, 99n66
kingdom of God, xvii
    and church, 16–20, 16 (identical in
        Jesus)
    definition of, xvii
    and Jesus Christ, 4–8, 7n11, 11–12,
        14–17, 20–21, 25, 28–29, 53, 56,
        68, 132
    one with church, 17
    present reality, 17
    and redemptive history. See
        redemptive history
    and redemptive work. See
        redemptive work
Kline, M. G. 59n104, 61–62n112,
    62–63n114
    on Hittite culture, 59n104
    on suzerain and vassal, 58–59,
        59n104
    on works principle, 62n112,
        62–63n114
knowledge, xiii,
    and activities of heart, 126
    beginning of, 142
    and Bible, 136
    biblical virtues of, 43, 46
    and corruption, 46n69
    developing of, 44

of God's saving grace, 134
and God's word, 136
of good and evil, 35, 88
growth of, 142
highest standard of, 43 (God)
and human creation (pre-fall),
    44n59
as image of God (narrow sense:
    biblical sense), xxi, 42, 42n55,
    43, 140–41
and Jesus, 151 (1 Cor 1:3)
of Jesus Christ, 12, 148
and knowing Jesus, 138
as marred knowledge, 43n58
and new creation, 143
and new self, 143
renewal of, 148
as restored, 142–43
and wise person, 144
of word, 24
of world, 133, 136, 145
knowledge of God. See God's
    knowledge
knowledge of word, 24

language
    of David (soldier), 157
    as dead language, 121
    of faith, 128
    of world, 117, 119, 122
law
    of God, xix, 45, 60, 81
    of God's love, 64
    of God's righteous nature, 80, 124
    of God's righteousness, 4, 45
    of God's word, 83
    and gospel, 32, 36n38, 87n32,
        122n68, 127
    of Israel, 60, 64, 81–82
    of kingdom of God, xviii, xix, xix,
        26, 48, 60, 73, 76, 81, 132, 146,
        155
    of Moses. See Mosaic law
    and Prophets, 61, 87, 92, 161
    and Ten Commandment, 45n63
liberal theology, 104n14
life
    and blessings, 166

SUBJECT INDEX

and death, xix, 66, 119, 165
as eternal. See eternal life
as good. See good life
as human, 97, 108, 154–55
and perfect obedience. See perfect obedience
power of. See power of life
as present, 117
as righteous, holy, and good, 97
word of. See word of life
love
  as attribute of God, 103
  as fulfilling Mosaic law, 61, 99
    (Rom 13:10; Gal 5:14)
  for God, 61–64, 73, 165–66, 189
  of God. See God's love
  Jesus' teachings on, 149
  and Mosaic law, 61
  for neighbors, 61–64, 148–49, 166
Lordship attributes (word: 104–18), 117, 124, 132, 148, 154, 156, 175–76, 180–81, 188; see also control, authority, and presence
Luther, Martin
  on Mosaic law. 61n110

marred image. See image of God
marred intellectual excellence, 140
marred moral excellence, 141, 152
Mediator, 32–33, 39n43
  of Adamic and Davidic covenants, 67
  of all covenants, 32
  Bavinck on, 39n43
  of covenant of grace, 57, 66–67, 159
  Jesus Christ as, 35, 39n43
  of new covenant, 22, 33, 47, 185
  of reconciliation, 39n43
  of redemption, 66–67
  redemptive history of, 33
  Son as, 31
  of union, 39n43
medical knowledge, 140–41
medieval theology, 62n112, 63n114
merit
  of human autonomy, 133
  human merit, 63n114
  of human works, 62n112
  of Jesus, 69

meritorious obedience, 62n112
meritorious works, 62n112, 62n114, 89
Messiah. See Jesus Christ
millennium, 11
mission
  to church, 20
  to disciples, 20
moral ability, 42, 47
moral excellence. See image of God
moral law, 61, 73n142
  Calvin and Luther on, 61n112
  and love God and neighbor, 61, 63
Moses
  and blood covenant, 36
  and coming Messiah, 37
  and covenant, 35
  and covenant of works, 39n43
  and covenantal words, 28
  and justification, 38n41
  and law, 62
  and Mosaic law. See Mosaic law
  and Pentateuch, 58
  and redemptive history, 132
  and salvation, 72
  and Ten Commandments, 58
Mosaic covenant (57–66)
  and blessings and curses. See blessings and curses
  and blood covenant, 65
  and blood of Jesus, 65
  and continuity, 59n104
  and covenant of grace, 66
  and covenant relationship, 59
  and covenant of works, 61n112
  fulfilling of, 71
  and God's grace, 57
  and God's kingdom, 57
  and God's legal administration, 59, 59n104
  and God's righteousness, xix, 84
  and grace and law, 59
  as highest authoritative law, 108
  and legal framework, 60
  and meritorious obedience, 62
  and Mosaic law. See Mosaic law
  and Old Testament, xviii, 58
  at Sinai, 39n43

Mosaic law (60–64), 45, 78–79, 87, 98
    and blessings and curses, 73
    Calvin on, 61n110, 73n142
    and Christian life, 73n142
    and Christians, 73
    and covenant of works, 61
    and covenantal relationship, 58
    and curses, 61
    and external actions, 61
    and God's grace, 63, 166
    and God's righteousness, xix, 45n63, 60, 63, 65, 78, 98
    and good life, 97
    as good news, 121n68
    and gospel, 64, 66, 86, 88, 159
    as holy, righteous, and good law, 70, 81, 88
    human meritorious works of, 62
    and inability of sinners, 63, 88
    and internal aspect of obedience, 62
    as judging law, 88n33
    and judging righteousness, 82, 85–86, 88
    and justification, xix, 66, 88–89
    and kingdom of God, 85
    as law to rule, 64
    as legal covenant, 60
    and legal obligations, 58
    and love (fulfilling Mosaic law), 61, 99 (Rom 13:10; Gal 5:14)
    Luther on, 61n110
    and Messiah, 63, 66, 85–86, 88
    as moral law, 61
    and necessity of Jesus' perfect obedience, 62n114
    as our guardian, 61
    and perfect obedience, 65
    and promise of life and blessings, 166
    and redemptive history, 64–65
    and requirements of, 61, 66, 89, 92
    as role of governing, 85
    as sacrificial law (ceremonial law), 61
    and saving righteousness, 64, 85–86, 88
    and sinners, 64, 89
    and sins, 62, 85, 88
    as social law (judicial law), 61
    as social moral judgment standard, 60
    as standard, 63, 81, 125
    as structure of God's righteousness, 63
    summary of, 64
    as teacher, 73
    as type of law, 60
    as word of God, 121n68
    and works righteousness, 62n114
Mountain Sinai, 22n62, 39n43, 60

natural revelation, 102n3
nature preservation (covenant of), 52
new covenant (70–75)
    blood of, 37, 72
    and change in status, 74
    and eternal immutability, 73
    Fulfiller of, 75
    fulfilment of, 70–75
    and God's faithfulness, 73
    and God's family, 75
    and God's grace, 73, 75
    and God's promises, 75
    and God's righteousness, 73
    and good news, 133
    and justification, 63n114
    Mediator of. *See* Mediator
    and Messiah, 69
    and Mosaic law, 73
    and perfect obedience, 74
    Representative of. *See* Representative
    and salvation, 75, 133
    and sanctification, 63, 74
new creation, 142–43
new heart, 163n128
new life, 119, 174–75
new self, 43–44
    in Jesus, 143, 146, 150, 152, 182
    and Jesus as the greatest teacher, 153
    judgment standard of, 146, 149
    and justification, 142
    and necessity of growth, 142
    as new identity, 149
    and restored image, 140
Noah

and covenant of grace, 50
and God's grace, 50n79, 53
and God's promise to, 52
and Messiah, 53
and not justified by works, 55
Noahic covenant, 49–53
covenant of grace. *See* covenant of grace
Noahic flood
and baptism and union, 51
as flood judgment, 50
and imputation, 51
and Jesus' baptism, 50
and judging righteousness, 85
as sign and seal of covenant of grace, 50
as type of God's final judgement, 50, 52

obedience
of Adam. *See* perfect obedience
alive and active, 50
of faith, xx-xxi, 3, 5, 36–38, 41, 50, 53, 56–57, 59, 69, 74–75, 102, 108, 110, 117, 173, 177
of Jesus Christ. *See* perfect obedience
as meritorious, 62n112
and perfect obedience. *See* perfect obedience
of the righteous, 74
offering of Isaac, 57n99, 84
offspring of woman, 35, 65, 67, 69, 84
old self, 51, 143, 146, 150
omnipotence, 103
original sin
doctrine of, 39n43, 46n69
and justification, 39n43
and marred image, 46n69
and soteriology, 39n43
Osiander, 94n44
outside of us (*extra nos*), 93

pactum salutis, 31n18
parable
of kingdom of God, 7n12
of sower, 112
of vine (John 15), 112, 114, 177–82

Paul the Apostle, 182–86
conversion of, 182–85
peace, 26n75
counsel of, 31n18
as fruit, 164, 170
God of, 186
of God, 168
with God, 24
and Holy Spirit, 124, 148
of Jesus, 168
of the Lord, 148
Pentateuch, 58
perfect obedience
and Abraham, 56
and of Adam, 39n43
and all the words, 91
and God's righteousness, xix, 90, 92
and gospel, 15, 23
and imputation, 46
and invitation to God's family, xiii
and Jesus Christ, xiii, 15, 23, 49, 56, 74, 86n30, 90, 153
and judging and saving righteousness, 92
and justification, xx, 22, 49, 66, 90, 99
and life of Jesus, 135, 153–54
and model for our lives, 153
and Mosaic covenant, 62
and Mosaic law, 61–63, 65, 82, 85, 92
and necessity of (85–86), 34, 62n114
and new covenant, 74
and perfect righteousness (92–95), xx, 23, 89, 92
and perfect sacrifice, 75
and redemptive work, xx, 99
and remission of sins, 92
and restored image, xii, xviii, 22, 49, 83, 140, 153
and restored kingdom, 63
and salvation, 12, 37
perfect righteousness (92–95)
of believers, 93–94
imputation of, 56–57
of Jesus Christ, xii, 86n30, 23, 66, 92, 94

perfect righteousness (continued)
   and judging and saving righteousness, 92
   and justification of sinner, xii, xx, 23, 66, 93
   and perfect obedience. *See* perfect obedience
   and salvation, 56
   standard of, 84
   as your perfect righteousness, 66
perfection as God's attribute, 103
Peter
   and Christian life, 51
   and flood judgment, 51
   and Noahic covenant, 52
philosophical knowledge, 140–41
philosophy
   as deceptive, 147
   as general, 99
   as moral, 99n66
   as political, 84
   warning against, 147–48
   as worldly, 142–43
politics, 99n66
pollution of sin. *See* guilt and sin
postmillennialism, 10n22
power of judgment (word, Heb 4:12; 124–30), 181
   on behalf of God, 125
   from God's attribute, 124
   as judging hearts, 126–28
   from perspective of good life, 124
   from perspective of salvation, 124
   concerning salvation, 126–28
   concerning sanctification, 127–28
power of life (word, Heb 4:12; 118–22), 128–30, 148, 156, 176, 180–81, 188
   as life-giving, 118
   as light of life, 119
   as living, 118, 120–21
power of (to) work (word, Heb 4:12; 122–24), 128–30, 181
   as active power (energeia, ἐνέργεια)), 122–23
   and controlling power, 123
   as power to save, 124
   as sufficient power to keep promises, 123–24
   as working power, 123
presence (dwelling of word: 111–16), 187
   as abiding, 113
   as dwelling of Christ, 113
   as dwelling in hearts, 111
   fruit of, 114n50,
   as God's personal presence, 111, 188
Prayer, xviii,11 (blessing), 25, 84n28 (Ps 72), 147, 167, 189
premillennialism, 10n22
present reality
   definition of, 6–7
   of God's word, 117, 156
   as historic, 8
   of Jesus, 13
   of kingdom of God, xx, 1, 6–9, 12, 17, 20–23
   meaning of, 14
   of our lives, 12
preservation,
   of humanity, 51, 53
   as nature, 52 (Noah)

ransom, xiii, 8, 160
rational ability (human), 47
reason
   as human, 104n14
   as marred, 145
reconciliation, xii, 8, 39n43, 160
Redeemer, 14, 35, 49, 57, 85
redemption, xii, 8, 160
   and covenant of redemption. *See* covenant of redemption
   as historical event, 29
   as our redemption, 151
   plan of, 32
   of sinners, 30
   word of, 161
   work of, 31, 109, 115, 181
redemptive history, xii, 35, 49, 71, 102, 132
   and Bible, 35
   and church, 16, 17 (one with kingdom of God)
   definition of, 101, 131–32

and God's covenant, 132
and grace, 131–32, 134
and Holy Spirit, 134–35
and human history, 32, 131–32
importance of, 132–33
and Jesus Christ, 71, 101, 132
and kingdom of God, xvii, xviii, 15, 16, 17, 131
and Mediator, 33
and Messiah, 64
and salvation, 133–34
redemptive work, 6, 14, 66, 68, 72, 76, 105, 108–9, 115, 131, 134, 160, 167
and covenant of grace, 33–34, 69
and covenants, 30
and eternal value, 3
and flood judgment, 50
and God's love, 166
and God's righteousness, xix, 76
and gospel, 145
and guilt, 10
and Holy Spirit, 134
and human creation, 5
and human history, 131
and image of God, 41
and judging and saving righteousness, 86, 88
and justification, 11–12, 91
and kingdom of God, 8, 12, 15–16, 18
and necessity of, 155
and perfect obedience, xx, 99
and restoration, 29
and salvation, 69–70
and the Son, 31
and soteriology, 8
and word, 23, 133, 135
Reformers, 62n112 (on indwelling grace)
remission of sins
in justification, 89, 95
repentance
and life, 121n65
and salvation, 121n65
of sin, 4, 85
representative. *See* Adam and Jesus Christ
Representative
of all believers, 54, 91

as covenant Representative, 17, 54
of God's children, 152
of new covenant, 5, 15, 29n11, 31, 34, 66, 69–72, 133
restoration
of God's image, 43
of God's kingdom, 5
of identity, 155
of marred goodness, 43nn58
of marred holiness, 43nn58
of marred image, xi, xx, 5, 48, 155
of marred knowledge, 43nn58
of marred moral excellence, 141
of marred righteousness, 43nn58, 49, 83n24
of marred whole person, 43nn58
of marred wisdom, 43nn58, 141
of relationship, 29
resurrection
of dead, 119
death and, 13, 51, 161
and eternal life, 121
power of, 122n71
and victorious church, 19
revelation
and kingdom of God, 53
of Messiah, 66
reward
for Adam's efforts, 41
as meritorious reward (medieval theology), 63n114
for obedience to Mosaic covenant, 62n112
for the righteous, 11
righteousness
alien righteousness, 93
as human, 89
of Jesus Christ, 14, 51, 62n114, 83n225, 91, 93–94, 141
perfect righteousness. *See* perfect righteousness

sacrifice
as animal, 57n99, 65, 84
Isaac as, 57
of Jesus Christ, 5, 13, 57, 74, 118, 144
as living, 118
as perfect sacrifice, 57, 75

sacrifices, 36, 84–85
salvation
   and covenant of grace, 35
   and covenant of redemption, 33–34
   before creation, 31
   of fallen humanity, 5, 31, 63, 71, 133
   as gift, 69
   God's righteousness as standard for, 81–95
   by grace alone, 33–34, 54n92
   as human, 30–31
   and justification, 49, 94–95, 112
   as present reality, 6
   and sanctification, 112–13, 116
   of sinners, 6, 28, 31, 35, 41, 56, 70, 131, 178
Sandel, Michael
   on justice, 84n28, 99n66
saving righteousness, 77n3, 82, 82n20, 83
   in Abrahamic covenant, 84
   Adam, 83n25, 84
   and animal sacrifices, 84
   concept of, 78n4, 81n20
   in Davidic covenant, 85
   and gospel, 64, 86–88
   and Messiah, 60, 84
   in Mosaic covenant, 84
   in Mosaic law, 64, 85–86, 88
   necessity of, 64
   in New Testament, 81n20, 86
   in Noahic covenant, 84
   in Old Testament, 82, 86
   and perfect obedience, 92
   and perfect righteousness, 92
   and redemptive work, 86
   and salvation, 91
   standard of, 81, 87
Savior, 13, 109
scientific knowledge, 140–41
Scripture
   characteristics of, 108
   clarity of, 108
   coherence of, xii
   comprehensiveness of, 108 (meaning)
   inerrancy of, 108
   infallibility of, 108
   inspiration of, 108
   necessity of, 108
   sufficiency of, 108 (meaning)
seed, 7n12, 163
semi-eschatological, 9n16
Shreiner, Thomas
   on saving and judging righteousness, 81n20, 86n30
signs, 11
sin
   definition of, 45
   of Adam. See Adam
   forgiveness of sins, xi, 65, 68, 72, 87, 107, 150, 160, 178 179; see also forgiveness of sins
   and guilt, xx, 10 (meaning of), 45, 47n74 (imputation), 72, 83 (meaning of), 178–79
   pollution of, xx, 10 (meaning of), 23, 23n69 (meaning of), 47n74 (imputation), 72, 83
sinful nature, 10, 23n69, 48, 179, 189
slavery, 84, 97
Son, 13, 31
   and covenant of redemption, 31
   as Mediator, 31
Son of God, 41n51, 110, 127, 129, 137, 150
Son of Man, 9
soteriology, 8, 11–12, 35, 39n43, 76
speech, 103 (God's)
suzerain, 58–59, 59n104
suzerainty treaty, 59n104

tabernacle, 36
temple, 36, 175 (heart)
temptations
   in human lives, 20
   of world, 189
Ten Commandments, 28, 45n63, 58, 60, 60n106 (summary), 97; see also Decalogue
theology of grace, 182
Thiselton, Anthony C., 36n39
Trinity
   and covenant of grace, 32–33 (external work of)

and covenant of redemption, 30–31
(internal work of), 32–33
and creation, 105
and salvation, 30
work of, 178, 178n141
tree of the knowledge of good and evil, 35, 44, 88
trust, 14, 115, 161
   in authority of words, 109
   of faith, 157
   in God, 160, 168
   in God's grace, 24, 160
   in gospel, 160
   in Jesus, 129
   in the Lord, 133–34
   purpose of (assurance), 157–61
   in words, 158, 160
   words of (assurance), 157–59

unbelief, 110, 128, 151
union with Adam
   with all humanity, 38, 39n42
   and covenant breakers, 40
   after covenant of redemption, 46n68
   for understanding union with Jesus, 38
union with Jesus Christ
   in baptism, 51
   with believers, 39n42–43
   and believers in the Lord, 167
   in Christ's death and resurrection, 51
   and covenant keepers, 40
   in covenant of redemption, 39n42, 46n68
   in imputation, 51, 94, 94n45
   in justification, 56, 74
   in sanctification, 74
   and union with Adam, 38
unity in diversity, xii, xiin1, 30, 42, 73, 138, 167
unrighteousness, 4, 62n114, 63, 82, 83n26, 85, 92
Ur of the Chaldeans, 54

vassal, 58, 59, 59n104
vassal state, 58

violation of God's law, 82n21
virtue, 84n28
Vos, Gerhardus, 9n16 (eschatology)

Westminster Confession of Faith, 38n41
will of God, 169 (transformation)
wisdom
   of believers in Jesus, 141
   of God. *See* God's wisdom
   human wisdom. *See* human wisdom
   of Jesus, 139, 140–41
   Jesus as God's wisdom, 137
   of world, 140
wisdom of the world, 140
word of God (101–186), xix–xxii, 3, 11, 21–24, 29, 37, 44, 48, 58, 65–66, 70, 85, 100, 112, 144, 187
   and application, 102, 114, 116
   assurance of, 109
   characteristics of (103–30); *see also* power of life, power of work, and power of judgment
   as commandment to love yourself, 148–52
   as commonality (foundation), 102
   and creation, 52
   and encountering God, 111, 116, 144, 182, 188–89
   as eternal result, 3
   as eternal wisdom, 148
   as eternal word, 23–24, 188–89
   as foundation, 134
   as God, 21n60, 188
   and God's attributes, 28
   and God's righteousness, 76–100; *see also* God's righteousness
   and gospel, 160–61
   highest importance of, 131
   as holy, righteous, and good, 75, 88, 152, 189
   and Holy Spirit, 21, 23, 148, 174–82
   as human responsibility, 135–36
   importance of, 102, 130–44, 132–32 (for God's grace), 137–44 (as wisdom and salvation), 178
   as knowledge, 136–38, 140–42

word of God (continued)
    as language of faith, 128
    as law, 48
    as living God, 118, 188
    as Lordship attributes (word: 104–18); *see also* Lordship attributes
    to Paul, 182–86
    as power of judgment (word, Heb 4:12). *See* power of judgment
    as power of life (word, Heb 4;12). *See* power of life
    as power of (to) work (word, Hb 4:12). *See* power of (to) work
    purpose of, 155–73, 157–59
        (assurance), 165–68
        (obedience), 168–70 (presence of the word of obedience)
    and redemptive history. *See* redemptive history
    as standard, 108, 131, 146, 152, 154, 189
    as standard of deeds, 152–55
    as standard of judgment, 145–48
    as standard of knowledge, 189
    and vine (John 15), 177–82
    as wisdom, 137–44
word of life
    for all believers, 118
    given by God, 181
    as living word of life, 117
    to sinners, 119
    as word of living Jesus, 120
    work of, 185
work of Christ, xii, 12
    as source of salvation, 72

works principle, 61–62n112, 63n114
works righteousness, 62n112, 62n114
world
    after Adam's fall in, 47
    and church, 18
    and creation, 4
    before creation of, 31
    elementary principles of, 147
    false gods of, 103
    God's children in, 20, 23, 26, 102n3
    God's word as controlling power of, 106
    and healthy relationship with, 150
    Judge of, 78, 124
    judgment of, 50
    King of, 12–13, 20, 77, 79
    kingdom of, 27
    and kingdom of God, 7, 15–16, 19–20, 23, 26, 70
    knowledge of, 133, 136, 140
    lawlessness in, 45
    light of, 119–20
    no hope in, 47
    overcomers in, 164, 173
    sins and curses in, 62n114
    wickedness in, 51
    words of, 115, 122, 128
    wrong knowledge of, 24
worship, 20, 22n63, 41, 74
    of angels, 148
    self-impose, 147–48
wrath of God, 48

Scripture Index

Genesis

Reference	Pages
1:1	105
1:26–27	40, 43
1:26–28	40–41
1:26–30	40
1:28	40
2:16–17	40, 44
2:17	152
3:14–15	35
3:15	36, 56, 84
3:15–19	40, 44, 49, 65, 67
3:17	102n3
3:21	36, 65, 84
6:1–4	49
6:5	47
6:5–7	50
6:8	50n79
6:8–9	50
6:10	52
6:13–22	53
6:13–7:6	84
6:22	50
7:6–8:19	50, 84
8:20	84
9:1–3	51n86, 51
9:6	44, 102n3
9:7	52
9:9–11	52
9:9–13	52
9:26–28	52
10:32	67
11:1–9	53
11:10–21	52
11:10–32	67
12:1–2	53
12:1–3	168–69
15	53
15:5–7	50n79, 54–55
15:6	56
15:9–17	36n37
15:9–21	57n99, 84
15:18	36n37
17	56, 57n99
17:4–7	54–55, 169
17:11	36, 65
17:14	36, 65
18:3	50n79
18:14	103
19:19	50n79
22	57n99
22:1–9	84
22:17–18	54, 56, 67, 169
26:4–5	56
32:12	54n91

Exodus

Reference	Pages
2:24–25	59
9:21	111
19	57
19:4–5	60
19:4–20:20	60
20:1–7	60n106
20:1–17	60–61
20:6	29
21:1–23:13	61
24:7–8	65

Exodus (continued)

24:8	36, 65
25:1–30:38	61, 85
33:12–13	50n79
33:16–17	50n79
34:9	50n79

Leviticus

1:1–8:36	61, 85
16:1–34	85

Numbers

11:11	50n79
11:15	50n79
15:1–31	61

Deuteronomy

1:6	60
4:7–8	113n49
6:3	165
6:4	165, 165n131
6:4–5	165
6:4–9	37
6:6	111–12
8:3	58, 147n112
6:6	111–12
6:17–18	165
6:17–19	165
6:24	166
15:1–31	85
16:18	78, 78n4
16:20	77n3, 78, 78n4, 80
27–28	106n21
27:26	61, 165
28:1–6	61
28:1–14	165
28:15–19	61, 165
30:11–14	113n49
30:14	111, 113n49
30:14–16	110
32:46	111–12
33:21	78n3

Judges

5:11	78n3

1 Samuel

12:7	78n3

2 Samuel

7:12–16	67n124
7:28	143
22	157, 158n121
22:1–3	158
22:2–3	158
22:32–33	158
22:29	158
22:30	158
22:31	158
22:33	158

1 Kings

17:24	143
18:24–46	103

1 Chronicles

17:11–14	67, 85

Job

22:22	111

Psalms

1	182
7:8–9	127
9:7–8	77–78, 78n4
10:14	84n26
16:6	41n51
18	158n121
18:2	158
18:28	158
18:29	158
18:30	158
19:7–11	103
23	158n12, 158–59, 182
23:3	77n3
26:1–2	127
27:1	158–59
32:1–2	68n128
34:15–22	95
35:10	84n26

40:10	82
50:6	83
65:6	77n3, 79n10
68:5	84n26
72	84n26
72:1–4	84n26
82	84n26
85:9–10	82
90:1–2	xviii
95:7–8	121n67
98:2–3	82
104	105
107:15	106
107:19–21	106
107:31	106
108	106
110:10	136
111	84, 106
113:7	84n26
115:5–8	103
118:14	158, 158n122
119:7	103, 145n108
119:43	142
119:86	103
119:89	103
119:89–90	143
119:129	103
119:142	103, 143
119:151	143
119:160	103
135:15–18	100
140:12	84n26
146:7–9	84n26

Proverbs

1:7	136–39
2:6	137–38
7:18	100
9:10	136–39
15:17	100
16:1	126n82
17:3	126n82
19:21	126n82
21:2	126n82
22:17	111–12

Ecclesiastes

2:26	144
3:17	83
11:9	83
12:14	83

Isaiah

11:2	136
24:5	40, 44–45
26:10	48
32:1	77n3, 79, 79n8
32:16	78n3
42:6	91n37
45:8	82
46:12–13	84
48:18	78n3, 79n10
51:5	77n3, 79n10, 82
51:7	77n3, 78, 78n4, 81
51:8	78n3, 79n10
55:3	68n127
55:6–9	xxii
55:7	48
55:11	27–28, 103, 105–107
56:1	78n3, 79n10
61	4
61:10–11	78n3, 79n10

Jeremiah

11:20	127
12:3	125, 127
17:10	125, 127
20:12	125, 127
22:16	84n26
31:33	xviin2, 162
31:31–33	70

Ezekiel

3:20	78n3, 96
18:24	78n3, 96
33:13	78n3, 96
37:1–14	163n128
37:4–5	163
37:14	163n128
44:7	36, 65

Daniel

2:20	136
2:23	144
9:24	77n3

Hosea

6:7	38n41, 40, 44–45

Amos

5:7	78n3
5:24	78n3
6:12	78n3

Micah

6:5	78n3

Zechariah

9:11	36, 65

Matthew

1:1	52
1:1–17	54, 68n127, 71n137
1:23	176
3:15	90
4:4	58, 147, 162
5:17–20	154
5:20	89–90
5:43	148–49
6:33	xiii, 15, 22, 89
7:24–29	164
9:15	4, 9
9:17	146
9:27	68n127, 69
9:35	4
11:11	4, 9
12:23	68n127, 69
12:32	9–10, 15
13:1–23	7n12
13:14–15	48
13:15	48n77
13:16–17	4, 9
13:18–23	112
13:23	112, 112n46
13:31–21	7n12
13:33	7n12
15:19	63n116
16:16	118
16:18–19	16
16:19	18
16:28	21
19:16–17	95, 95n50
19:19	148–49
19:23–30	7
19:25–26	141
20:28	xiin1, 160
20:30–31	69, 68n127
21:9	68n127, 68–69
21:15	68n127, 69
22:34–40	61
22:39	148–49
22:42	68n127, 69
23:13	4, 9
24:14	4
24:37–39	50
25:31	13
26:28	37, 65, 72
28:18–20	13–14, 19, 20–21, 23, 166–67
28:19–20	20
28:20	176

Mark

1:15	4, 6–7, 10
2:22	146
4:1–9	7n12
4:13–20	7n12
10	6
10:15	4
10:17–31	6
10:23	7
10:23–31	7
10:25–26	4
10:26	7
10:27	141
10:30	7
12:28–31	61
12:31	148–49
14:24	37, 65n118
16:16	100

SCRIPTURE INDEX

Luke

1:37	103
1:77	160
2:40	137n102
4:16–22	6
5:37–38	146
8:1	4
8:4–15	7n12, 112
8:10–15	75
8:12	112
8:15	16, 112, 171, 173
10:25–27	92, 165
10:27	148–49
13:9–10	61
13:21	7n12
14:15–24	75
17:20–21	7
17:21	4, 9–10
17:26–27	50
18:18–30	7
18:27	7n11
19:38	21
22:29	20
22:20	37, 65n118
24:25–27	71

John

1:1	105, 111, 115, 177
1:1–2	xix, 21, 103, 181, 187–88
1:1–3	105
1:1–14	177
1:4	119–20, 182
1:12	116, 130, 161, 181
1:14	105, 115, 120, 177, 181, 188
3:3–5	7
3:3–8	7
3:8	182
3:15–16	20, 100
3:16	4, 87n31, 116, 119–20, 130, 152, 161, 166, 179, 181
3:16–18	7
3:16–21	7, 150
3:18	126–27
3:36	120
4:10–11	118–19
4:10–14	119
5:24	87n31, 120, 126–27, 182
5:26	182
5:29	182
5:38	113, 113n48
5:39	109
5:40	120
6:33	182
6:35	119, 182
6:35–40	119
6:36	119
6:40	119–21
6:47	120
6:48	119–20, 182
6:51	119–20, 182
6:53	120
6:56	113n48
6:57	118
6:63	120n63, 159, 182
7:38	113
7:38–39	113, 118–19
7:39	182
8:12	119–20, 182
8:31	113n48
8:31–32	114, 142, 148
10:7–9	95
10:7–18	159
10:10	120, 182
10:14–15	159
11:25	119–20, 182
12:25	121
12:48	125
12:50	121n66
13:34	100, 166
13:34–35	98, 166
13:35	100, 172
14–15	115n54, 178
14–17	105, 176
14:6	109, 118–20, 142, 182
14:9	176
14:15	29
14:16	115
14:16–17	13, 166, 175, 181
14:17	142
14:18	176, 182
14:20	21, 115, 181–82

John (continued)

14:20–21	166, 172, 176
14:21	176
14:23	176, 181–82
14:26	100, 166, 182
15	171, 177, 178n142, 179
15:1	178
15:1–4	178n141
15:1–17	112, 114
15:2	178n142, 179, 181
15:2–3	176–77, 180–81
15:3	178–80, 178n142
15:4	166
15:4–5	113n48, 180
15:4–7	181
15:4–8	175
15:4–17	179
15:7	21, 113n48, 114–15, 162, 180–82
15:9	114n53, 166
15:10	166, 172
15:11	109
15:12	98
15:13	174
15:17	100, 166
15:26	100, 142, 144
16:1	109
16:7	175
16:13	142, 144, 175–76, 182
16:25	176
16:29	176
16:33	110
17:3	4, 7–8, 20–21, 137–39, 141
17:5	32
17:6–8	178n141
17:17	103, 142–43, 178n141
17:19	142
17:24	32
20:31	120–21, 182

Acts

1:3	4
1:24	125
2	19, 175
4:11–12	163
5:20	119, 119n62
8:4	23
8:12	4
9:3–5	183
9:10–12	184
9:11–14	184
9:13	184
9:17–18	184
9:22	184
9:28	184
11:18	121n65
14:15	118
14:17	102n3
15:7	23
15:8	125, 174
16:31	87n31, 100, 160
19:8	4
20:25	4
28:23	4
28:31	4

Romans

1:7	26n75
1:16	105, 139
1:16–17	xi, 100, 107, 144
1:17	xiii, 14, 46, 64, 77, 78n3, 82, 87, 93, 96, 116, 124, 129–31, 161–62, 167, 181, 188
1:18–21	102n3
1:18–3:20	62n114, 64, 70
1:29–32	84n26
2:4	xx
2:10	26n75
2:12	62, 88
2:12–3:20	88
2:13	88
2:16	127
3:4	91
3:5	47
3:9–10	88
3:9–12	70, 89
3:10	62–63, 74
3:10–12	34, 83, 96–97
3:12	95n50
3:19	125, 127n85
3:19–20	88, 166

3:20	62–63, 74, 88	7:12	34, 48, 63, 70, 74–75, 81, 88–89, 98, 152, 155, 189
3:21	77		
3:21–22	14, 46, 78n3, 82, 87, 91–93, 95, 102n3, 116, 130–31, 161–62, 181	8:1–2	116, 120, 130, 133, 165
3:21–26	96	8:1–4	98–99
3:21–31	54, 64	8:4	74
3:22	55n93, 55	8:5–7	48
3:24	xiin1, 91, 160	8:8	48
3:25	72	8:11	169
3:26	87n31, 91, 91n38	8:26–27	25, 100
3:28	91	8:28–29	xi
4	163n128	8:26–30	24
4:1–25	54	8:28–39	25, 162
4:3	55	8:29	189
4:5	96	8:29–30	32
4:6–8	68	8:31–39	24
4:11	55	8:35–39	xiin1, 13, 160
4:16	169	8:38–39	166
4:20	110	9:3–5	183
4:22–24	54	9:6	118
4:25	93n42	10:3	90n34
5:1	xiin1, 160	10:4	87
5:5	xiin1, 17, 21, 160, 166, 174–75, 175n137	10:8	113n48
		10:9	160
5:8	150	10:9–10	7, 114
5:9	72, 91	10:17	114, 151n116
5:9–11	xiin1, 160	12:1	118
5:12	83	12:2	169
5:12–21	38, 46, 62n114, 70	12:10	100
5:13	88	12:12	25, 169
5:17	92, 94	12:17	100
5:18	121	13:8–10	74, 99
5:19	62	13:9	148–49
6:1–2	153	13:9–10	113
6:1–11	51	14:15	97
6:3–10	163	14:16	96–97
6:4	119	14:17	26n75
6:5–7	51n83	15:13	26n75, 124, 195
6:6	143, 146, 150	16:26	140
6:7	91		
6:11	162–63, 162n127	**1 Corinthians**	
6:18	xiin1, 132, 160	1–2	140
6:19	80	1:17	140
6:22	80, 132	1:18	138–39
7:10	121, 166	1:19–22	140
		1:24	137–39

1 Corinthians (continued)

1:24–27	140
1:30	92, 97, 139–43, 151
1:30–31	104
1:31	151
2:1	140
2:4–8	140
2:5	144
2:7	32, 140
2:9	141
2:10	142
2:13	142
3:16	175, 175n137
4:3–4	151
5:7	xiin1, 160
6:11	91
6:20	15
10:31	15, 25
11:25	37, 65n118, 72
13:12	74, 74n145
15:22	39
15:24–28	20
15:45	118–19, 159
15:57	xiin1, 160

2 Corinthians

1:6	123
1:22	7, 21, 166, 174
2:15	14
3:3	118, 162
3:6	159
3:18	74
4:10–12	112, 113n47, 124
5:14	25
5:17	143, 149, 152
5:21	xiin1, 14, 160
7:4	26n75
10:17	151
11:10	142
13:11	26n75

Galatians

2:16	87n32, 88
2:20	150
3:5	112–13, 123–24
3:8–9	91, 93
3:10	xiii, 174
3:24	29, 61
3:24–25	88
4:6	128
4:21–31	54
4:28	54n92
5:13–14	73–74, 98–100
5:14	61, 148–49
5:16	169
5:22	166
5:22–23	144, 170, 173
6:16–24	100

Ephesians

1:3–6	31
1:7	72, 160
1:11	123
1:13	23, 25, 142
1:17	104
1:19	122n71
1:20–23	16, 18, 20
2:8	87n31, 144
2:8–9	xiin1, 92, 122n69, 160
2:8–10	144
2:10	100
2:15	140, 143, 149, 152, 183
2:20	17, 20
3:4	140
3:7	122n71
3:9	32
3:10–11	18
3:11–21	32
3:17	21
3:18	104
3:20	123
3:20–21	xiii
4:13	97
4:15–16	104
4:16	122n71
4:21	142
4:22	143, 146, 150
4:23–24	116, 130, 143, 166
4:24	43–44, 104, 140, 142–43, 149, 152, 181, 183
5:2	xiin1, 98, 104, 160

5:8–9	14, 104	2:8	142, 147
5:22	25	2:8–23	150
5:22–6:9	25	2:9–15	148
5:26	179n143	2:12	50, 122n71
5:26–27	18	2:13–15	xiin1, 160
5:32	140	2:16–18	147
6:17	179, 179n143	2:18	147
6:19–20	25, 140	2:20	147
		2:23	147
		3:3	148

Philippians

		3:9	143, 146, 150
1:9	75, 186	3:10	43, 104, 116, 130, 140–41, 143, 148–50, 152, 167, 181, 183
1:16	186		
2:1	186		
2:5–8	155		
2:9–11	20	3:15	26n75, 148
2:12–13	20	3:16	26n75, 100, 164
2:13	123	3:16–17	148
2:16	119–20, 186	3:23	26
3:6	89	4:2	100
3:8	150	4:3	140
3:9	87n31, 91, 94		
3:21	122n71	## 1 Thessalonians	
4:4	25, 94, 186	1:5	105, 107
4:4–6	167, 173	1:6	124, 124n75
4:4–7	168	2:8	174
4:6	26n75, 100	2:13	120–21
4:6–7	128	4:9	100
4:7	26n75, 168	5:17	100
4:8	186	5:18	26n75
4:8–9	168, 186		
4:9	26n75, 186	## 2 Thessalonians	
4:13	186	1:3	100
		2:12	48
## Colossians		2:17	100
		3:16	26n75
1:5	23		
1:10	97, 100	## 1 Timothy	
1:11	xiin1, 26n75, 160		
1:13–14	xiin1, 160	1:8–11	98
1:24–25	185–86	2:4	142
1:26	140	2:6	xiin1, 160
1:29	122n71	2:15	114n53
2:1–3	147–48	3:16	20, 91
2:2	140	3:16–17	91n38, 97–98
2:2–3	151	4:5	26
2:3	104, 141	4:5–6	147
2:7	26n75	4:5–8	147

1 Timothy (continued)

4:15–16	147
5:10	100
6:15	21

2 Timothy

1:9–10	32
2:5–6	173
2:7	168
2:15	142
2:21	100
3:14	114n53
3:16–17	98, 100–111, 173, 177, 189
3:17	100
4:4	173
6:12	173

Titus

1:15–16	96–97
2:14	xiin1, 160
3:1	100
3:7	91

Hebrews

1:18	22n62
1:22	22n62
2:18–20	103, 128
3:7–19	128
3:8–9	128
4	121n68
4:2	121n68, 121–22, 128
4:6	121, 121n68, 128
4:11	121
4:12	21, 24, 105, 119–28, 181
4:12–13	111, 117–18, 122n70–71, 123n72, 125n78, 127–30, 156, 188
4:12–16	128
4:14	128n87
4:14–15	128
4:14–16	128–29
4:15	128
4:16	22n62
5:1–10	128
5:8	154
6:1–2	129
6:11–12	129
6:11–18	129
6:20	128
7:1–28	128
7:25	22n62
8:1	13, 20
8:1–2	19
8:10	xvii, 162
9:11	65
9:12	72
9:14	72
9:15	65, 67
9:18	37, 65n118
9:20	37, 65n118
9:22	72
9:26	xiin1, 15n34, 160
10	128n87
10:1	22n62
10:10	129
10:16	162
10:19–22	22–23
10:22	22n62
10:24	100
10:29	37, 65n118, 72
10:31	118
10:36	129
10:38	129
10:38–39	22–23, 54
11	21, 86, 128n87
11:1–2	54, 129
11:6	22n62, 54, 110, 116, 129–30, 156, 167, 172, 181
11:7	50
11:8–12	54, 56
11:17	50, 128
11:17–19	54, 56
11:29	128
11:36–37	128
12	21
12:1	21
12:1–2	19
12:2	13, 20–21
12:11	26n75
12:18	22n62

12:22	21	3:5–6	50
12:22–24	22	3:6–7	52
12:24	22, 37, 65n118, 72	3:14	26n75
12:28	22		
12:28–29	22n63	**1 John**	
13:18	100	1:1	119–20
13:20	65n118	1:4	26n75
13:20–21	37	1:5	120
13:21	100	1:7	72, 160
		1:9	48, 95
James		2:1	13
1:5	144	2:4	142
1:18	175	2:6	113n48
1:21	162	2:14	113n48, 114n50
2:8	148–49	2:18–19	25
2:21–23	56	2:24	113n48
3:9	44	3:4	45
4:8	115n54	3:11	172
4:11–12	79–80	3:14	121
5:13	100	3:15	120
		3:16	174
1 Peter		3:20	125
1:2	72	3:21	172
1:20	32	3:22	172
1:23	24, 117, 118, 156, 175	3:23	100
1:25	23, 103, 175	3:24	113n48
2:2	100	4:7	100
2:4	24	4:10–11	98
2:4–12	24	4:11–12	100
2:9	41n51	4:12	113n48
2:24	51	4:15	113n48
3:12	51	4:16	151
3:18	47, 51, 97	5:4	152, 164
3:20–22	50–51	5:5	110, 173
4:8	51n85, 100	5:7	142
4:18	51, 51n85	5:12	121
		5:12–13	120
2 Peter		5:20	137–39
1:1	51		
1:3	121n66, 188	**2 John**	
2:5	50, 51	1:5	100
2:7–8	51	1:9	114n53
2:12–16	47–48	1:11	100
3:1–7	52		
3:4–5	52n88	**3 John**	
3:4–7	52	1:3	142

Jude

1:15–16	47

Revelation

1:3	173
1:5	26n75, 132
1:6	18
2:1–3:22	18, 20
4:3	53
5:5	69
7:14	72
11:15	21
11:17	21
12–19	18
15:3	21
17:14	21
19:11	99
19:16	21
20	11
21–22	19
21:1–4	19
21:3	75
21:5	13
21:7	173
22:3–4	74
22:7	173
22:11–12	99
22:12	173
22:16	69

www.ingramcontent.com/pod-product-compliance
Lightning Source LLC
Chambersburg PA
CBHW051637230426
43669CB00013B/2332